SHARKS OF ARABIA

SHARKS of ARABIA

DR. JOHN E. RANDALL

IMMEL
Publishing

SHARKS OF ARABIA

IMMEL Publishing
Ely House, 37 Dover Street
London W1X 3RB
First published 1986.

©1986 John E Randall.

All rights reserved. No part of this publication may be reproduced, stored in a retrieval system, or transmitted in any form, or by any means, electronic, mechanical, photocopying, recording or otherwise, without the prior permission of the copyright holder.

Phototypeset in Bembo by
The Typesetting Company, London, England.
Printed and bound in Japan by
Dai Nippon Printing Company, Tokyo.
Design and artwork by
Patrick O'Callaghan Graphic Design.

ISBN 0 907151 09 4

Page 1:
Blacktip Reef Shark
Carcharhinus melanopterus
Photo by J. Randall

Pages 2 & 3:
Whitetip Reef Shark
Triaenodon obesus
Photo by J. Randall

CONTENTS

FOREWORD 7

INTRODUCTION 9

FORM AND FUNCTION 14

EVOLUTIONARY HISTORY . . 43

MAN AND SHARKS 52

CLASSIFICATION 67

GLOSSARY 133

BIBLIOGRAPHY 137

Jaws of Tiger Shark
Galeocerdo cuvier
Photo by J. Randall

FOREWORD

SHORTLY AFTER MEETING JACK RANDALL more than twenty years ago I had the pleasure of his company on a small research vessel working off the Bahamas. Among the fishes caught on that cruise were some largish whaler sharks, species which I had recently begun to study. Like most people who rarely have the opportunity of seeing these splendid, sometimes dangerous predators either in their natural habitat or freshly landed, I found them fascinating and awesome. Jack Randall did too, but that didn't deter him from scuba diving in the area where they had been caught to look for the smaller bony fishes which are his primary research interest. He still does the same, and even nearly being bitten by dangerous sharks on at least two occasions has not discouraged him from entering their realm. Admittedly he tries to tip the scales in his favour by learning as much as possible about sharks – how to recognise the species, their behaviour and habits, their reputations and how they live up to them. Such seeking of knowledge comes easily and natural to Jack, whose able and enquiring mind covers a broad spectrum of natural history. It is not surprising that as a result he has considerably extended our knowledge of sharks and their biology, essentially as a side-line to his main interest in tropical bony fishes.

In writing this present book on sharks his aim has been to share his knowledge and provide background information that will enable and encourage others to extend our understanding further. The geographical area he has chosen to encompass – the seas around the Arabian peninsula – is a rich one in terms of its shark fauna, and because many of the species found there have much wider, sometimes worldwide distributions, his accounts of them have much greater applicability than the title of his book might suggest. I commend him, too, for his substantial introductory chapters which deal with sharks generally, including their anatomy, biology, fossil history and their use and relationship to man. This book deserves to be a success.

Jack Garrick

DR. J.A.F. GARRICK PROFESSOR OF ZOOLOGY
VICTORIA UNIVERSITY OF WELLINGTON NEW ZEALAND

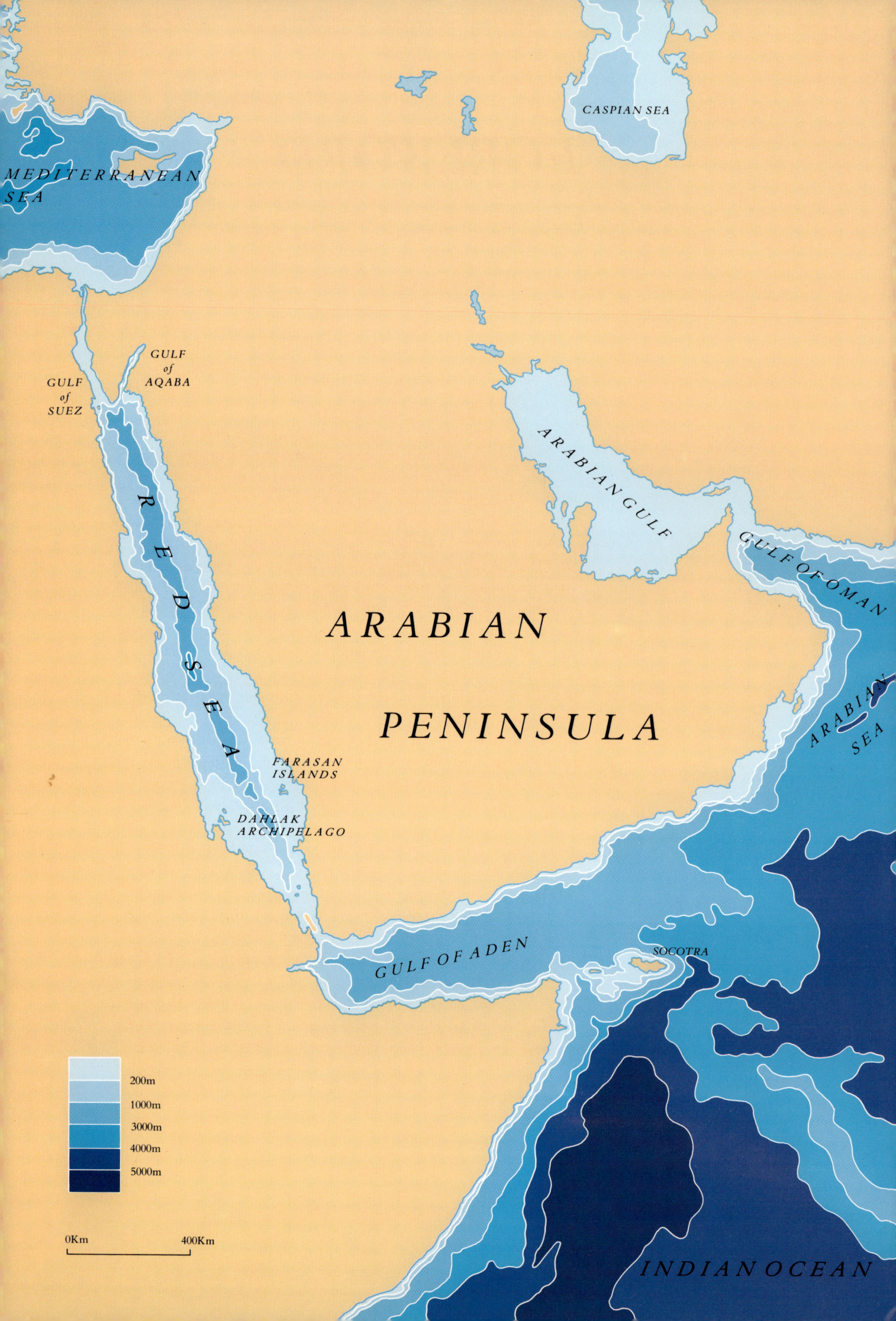

INTRODUCTION

There is something special about sharks. The mere mention of the word shark guarantees immediate attention from all within earshot. It is difficult to fully understand the basis for the combination of fear and fascination with which most people react to sharks. In part it is the contemplation of being a victim of a shark attack – the sudden unpredictable nature of such an attack and the helplessness of the victim; the awareness that it can happen if one is swimming near shore or floating in a life jacket in midocean; the total horror of being eaten alive. In part it is the aura of mystery about sharks.

We need to know more about sharks. Which ones are dangerous? What is the normal diet of sharks? How far do they range in search of food? How do they find their prey? How do they reproduce? How fast do they grow and how long do they live? What controls their populations? What do we know of their behaviour? Fundamental to finding answers to all these questions is a sound system of classification. We must start with the correct scientific name for each species and have an accurate and concise way of identification.

This book is primarily a guide to the species of sharks that have been found in the waters that surround the Arabian Peninsula: the Red Sea, Gulf of Aden, northern Arabian Sea, Gulf of Oman, and Arabian Gulf (often called the Persian Gulf). The sea is continuous around the peninsula, and one would presume that highly mobile animals like sharks, if they occur in any of these bodies of water, would range into all of them. Many do. But there are species in the Red Sea that are not found in the Arabian Gulf and vice versa. Although the Red Sea and the Arabian Gulf lie at the same latitude, there are major differences in their physical environments. Though narrow, the Red Sea is deep, the average depth about 490 m, the maximum at least 2,750 m. By contrast, the Arabian Gulf is shallow; in only a few places does it exceed 90 m, and most of it is less than 40 m. Because it is shallow, temperature is more susceptible to change with the

atmospheric temperature (which varies greatly from winter to summer). The Gulf also has a wider range of salinity, the northern part influenced by run-off from the Tigris and Euphrates Rivers and the southwestern part subject to high evaporation. To live in the Gulf an organism must therefore tolerate a wide range of temperature, and depending on locality, considerable variation in salinity. The Red Sea has about twice the number of species of fishes as the Arabian Gulf.

The scientific name of every animal and plant that has been described consists of two parts, the genus (capitalized) and the species. A genus (plural, genera) is a group of similar species. If an organism does not have any close relatives, it may be in a genus by itself; we refer to such taxa as monotypic. The two

INTRODUCTION

Blacktip Reef Shark
Carcharhinus melanopterus
Photo by J. Randall

words of a scientific name are in Latin, or Latinized from the Greek (or other languages). They should be italicized. Ideally, scientific names are based on the most important characteristic of an organism (or group of organisms). Thus the Blacktip Reef Shark was called *Carcharhinus melanopterus*. *Carcharhinus* means sharp-nosed (from the Greek) and *melanopterus*, black-finned. Many organisms are given names for the locality where they were found; thus *Carcharhinus amboinensis* was named for the island of Ambon in Indonesia. Others honor individuals, an example being the Tiger Shark (*Galeocerdo cuvier*), named for the famous French zoologist Baron Georges Cuvier. Usually a patronym (as such names are called) ends with *i* if honouring a man and *ae* if honouring a woman.

The systematic part of this book (commencing on p. 67) is organized in the traditional hierarchical system in biology: class, order, family, genus, and species. The class for sharks, rays, and chimaeras is Chondrichthyes (meaning cartilaginous fishes). This is divided into major groupings called orders; the ordinal names end in *iformes* (an example, the Carcharhiniformes). The orders in turn divide into families, the names of which end in *idae* (hence Carcharhinidae). Within a family in this work the genera are arranged alphabetically, as are the species within a genus. The most important characteristics (also called characters) of each family are given under the heading Diagnosis. These characteristics apply to all species in the family (though exceptions may be noted) and are usually not repeated in species diagnoses.

The species accounts are headed by the English common name in boldface type. Below this, the scientific name in italics, followed by the name of the person or persons who described the shark and the date of the description (the complete reference for each author is given

Silvertip Shark
Carcharhinus albimarginatus
Photo J. Randall

in the bibliography at the end of the book). When the name of the author or authors of a species is placed in parentheses, it means that he, she, or they used a different generic name in the original description. Species accounts are divided into Diagnosis and Remarks, the latter for geographic distribution, information (when known) on food habits, reproduction, etc., listing of invalid scientific names that have been in recent use (when a name is given to an organism that is already described, it is called a synonym and cannot be used), and other remarks such as how dangerous the species might be to man. Every species is illustrated, mostly from the author's photographs. Because teeth are so important in identification, these are also figured for most species. A Glossary of technical terms is given after the systematic section.

Sharks have proven difficult to identify, even by well-trained ichthyologists. Bony fishes have many features which can be counted: the spines and rays of the various fins, the scales in different series, gill rakers, vertebrae, and teeth. For sharks there are just the vertebrae (counts of which require laborious dissection or x-rays) and teeth. The form of sharks, in general, is similar from species to species. Most bony fishes exhibit distinctive colour patterns, whereas sharks are often uniformly coloured. Still another problem is the availability of specimens for study. Because many species of sharks are large in size, they are often not preserved, or just the head or jaws are retained for museums.

Only in recent years have definitive monographic studies been completed of various groups of sharks, notably those of the carcharhinid genera *Scoliodon*, *Loxodon*, and *Rhizoprionodon* by V.G. Springer (1964), the Hammerhead Sharks (Sphyrnidae) by C.R. Gilbert (1967), the Bullhead Sharks (Heterodontidae) by Taylor (1972), the large triakid genus *Mustelus* by Heemstra (1973), the Catsharks (Scyliorhinidae) by S. Springer (1979), the Requiem Sharks (*Carcharhinus*) by Garrick (1982), and the Bamboo Sharks (Hemiscyllidae) by Dingerkus and DeFino (1983). Among regional investigations, the monumental shark volume of *Fishes of the Western North America* by Bigelow and Schroeder (1948) and the excellent series of papers by Bass et al. (1973-1976) on sharks of the east coast of southern Africa are noteworthy. And finally, mention should be made of the recent papers on shark classification by Compagno (1970-1981), culminating in his *Sharks of the World* (1984a,b). Without all these studies the present book could not have been written.

Prior to the systematic section, chapters are presented which summarize the evolutionary history of sharks, the anatomy of sharks and how this relates to function, and the importance of sharks to man.

Oceanic Whitetip Shark
Carcharhinus longimanus
Photo by Chris Newbert

FORM AND FUNCTION

University courses in comparative anatomy traditionally devote an early laboratory to the dissection of a shark – usually the Spiny Dogfish (*Squalus acanthias*). This provides a basic introduction to the morphology of a generalized vertebrate. It is also fundamental to discussions of evolution. The student begins to comprehend the concept of homology when he perceives the similarity in the structure of the early mammalian embryo to a shark. The gill slits, multiple aortic arches, and simple heart (one auricle and one ventricle) of the developing mammal are much like these features in the adult shark. He learns that the spiracle of the shark, itself a vestige of a gill opening of an ancestral fish-like vertebrate, is homologous to the eustachian tube of mammals; also that structures like the tiny bones of the middle ear and the thyroid cartilages of mammals are derivatives of primitive jaws and gill arches.

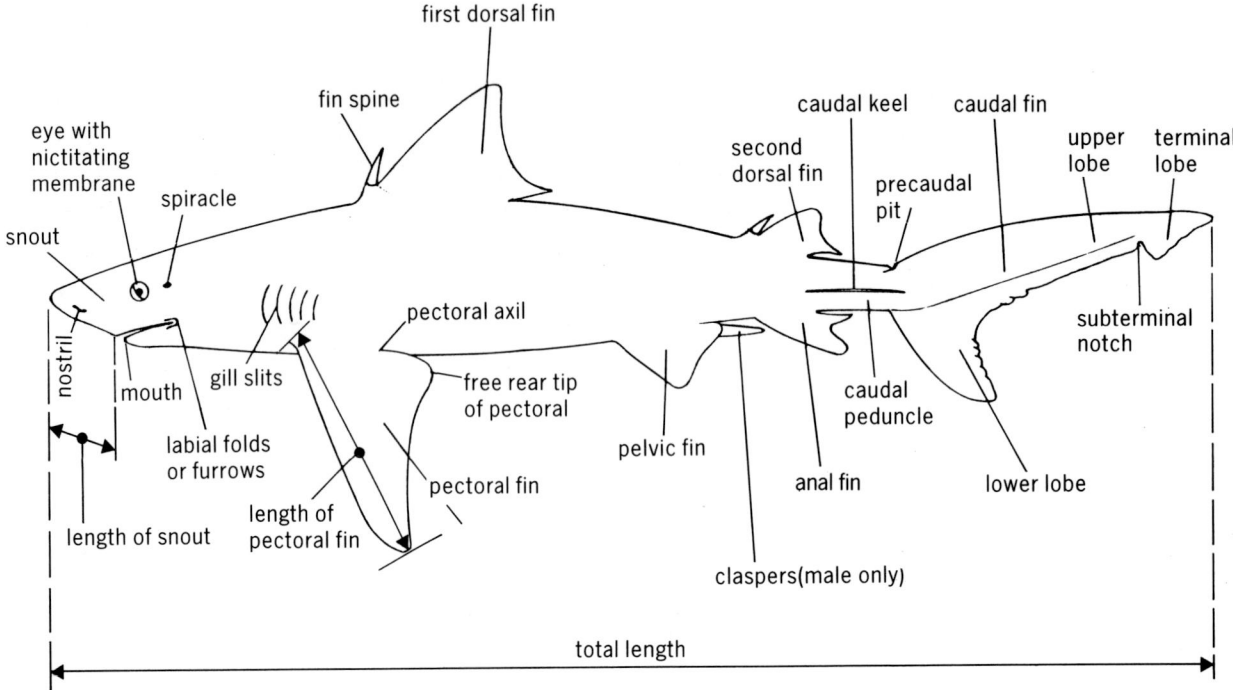

External Anatomy

Figures 1 and 2 provide the names of the principal external features of a composite shark. It is necessary to know this terminology to be able to understand the diagnoses given to differentiate the species which are presented in the systematic section of this book. Also shown are the way measurements are taken for total length, preoral length of snout, and pectoral fin length. Not diagramed are the heights of the dorsal and anal fins; these are measured vertically from the fin apex to the fin base.

Figure 1
A composite shark to show the principal external parts and measurements (after Castro, 1983, slightly modified).

FORM AND FUNCTION

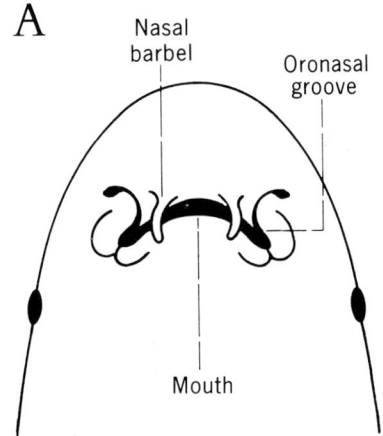

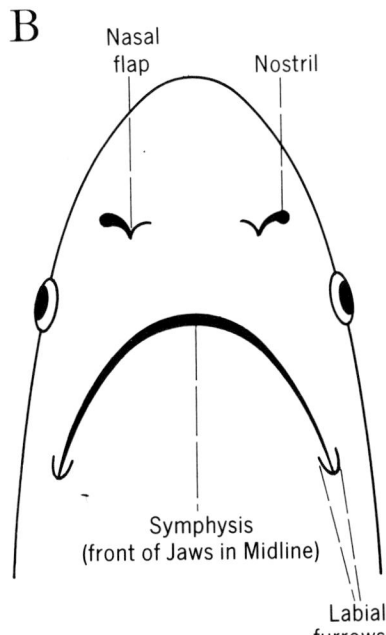

Figure 2
Underside of anterior part of heads of sharks to show mouth and nostrils. A. Nurse Shark B. Requiem Shark (drawing by Helen A. Randall).

Shark workers relate the body and fin measurements to total length (in contrast to ichthyologists studying bony fishes who use standard length, i.e. the length from the tip of the snout to the base of the caudal fin). This is unfortunate because not all measure total length in the same way. Some measure with a tape of the curvature of the shark, others in a straight horizontal plane (adopted here). Some measure to the distal end of the caudal fin after pulling the upper lobe down to the horizontal axis of the body, others by leaving the caudal fin in the normal position. The latter is used by the author as it can be more accurately compared to photographs or drawings of sharks.

Fins

Free-swimming vertebrates have fins for propulsion, stabilizing, steering, and braking. It is interesting to note the similarity in the fins which have independently evolved in fishes, certain extinct reptiles such as *Ichthyosaurus*, and cetaceans. The caudal fin provides the forward thrust (whether vertically oriented as in fishes or horizontally as in whales and porpoises). This fin of sharks is of the heterocercal type; the vertebral column is bent upward into the upper lobe which is longer than the lower (most bony fishes have a homocercal tail which is externally symmetrical above and below). The standard explanation of the locomotion of a shark involves a balance of forces forward and behind the center of gravity. Because of the longer upper lobe, the thrust of a shark's caudal fin has a downward as well as a forward component which imparts a lift to the tail. This would tend to depress the head during swimming were it not for the widely spread and slightly inclined pectoral fins and the inclined flattened lower part of the snout which counterbalance the tail lift. Thomson and Simanek (1977), however, have shown that there is also a rotation of the tail and an effect of the lower lobe which aid in bringing the different forces into balance. The upper lobe of the caudal fin of a few sharks, notably the Mackerel Sharks (Lamnidae), is only slightly larger than the lower. The lamnids swim differently from other sharks. Instead of the long sinuous movement of the body and wide sweep of the caudal fin, the body is stiffer, and there are rapid short lateral movements of the tail, much like the locomotion of the tunas and mackerels. Like the scombrid fishes, these sharks have a need to strengthen the narrow caudal peduncle and base of the caudal fin with a horizontal keel (or in some, two keels). Most sharks have a small triangular terminal lobe at the end of the upper lobe of the caudal fin. Many have a distinct notch at the juncture of the caudal fin and the caudal peduncle termed the precaudal pit; there may be one in front of the lower lobe as well as the upper, though the upper one is more distinct.

The dorsal fins (and anal fin when present) counteract rolling and lateral movement from tail thrusts. Most sharks have two dorsal fins. On some there is a narrow median ridge on the back between these two fins which is called the interdorsal ridge; it is a useful character in the classification of the large genus *Carcharhinus*. *Heterodontus* and many of the squalid sharks have a stout spine at the front of each dorsal fin; these spines are venomous in at least some species. The pectoral fins of bony fishes function for steering and braking. In sharks they are held to the side and serve as horizontal stabilizers and provide lift as mentioned above. The pelvic fins are relatively unimportant in swimming (cetaceans have nothing comparable) but aid in stabilizing and perhaps in steering. In male sharks they are modified along their medial edge into claspers, the intromittent organ of these fishes.

The fins of sharks are supported by parallel rods of cartilage, those most proximal are called basals and more distally radials; in the outer more flexible part of the fin the support is from the slender, fibrous, ceratotrichia.

Skin

The rough texture of the skin of sharks is due to the presence of small dermal denticles (or placoid 'scales'). These are not broadly overlapping like the typical scales of bony fishes. They are like small teeth, the main mass being dentine with an inner pulp cavity and a hard outer layer of vitrodentine or enameloid (because the vitrodentine is epidermal in origin, in contrast to the dermal derivation of the rest of these structures, dermal denticle should more properly be called cutaneous denticles). These scales appear to be remnants of the bony armor of ancestral fish-like vertebrates. They are often distinctive in shape and may be useful in species identification. Figure 3 shows the dermal denticles of the Bull Shark. The scales function as protection (sharks, in general, are more resistant to injury than bony fishes because of their tough hide); this includes protection against external parasites as well. On a few sharks such as the Angelsharks (*Squatina*) and Swell Shark (*Cephaloscyllium uter*) the denticles are well-spaced and sharp and probably serve as a deterrent to predators. A hydrodynamic function has also been suggested for the dermal denticles of sharks, minimizing the friction of the current flow past the skin. One reason for the toughness of the

Figure 3
Dermal denticles of the Bull Shark (*Carcharhinus leucas*) (after Bigelow and Schroeder, 1948).

skin of sharks is its role in locomotion. The outer muscles are strongly attached to the skin which acts as an overall external tendon transmitting a major part of the muscular force to the tail. The elasticity of the skin also contributes to the propulsive force. When the contracted muscles of the concave side of the body relax, the stored energy in the strongly stretched skin on the convex side is released, thus accelerating the unbending. Wainwright, Vosburgh, and Hebrank (1978) found that the internal hydrostatic pressure of a shark increases more than tenfold from slow to fast swimming. When the pressure is higher, it stresses the skin, causing it to become stiffer. In this form it is better able to transmit the force of the stronger muscular contractions of fast swimming.

Compared to bony fishes, in general, sharks are surprisingly drab in colour. A typical colour description reads: grey or brown above, shading to whitish below, without markings. When there are markings, they are usually in shades of black or white. Chromatic colours are rare in sharks, though Makos (*Isurus*) and the Blue Shark (*Prionace glauca*) are blue on the back; olivaceous or yellowish hues are not uncommon in some groups.

The skin of sharks is the site of the lateralis system, the pit organs, and the ampullae of Lorenzini. The lateralis system of sharks (and bony fishes) consists of a complex of canals on the head and one along the side of the body with pores connecting to the surface. Neuromasts in the canals are the receptors of low frequency vibrations, thus enabling fishes to detect an object at some distance either by a reflection of the movements of the receptor fish from the object or of the object's movements if it is in motion. A pit organ is a bud-like structure containing a neuromast; it is located between the bases of two modified dermal denticles. Most, if not all, sharks have a pair of these organs in front of each endolymphatic pore on the top of the head, a row across the ventral part of the head behind the mouth, another transverse row near the base of each pectoral fin, and in a variable pattern on the body; usually there is a single row above the lateral line or a broad scattering dorsally on the body (Tester and Nelson in Gilbert et al., 1967). Dijkgraaf (1963) has hypothesized that the pit organs act together with the canal neuromasts to locate objects away from the shark. Since canal neuromasts can respond only through pressure changes communicated via the pores from the surface, the neuromasts of pit organs could receive a different response depending on the orientation of the movements. The ampullae of Lorenzini are sac-like structures that link to the surface through tubules filled with a viscous jelly-like substance. The ampullae contain sensory cells which are innervated by about five afferent nerve fibers of the facial nerve. They are found over the head of all elasmobranch fishes. Although the ampullae are sensitive to mechanical, thermal, and salinity stimuli, it is their role as electroreceptors that is the most important. Experiments have shown that elasmobranchs are able to located prey entirely by detection of the bioelectric fields of these animals. Also it has been shown that some of these fishes can orient with respect to the earth's magnetic field, thus aiding them in migrations (Kalmijn in Gilbert et al., 1967).

Equilibrium Organ

In sharks this consists of three semicircular canals (as in higher vertebrates), joined ventrally to three sacs, the utriculus, sacculus, and lagena; it is protected by the cartilage of the otic capsule. Each semicircular canal lies in a different plane, each at right angles to the other two. Each is filled with endolymphatic fluid; in an enlargement (ampulla) there is a patch of sensory epithelium called the crista. The sensory cells of the cristae have cilia which project into a small mass of mucus. Acceleration by the shark will cause the endolymphatic fluid in the canal of the plane of movement to shift, pulling the mucus with it, and stimulating the sensory nerve endings linked to the cilia. The utriculus, sacculus, and lagena each have a large concretion of calcium carbonate, the lapillus, sagitta, and astericus, respectively, better known collectively as otoliths. The otoliths are in contact with a sensory area called a macula. The otoliths stimulate the maculae from the effect of gravity or accelerations. In sharks there is a narrow passage, the endolymphatic duct, which runs from between sacculus and utriculus to the exterior on top of the head (this duct is closed in bony fishes). Experiments have shown that the sacculus and lagena are involved with hearing as well as equilibrium (though not with the refinement of birds and mammals which have a cochlea in the inner ear, a structure lacking in fishes, amphibians, and reptiles).

The otoliths of fishes gradually enlarge peripherally with growth; thus external rings are laid down which are comparable to the rings of a tree trunk. These rings have been used in many bony fishes to assist in age determination, particularly in areas of large seasonal variation in water temperature where the growth rate may vary greatly from summer to winter. The otoliths of sharks have not proven useful in ageing, but sections of vertebrae of some sharks have (see, for example, Tanaka and Mizue, 1979).

Eye

The eye of sharks is basically the same as other vertebrates with cornea, iris, lens, retina, etc. It tends to be more compressed laterally. It can vary from 1% of the total length (in adult *Ginglymostoma*) to as much as 10% (in deep-sea squaloids). The lens is spherical, as in bony fishes, because it must account for most of the refraction. In terrestrial animals the cornea is the main refracting element (in humans it takes care of 75% of the refraction) but in a liquid medium the refraction of the cornea is greatly limited. The pupil shape of sharks is highly variable, from circular to slit-like in different directions (i.e. horizontal, vertical, or diagonal). Unlike nearly all bony fishes, sharks are able to control the size of the pupil with the iris. Pupillary response is slow in most sharks but relatively rapid in a few (less than a minute for the complete response in *Carcharhinus*) (Gruber, 1977). Contrary to early reports, the retina of sharks can have cones as well as rods, and some species are believed to have colour vision. The shark eye is remarkable for the highly developed tapetum lucidum (the most efficient in the animal kingdom). The inner portion of the choroid layer of the eye next to the retina has been modified to form the tapetum, a strongly reflecting silvery surface due to the presence of tiny platelets containing crystals of guanine. When light is bright, melanin from a pigment cell at the base of each platelet masks the tapetum. When light is dim, it is reflected back from the tapetum, stimulating the retina a second time. When diving at night with a light, the diver's first awareness of the shark near the limit of visibility is the reflection of light from its eyes like those of a cat.

Many sharks have an eyelid, the nictitating membrane, which is strong and opaque and serves to protect the eye from injury. The Great White Shark (*Carcharodon carcharias*) lacks a nictitating membrane but protects its eyes by rolling the eyeballs backward as it strikes its prey (McCosker, 1981).

Nostrils

The paired nostrils of sharks are found on the underside of the snout near the front. They may be partially covered by a nasal flap. In some groups such as *Heterodontus*, Orectolobidae, and Hemiscyllidae, there is a deep oronasal groove linking the nostrils to the mouth, and some such as the orectolobids and hemiscyllids have a barbel extending from the medial edge of the nostril to the mouth. The olfactory organ of most sharks, however, lies in a blind sac. It consists of lamellae covered with olfactory epithelium. As indicated by the large olfactory bulbs and lobes of the shark brain, the olfactory sense is very acute.

Gill Slits

These consist of a series of vertical to near-vertical openings posteriorly on each side of the head. Except for the five species of the order Hexanchiformes and the Sawshark (*Pliotrema*) which have six or seven pairs of gill slits, all sharks have five pairs of such openings. These function in respiration as exits for the water that is drawn into the mouth and over the gill surfaces for gaseous exchange. The slits can vary from about 1% of the total length in some squalids to the full height of the head in the Basking Shark (*Cetorhinus maximus*). The latter and the Whale Shark (*Rhincodon typus*), the two largest species of sharks, use their gill slits also for filter-feeding; they have a screening mechanism over the internal gill openings.

Spiracle

This is a rudimentary gill opening which is found behind or below the eye in most elasmobranchs. It has been lost mainly in the most active, fast-swimming species. Even when it is very reduced, it has a small patch of gill filaments (hemibranch); aerated blood from the gills passes through these supplementary capillaries before going in a separate blood vessel to the eye and brain. The spiracle is large on some benthic sharks and on rays and skates. It serves as the incurrent opening for respiratory water instead of the mouth (which in these fishes is ventral and often buried in sediment).

Mouth

The mouth of the great majority of living sharks lies ventrally on the head, the snout overhanging anteriorly. Ancient sharks such as the long-extinct *Cladoselache* seem to have had a terminal mouth. Higher forms may have developed the ventral mouth for benthic feeding. As evolution proceeded, the mouth may have remained ventral even though some sharks diverged to feed on midwater and surface prey. That the overhanging snout is not an impediment to midwater feeding may be seen in the analysis of feeding behaviour of the Great White Shark (*Carcharodon carcharias*) by Tricas and McCosker (1984). An elevation of 30° to 40° of the snout above the horizontal axis of the body at the time of biting results in the gaping mouth approaching the terminal position. Also, the anterior snout still serves for streamlining, an anterior planing surface, and sensory functions. By being anterior to the mouth, the nostrils sample the environment directly in front of the mouth (in contrast to bony fishes where the nares are dorsally on the snout). The electroreceptors of sharks are also ventroanteriorly on the snout, thus providing a similar advantageous position in locating prey (Moss, 1977). The jaws of modern sharks have lost the direct connection to the chondrocranium (braincase), articulating posteriorly through the hyomandibular cartilage. This has allowed for jaw protrusion and a shortening of the jaws for a stronger bite (see following section on Evolutionary History). The mouth of sharks varies from a parabolic curve to nearly transversely straight and from moderately small to very large. Often there are grooves at the corner of the mouth which are termed labial furrows.

Teeth

The teeth of sharks are actually modified, enlarged dermal denticles, and the structure is basically the same, with a pulp cavity, dentine, and thin layer of hard, enamel-like vitrodentine. In contrast to the relatively homogeneous body form of the majority of sharks, the teeth exhibit a wide variety of size and shape. They can be sharp-edged and blade-like, with or without serrate edges (hence adapted for shearing or sawing pieces from large prey), long and raptorial (well-suited for seizing smaller slippery prey), or molariform (for crushing molluscs and other hard-shelled invertebrates). Some sharks have sharp teeth anteriorly and blunt crushing teeth posteriorly. The pointed projection of the crown of a typical tooth is called the cusp. Some species have teeth with one or more lateral small cusps (or cusplets). A few, such as the Six-Gill Shark (*Hexanchus*), have a row of cusps on a single tooth. Shark's teeth do not have roots, but the basal part is broadly attached in the jaws. Nevertheless, the teeth of sharks are relatively easily detached, and not infrequently those of the larger dangerous species are found in their human victims or imbedded in the wooden hulls of boats they have attacked. The teeth of many species are sufficiently characteristic that the identity of a shark can be determined from even a single tooth. Sharks have numerous rows of replacement teeth along the inner jaw margins behind the front teeth. As front teeth are lost, others move into place from behind. Species with small teeth usually have more than one functional row in the jaws. The number of teeth in the outer row in the jaws is also of importance in the identification of a species.

Respiratory System

The mouth of sharks, as in other vertebrates, leads to the buccal cavity and thence to the pharynx. For respiration, water is taken in through the mouth (except for those mentioned above that utilize the spiracle for this purpose) by a pumping action of the pharyngeal and branchial musculature. The intake of water is the result of the expansion of the pharynx with the mouth open and the gill slits closed; the mouth then closes, the pharynx is constricted, and the gill slits open for the release of excurrent water. The gills are supported by the gill arches which consist of five linearly conjoined rods of cartilage having the names, from dorsally to ventrally, of pharyngobranchial, epibranchial, ceratobranchial, hypobranchial, and basibranchial. The epibranchials and ceratobranchials bear the gills. The gills comprise numerous parallel gill lamellae; these are highly vascularized membranes where oxygen is taken up from and carbon dioxide released to the passing water. In sharks the gill lamellae are closely attached to the gill septum, a sheet of supportive connective tissue extending from the gill arch, only the distal ends being free (elasmobranch means 'plate gill'). By contrast, the gill lamellae of bony fishes are largely free from the septum. Respiration and feeding in fishes are closely linked. The suction used for the intake of water for respiration is also employed to engulf prey, although more strongly than during normal respiration. This type of feeding is especially well-developed in the Nurse Sharks (*Ginglymostoma* and *Nebrius*). The earliest archaic fish-like vertebrates are believed to have used the gill system for filter feeding as well as respiration. Secondarily, many Recent bony fishes and a few sharks have developed gill rakers on which to strain zooplankton from the water as it passes through the pharynx and gill chambers.

Digestive System

Food from the mouth goes through the pharynx and esophagus to the stomach in sharks as in most other vertebrates (in some teleost fishes the stomach is secondarily lost). The stomach of sharks is J-shaped, the lower part of the J curving to the left. The large upper part of the stomach is called the cardiac region and the narrow posterior part the pyloric region which ends in the pyloric valve at the entrance to the intestine. The stomach of sharks is very large. Like other large carnivores, sharks feed infrequently (one finds the stomach empty more often than with food). However, when they do capture a prey animal, they generally make a big meal of it. For this they need a capacious stomach. The intestine of elasmobranch fishes is very different from that of bony fishes and higher vertebrates. It contains the spiral valve, giving it a structure like an enclosed spiral staircase (Figure 4). In the Requiem Sharks (Carcharhinidae) and

Figure 4
Spiral valve of the Spiny Dogfish (*Squalus acanthias*) (after Jammes, from Storer and Usinger, 1965).

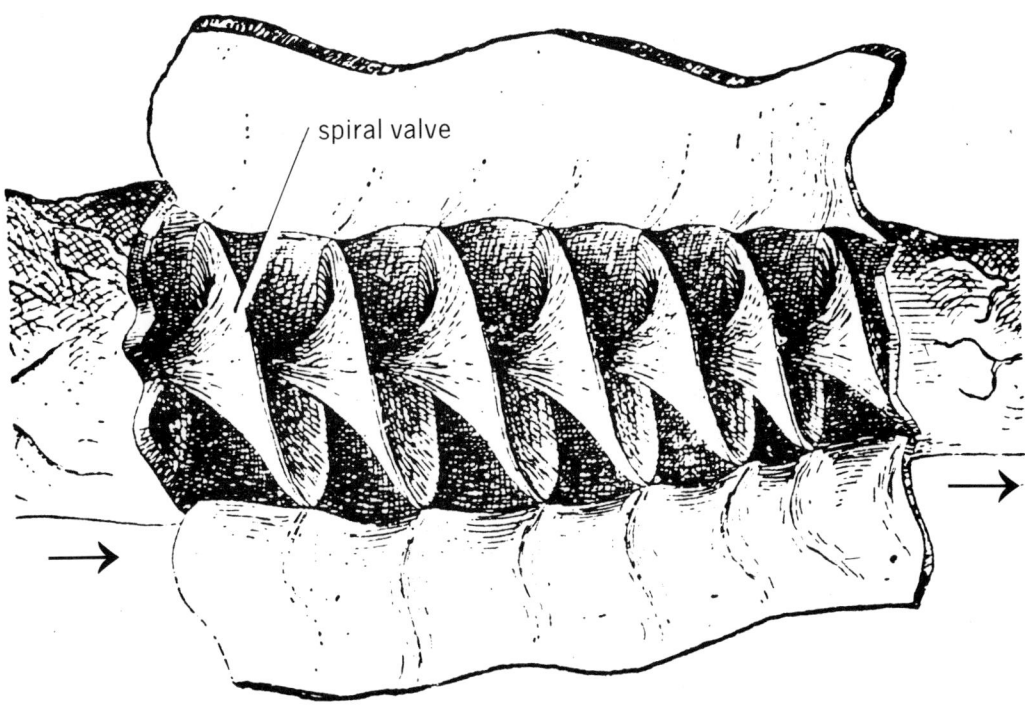

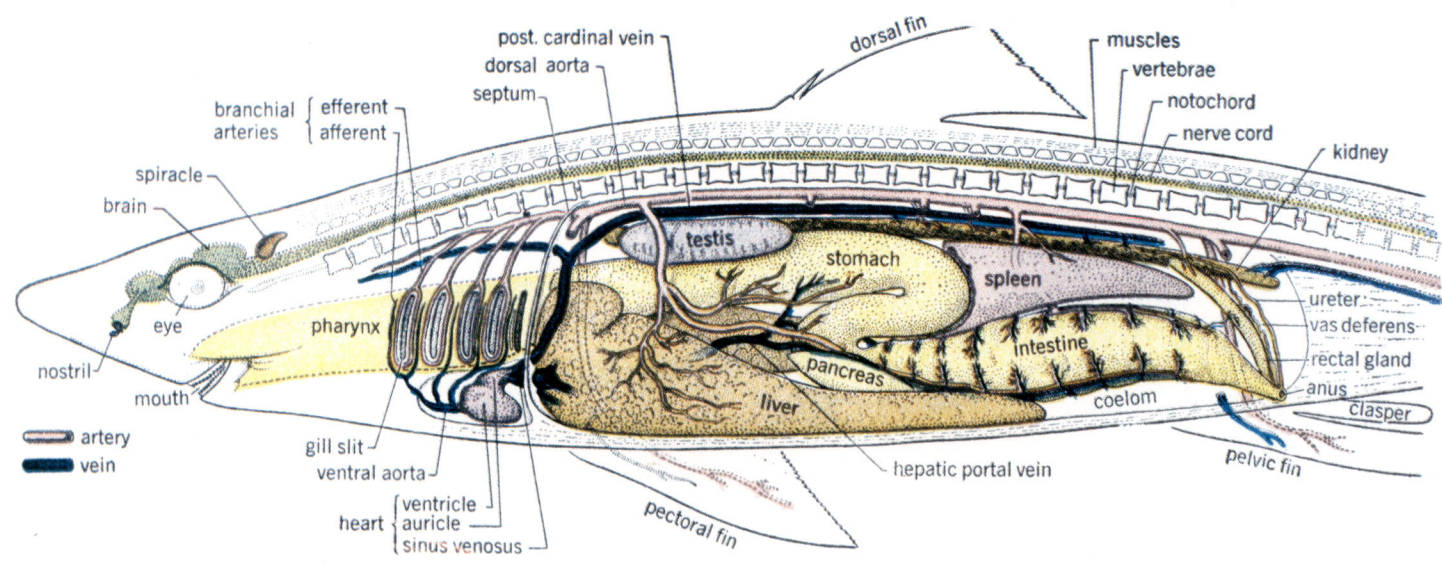

Figure 5
Internal structure of the Spiny Dogfish (*Squalus acanthias*) (after Storer and Usinger, 1965).

Hammerheads (Sphyrnidae) the valvular intestine has a different form, referred to as the scroll type in that it resembles a scroll rolled up on itself within the intestine. The spiral valve serves the same purpose as the long convoluted intestine of higher vertebrates: increasing the absorptive surface and allowing for a longer time for the food to pass through the intestinal tract. There is a disadvantage to the spiral valve, however. Large pieces of indigestible material such as squid beaks or mollusc shell fragments cannot pass through this type of intestine. They can go through the simple tubular intestine of bony fishes, which has a greater capacity for expansion. Sharks overcome this problem by regurgitating the indigestible parts. For telemetering the movements of a shark, Nelson (1974) has concealed a transmitter in a dead fish which is fed to the shark. After the fish is digested, the transmitter is regurgitated (if this takes place in shallow water, the transmitter can then be recovered). The spiral valve leads to the posterior part of the intestine which ends in the anus. The anus empties into an external cavity called the cloaca where the urinary and genital tracts also terminate. When one opens the body cavity of a shark, the largest and most conspicuous organ is the liver (Figure 5); it is generally reddish to olivaceous brown. It can account for as much as 25% of the total weight of a shark.

Among the many functions of the liver in vertebrates are: the secretion of bile which aids in fat digestion; the storage of excess sugar in the form of glycogen; the storage of fats; the production of proteins; the utilization of proteins as food through the deaminization of amino acids, resulting in the formation of urea; the destruction of worn-out red blood cells; and the detoxification of certain poisons. In sharks it has a very important hydrostatic function. The large amount of oily substance in a shark's liver decreases its overall specific gravity, thus partially offsetting the weight of the denser tissues such as calcified cartilage. Bony fishes have solved this problem very differently by the development of the gas bladder. The large size of the shark liver is of special importance in food storage in view of the long time between meals. Gohar and Mazhar (1964a,b) reported a pregnant female Whitetip Reef Shark (*Triaenodon obesus*) which survived six weeks in an enclosure without food. The relative weight of its liver had reduced to 46 g/kg body weight compared to 80 g for free-living sharks of this species. The pancreas of sharks is a triangular pale reddish bilobed organ lying next to the cardiac portion of the stomach with a duct to the anterior part of the intestine. It has well known digestive and endocrine functions. Other organs apparent within the body cavity of a shark are the deep red spleen, which is part of the lymphatic system, and the small slender rectal gland which excretes excess sodium chloride.

Circulatory System

The heart of fishes lies in the pericardial cavity which is ventral in the thoracic region (anterior to the pectoral fins). It consists of two principal chambers, the thin-walled auricle (or atrium) and the more ventrally located thick-walled ventricle. The blood leaving the heart from the contractions of the ventricle passes into the short muscular conus arteriosus which has valves to prevent it from re-entering the ventricle. It then moves anteriorly into the large ventral aorta which immediately gives off five pairs of lateral aortic arches (branchial arteries) which ascend to the gill region. These afferent arteries divide to arterioles and ultimately to capillaries in the gills for the uptake of oxygen and release of carbon dioxide. The oxygenated blood of sharks collects in a pair of efferent vessels in each gill arch (in bony fishes there is only a single efferent artery). One efferent vessel from the first gill arch passes to the hemibranch in the spiracle where still more oxygen is added; as mentioned, it is this blood which serves the eyes and brain. The other efferent arteries join to form the dorsal aorta which sends internal carotid arteries into the head but otherwise courses posteriorly in the dorsal part of the coelom (body cavity), giving off major branches: the subclavian arteries to the pectoral fins, the coeliac to the digestive system, the anterior mesenteric to the spleen, the posterior mesenteric to the rectal gland, several renal and gonadal arteries to the urogenital system, and the paired iliacs to the pelvic fins; the dorsal aorta then continues into the tail as the caudal artery. After serving all the organs and tissues in capillary networks, the blood collects in veins. It passes from the caudal vein to paired renal portal veins to the kidneys. Other lesser veins posteriorly collect to the postcardinal veins (which parallel the kidneys) and the lateral abdominal veins on each side of the body cavity. Venous blood from the head region is returned to the heart via the jugular and anterior cardinal veins. Blood from the digestive tract is carried to the liver in the hepatic portal vein where it breaks into capillaries for removal of sugar, etc. Blood from the liver passes to the heart via the hepatic veins. All these large veins (except the portals mentioned above) drain to sinuses which enter the large sinus venosus; it in turn delivers the venous blood to the auricle just below it.

Urogenital System

Because the excretory and reproductive systems of sharks are so closely associated, they are generally discussed together. The kidneys of sharks are long, slender, dark red organs which lie in the upper part of the body cavity, one on each side of the dorsal aorta. Kidneys must be functional early in development because the growing embryo is accumulating metabolic wastes. In the early embryo paired nephric units develop for each of a few anterior trunk segments; waste is removed from the coelomic cavity via peritoneal funnels, then passes posteriorly in the pronephric duct (formed from the fusion of nephric tubules) to the cloaca. This early kidney is termed the pronephros. It is soon replaced in the embryo with a more posterior kidney called the mesonephros ('middle kidney') and the same duct is now called the mesonephric duct (also known as Wolffian duct). In adult fishes this duct is often referred to as the ureter. Strictly speaking, it should not be, as it is not homologous to the ureter of higher vertebrates. For the same reason the kidney of adult sharks is more properly called the opisthonephros. Romer (1949) has proposed that the 'ureter' of adults of lower vertebrates be called the archinephric duct. Initially the mesonephros develops as a pair of tubules per segment, like the pronephros, but many more tubules are added. The later tubules lack the peritoneal funnels; they develop the renal corpuscle (or Malphigian body) which is the functional excretory unit of the kidney of adult fishes (and of the metanephric kidney of adults of higher vertebrates). A knot of capillaries called the glomerulus releases fluid of the blood (but not blood cells) by filtration pressure to the encapsulating Bowman's capsule which leads to tubules where essential elements of the fluid are reabsorbed, leaving the rest to pass out as urine.

The urine of sharks contains little urea. Sharks are unique in retaining a high percentage of urea in their blood and tissue fluids (2.0 to 2.5% compared to 0.01 to 0.03% for other vertebrates). They maintain this high concentration (and one of chloride) to overcome the osmotic problem that marine organisms have whose body fluids are hypotonic to seawater. Otherwise they would lose water over membranous surfaces, such as the gills, to the sea. Marine bony fishes combat this osmotic problem by oral intake of seawater and active excretion of the salt by special cells in the gills.

The testes of sharks are elongate, cylindrical, and whitish; they are located dorsoanteriorly in the body cavity. In many species they are found at the anterior end of the epigonal organ, the function of which is believed to be the formation of blood cells. The spermatozoa are produced in a multitude of seminiferous tubules in the testes. The anterior part of the shark kidney is not as well developed as the posterior. The testes of young sharks develop at this site, appropriating kidney tubules for sperm transport (becoming ductuli efferentes) to the archinephric duct and modifying kidney tissue for the production of spermatic fluid. That part of the archinephric duct devoted only to the genital system is now called the ductus deferens (old name, vas deferens) which becomes very convoluted in mature males. Posteriorly the archinephric duct serves both the excretory and male reproductive systems. In many sharks the duct is taken over entirely for sperm transport, the posterior part modified as the enlarged, straight, seminal vesicle which terminates in the sperm sac. The two sperm sacs unite to form the urogenital sinus which also receives the urine from an accessory urinary duct that develops for these sharks. The urogenital sinus opens to the cloaca in the urogenital papilla. The testes of elasmobranchs vary greatly in size with the species. Also they become larger in the breeding season. During mating the claspers of male sharks are bent forward, and one is inserted into the cloaca of the female to effect sperm transfer. This is aided by the action of the pair of siphon sacs which lie under the skin ventral to the base of the pelvic fins. The duct of each of these sacs empties proximally into the base of the clasper groove. The contraction of the siphon sac during copulation produces a current which forces sperm through the clasper groove. Females often bear scars from bites inflicted by males during courtship, particularly on the pectoral fins.

The ovaries of sharks are also in an anterior position in the body cavity, dorsal to the liver and digestive tract. They are small and smooth in immature females, but larger and with rounded protrusions (from the developing ova) on the surface in adults. Some sharks have only a single ovary which is at the anterior end of the long epigonal organ. Ova in various stages of development may be seen within the connective tissue of the ovary; each ovum is surrounded by a layer of nutritive cells called the follicle. When an ovum is ripe, it is discharged into the coelom by the rupture of the follicle. It is conveyed anteriorly by the action of ciliary tracts in the coelomic wall to the ostium, the ciliated funnel-shaped opening of the oviduct. In contrast to males, there is no connection between the kidneys and the female reproductive system. The archinephric duct of the embryonic shark divides longitudinally into two ducts, one of which continues to receive the waste material from the mesonephric tubules. The other is vestigial in males but becomes the oviduct (also known as Müllerian duct) of females. Its anterior end is expanded to form the ostium which develops from modified peritoneal funnels of the embryo. The oviducts are long; the posterior end of each is enlarged to form the uterus. The two uteri are united posteriorly and end at the cloaca. Near the anterior end of the oviduct is an enlargement known as the shell gland. Albuminous material is secreted around the egg in the upper part of the shell gland and the egg case in its lower part. After the female is inseminated, the sperm travel up the oviduct and fertilize the ova before they receive the layering in the shell gland.

Figure 6
A. Egg case of a Bullhead Shark (*Heterodontus*). B. Egg case of a scyliorhinid shark (after Castro, 1983).

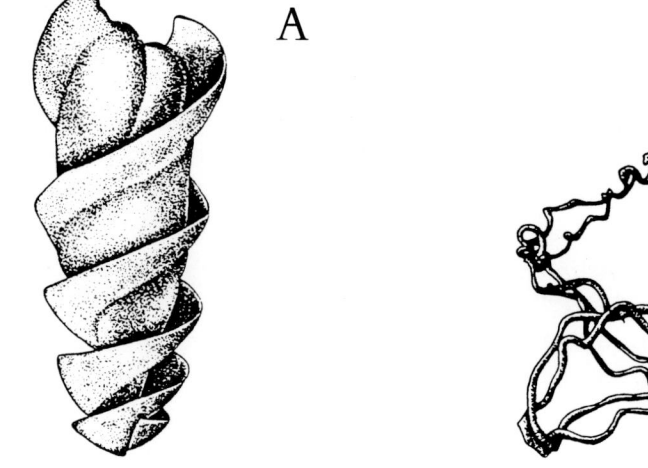

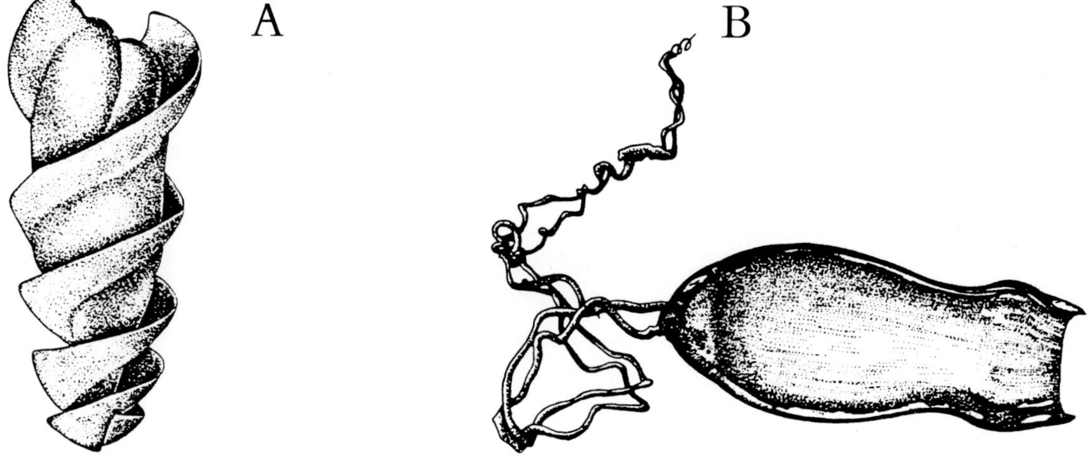

FORM AND FUNCTION

The following families of sharks have at least some species which are oviparous, i.e. they lay eggs which develop outside the female parent: the Bullhead Sharks (Heterodontidae), the Variegated Shark family (Stegostomatidae), the Collared Carpet Sharks (Parascyllidae), the Bamboo Sharks (Hemiscyllidae), the Catsharks (Scyliorhinidae), and possibly the Whale Shark family (Rhincodontidae). The eggs are large and well-supplied with yolk. They have tendrils with which they may become attached to objects on the bottom. When laid they are soft and light-coloured, but the shell hardens to a leathery texture and darkens after a few hours in the sea. The eggs of *Heterodontus* are shaped like a conical spiral (Figure 6A); those of scyliorhinids are rounded at one end, truncate to emarginate at the other and broadly oval in cross-section (Figure 6B).

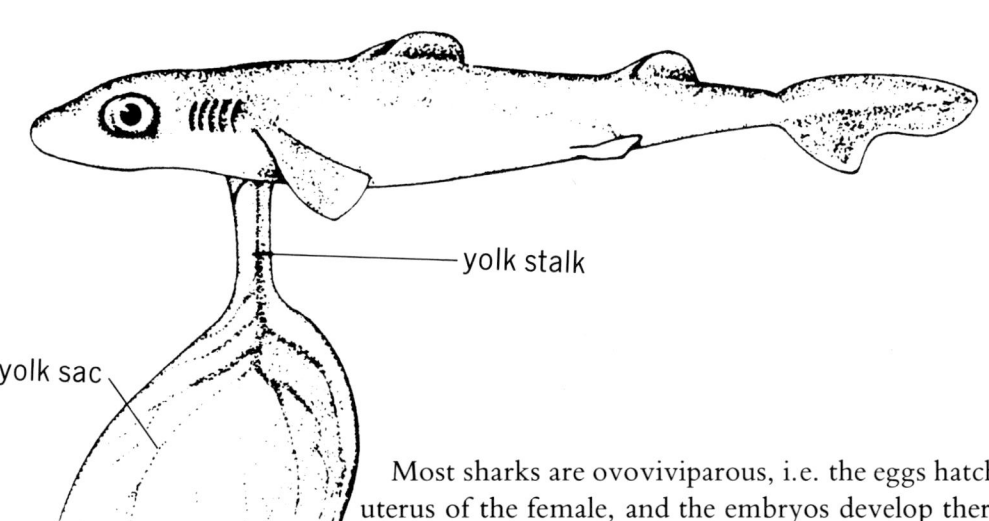

Figure 7
Typical embryo of an ovoviviparous shark (after Castro, 1983).

Most sharks are ovoviviparous, i.e. the eggs hatch within the uterus of the female, and the embryos develop there without a placental connection with the mother. Nourishment is provided after hatching by the large yolk sac that hangs down, pendulum-like on a narrow yolk stalk from the thoracic region (Figure 7). The developing embryos of most, if not all, of the lamniform sharks, such as the Sand Tiger Sharks (Odontaspididae), Mackerel Sharks (Lamnidae), and Thresher Sharks (Alopiidae) are oophagus after their reserve of yolk is used. They feed on other ova in the uterus or on their smaller litter mates as well (hence uterine cannibalism). Usually there is only one surviving pup in each uterus.

The Requiem Sharks (Carcharhinidae), the Hammerhead Sharks (Sphyrnidae), and some of the Houndsharks (Triakidae) have viviparous development, meaning there is a direct umbilical attachment from the developing embryo to the uterine wall of the mother after the yolk of the egg is utilized or that the uterus secretes nutritive fluid which is absorbed by the branched yolk stalks of the embryo.

SHARKS OF ARABIA

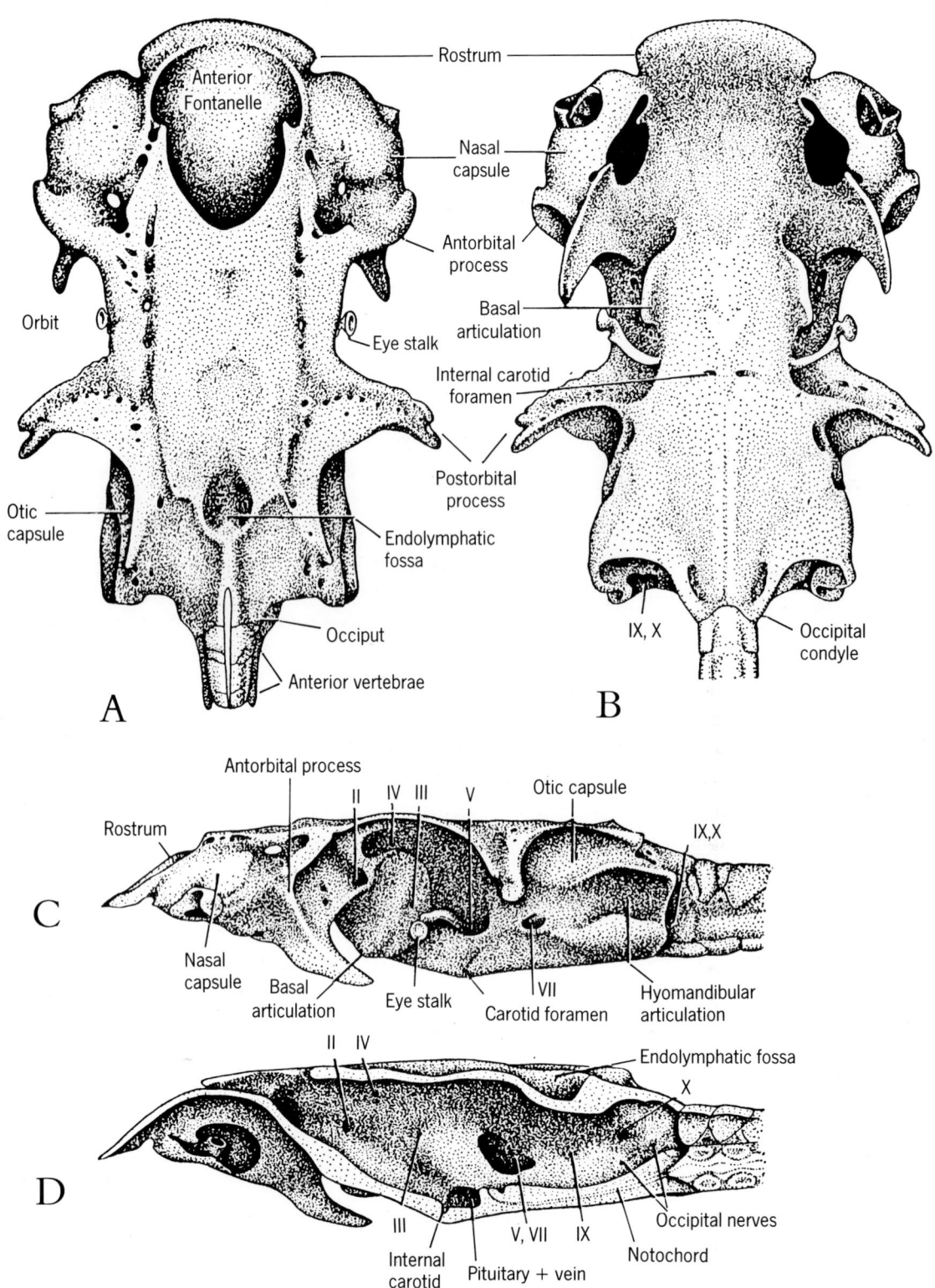

Figure 8
Chondrocranium of the Frilled Shark (*Chlamydoselachus anguineus*). **A** dorsal view. **B** ventral view. **C** lateral view. **D** sagittal section. Cranial nerve exits in Roman numerals (after Allis, from Romer, 1949).

Skeletal System

The axial skeleton of sharks is represented by the brain case (chondrocranium) (Figure 8) anteriorly, followed by the vertebral column. The chondrocranium develops in the embryos of all vertebrates from the fusion of individual cartilages, without any sutures. Sharks have retained this in the adult form, whereas bony fishes (Osteichthyes) and higher vertebrates have replaced it with bone. The chondrocranium is divided into four major regions: the ethmoidal front part with the large open anterior fontanelle dorsally and the laterally projecting nasal capsules which enclose the olfactory organs; behind, the narrow orbital region which laterally forms the socket for the eyeball and eye muscles and has a ventral depression for the pituitary gland; then the otic region with an otic capsule on each side for the protection of the inner ear; and posteriorly the occipital region with the foramen magnum at the back for the emergence of the spinal cord; the first vertebra articulates to the paired occipital condyles which are dorsolateral to the foramen magnum. Numerous openings (foramina) may be seen in the chondrocranium for the cranial nerves (designated by Roman numerals in Figures 8 and 13) and blood vessels.

The axial support of the body of the lower chordates and of the embryos of the higher chordates (vertebrates) is provided by the notochord (in the tunicates it is found only in the tail of the tadpole-like larva). This is an elongate rod dorsally in the body which is stiffened by a thick, tough layer of connective tissue. The phylum name Chordata is in reference to the universal presence of the notochord in this group. In most adult vertebrates it is greatly reduced or absent, being replaced by vertebrae which develop around it. The notochord is present in adult cyclostomes (lampreys and hagfishes), though lampreys have incomplete vertebrae associated with it. It was the longitudinal support for the body of primitive sharks, but the structural support in modern sharks has been taken over by the cartilaginous vertebrae (Figure 9). The notochord is still present in sharks between the vertebrae and constricted within the main central part (the centrum) of each vertebra. A cross-section through a vertebra reveals an arch of cartilage at the top (the neural arch) which encloses the spinal cord, and another arch below (the haemal arch) which protects major blood vessels (in the caudal vertebrae the caudal artery and just below it the caudal vein). During development, two half-vertebrae form per embryonic body segment. The anterior half of a vertebra develops in the posterior part of one segment, and its posterior half in the front of the following segment. The two halves fuse, the space between being in the middle of the segment. It is from

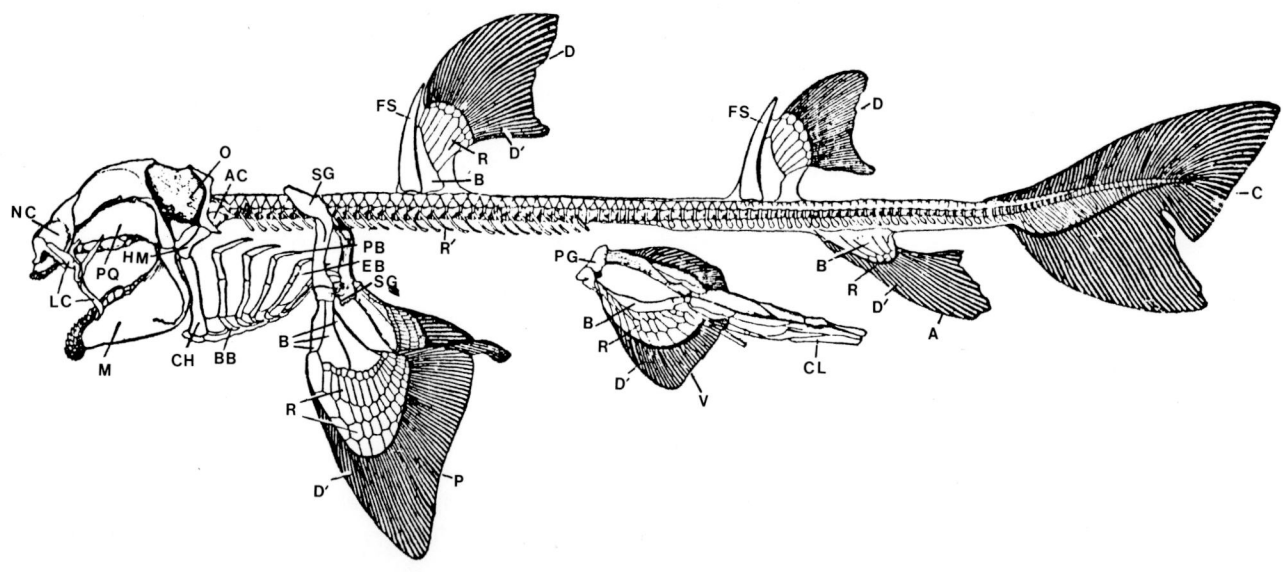

Figure 9
Skeleton of a shark (*Heterodontus*). **A** anal fin. **AC** auditory capsule. **B** basal elements of fin. **BB** basibranchial. **C** caudal fin. **CH** certohyal. **CL** claspers of male. **D** dorsal fins. **D'** dermal rays of fin. **EB** epibranchial. **FS** fins spines. **HM** hyomandibular. **LC** labial cartilages. **M** mandible. **NC** nasal capsule. **O** orbit. **P** pectoral fin. **PB** pharyngobranchial. **PG** pelvic girdle. **PQ** palatoquadrate. **R** radial elements of fin. **R'** ribs. **SG** pectoral girdle. **V** pelvic (ventral) fin (after Dean, from Romer, 1949).

here that the spinal nerves can develop unimpeded by cartilage. In the tail region of many sharks there are two vertebrae per segment, a result of the two embryonic half-vertebrae not fusing. This condition is referred to as diplospondyly. It provides greater flexibility to the tail. There need not be a uniform doubling of vertebrae throughout the tail, and in some species there can be partial diplospondyly in the trunk region.

The branchial skeleton was discussed above in reference to its supportive role in the respiratory system. The jaws have developed from primitive gill arches. The upper jaw in sharks is called the palatoquadrate cartilage and the lower the mandibular cartilage (or Meckel's cartilage). Anyone making a preparation of the jaws and teeth of a large shark will be struck by the bone-like hardness of the jaw cartilages. They, as well as other cartilages of the body such as the braincase and vertebrae, are hardened in modern sharks by the deposition of calcium salts.

The appendicular skeleton of sharks consists of pectoral and pelvic girdles and rods of cartilage basally in the fins. The U-shaped pectoral girdle is located anteroventrally in the trunk region. Each half (Figure 10A) consists of two bars of cartilage.

The ventral part medial to the fin is the coracoid, and the dorsal part the scapula (which may have one or more small suprascapular cartilages at the upper end). The proximal row of cartilages in the pectoral fin are the large, plate-like basals. Usually there are three: the inner (and longest) is the metapterygium, the middle one the mesopterygium, and the outer one the propterygium (Figure 10B). Articulating with these are series of radial cartilages. The pelvic girdle is a transverse ventral bar of cartilage. The major basal element of the pelvic fin (Figure 11) is the elongate basipterygium which articulates anteriorly with the girdle; the pelvic radials abut it along its lateral edge, and in males the basal cartilage of the clasper articulates to its distal end. The supporting cartilages of the dorsal and anal fins of elasmobranchs generally occur in three series, basal, median, and distal. In some such as *Heterodontus* and *Heptranchias* the basals may fuse to a single broad plate (Figure 9). Others like *Ginglymostoma* may show a segmentation of the distal cartilages to additional series. Or the distals may be absent, as in *Squatina*. The latter genus also serves as an example of sharks in which the basals come in contact with the vertebral column. The principal support for the caudal fin is, as mentioned, the vertebral column which extends into the long upper lobe. The neural spines of the vertebrae are prolonged above and the haemal spines even more below to give further support. The outer flexible part of all shark fins is strengthened by the slender horny fibers called ceratotrichia which are of dermal origin.

Figure 10
Skeleton of pectoral girdle (A) and pectoral fin (B) of the Seven-Gill Shark (*Heptranchias perlo*). **sc** scapula. **co** coracoid. **f.pt** foramen for nerves and blood vessels. **a.pl** process for articulation of pectoral fin. **pr.p** proterygium. **ms.p** mesopterygium. **mt.p** metapterygium. **ra** radials (after Daniel, 1934).

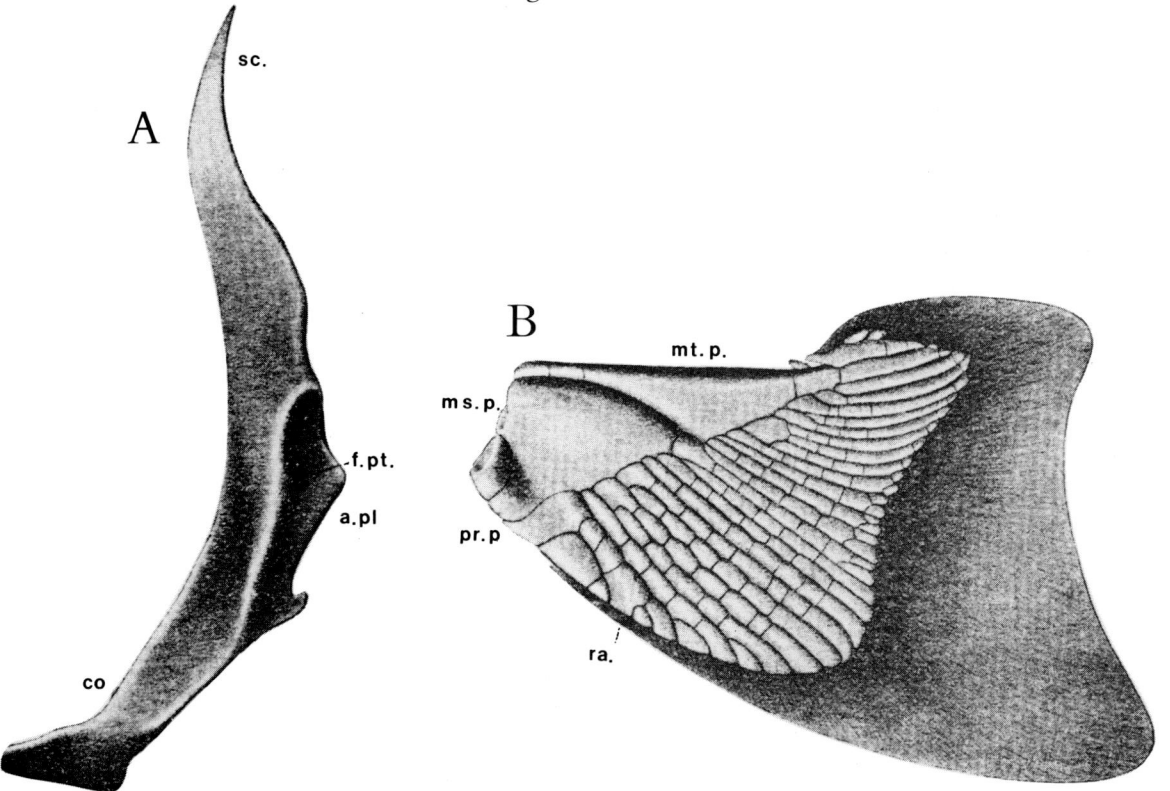

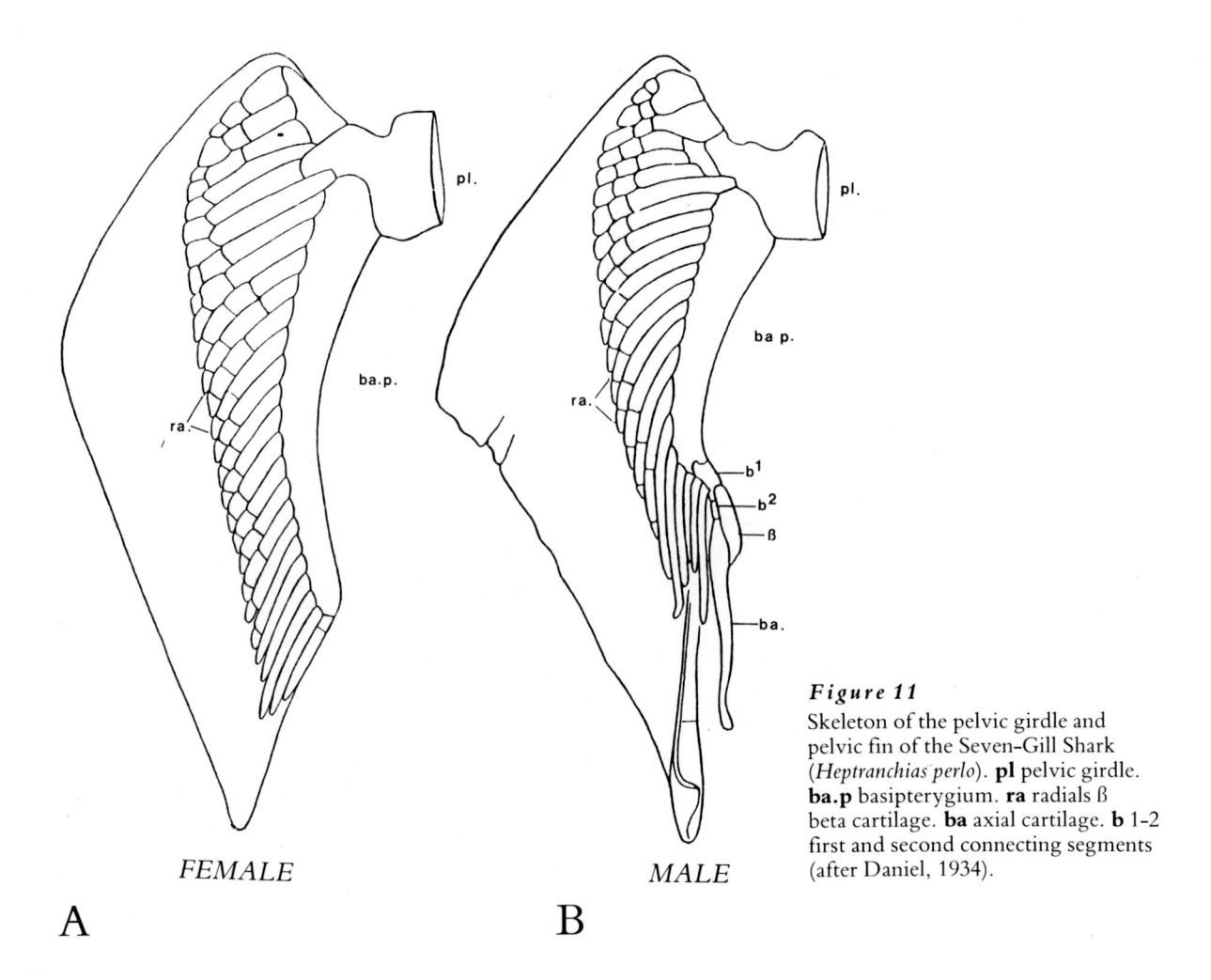

Figure 11
Skeleton of the pelvic girdle and pelvic fin of the Seven-Gill Shark (*Heptranchias perlo*). **pl** pelvic girdle. **ba.p** basipterygium. **ra** radials ß beta cartilage. **ba** axial cartilage. **b** 1-2 first and second connecting segments (after Daniel, 1934).

A FEMALE   B MALE

Muscular System

The main mass of muscular tissue of the shark which produces the propulsive force in swimming is segmentally arranged. Each segment of muscle, called a myotome, has a dorsoventral zigzag pattern when viewed laterally. The myotomes are separated from one another by a white partition of connective tissue called the myoseptum. Running longitudinally along the middle of the side of the body is another sheet of connective tissue, the lateral septum, which divides the musculature into the dorsal epaxial part and the ventral hypaxial portion. In most sharks the epaxial musculature is arranged in two main longitudinal bundles and the hypaxial in three. The epaxial bundles continue anteriorly above the gill region and attach to the posterior part of the chondrocranium. The hypaxial bundles end anteriorly by attachment to the pectoral girdle.

The fin muscles of fishes are outgrowths of the myotomes. Dorsally on the paired fins are broad, fan-like abductor muscles which elevate the fins, and on the ventral side the adductors

FORM AND FUNCTION

which depress these fins. The pectoral abductor originates on the fascia (overlying connective tissue) of the myotomes and on the scapula, and the adductor to fascia and the coracoid. The corresponding muscles of the pelvic fin also originate on fascia and the upper and lower parts of the pelvic girdle.

In the branchial region the most conspicuous muscles are the superficial constrictors (Figure 12). The fibers of each follow the curved dorsoventral path of the gill arch. The contraction of these muscles compresses the gill chambers, forces water out, and closes the gill slits; also it aids in opening the mouth. Dorsal to the constrictors are the levators (sometimes called trapezius) which run from dorsal fascia to the dorsal part of the gill bars (and on some sharks diagonally backward to the scapula); these serve to raise the gill arches. The intermandibular, a broad anterior extension of the ventral part of the first (hyoid) constrictor, connects the two rami of the lower jaw. Anterior and a little deeper to the superficial constrictors is the levator palatoquadrati which elevates the upper jaw. More important is the action of the large adductor mandibulae which strongly closes the jaws. A specialized portion of this muscle, the preorbital, passes forward to attach to the antorbital process of the chondrocranium; its function is to pull the upper jaw forward. Below the intermandibular and the adductor mandibulae is the hypobranchial musculature between the coracoid bar and the mandibles. These muscles assist in opening the mouth and the expansion of the gill chambers.

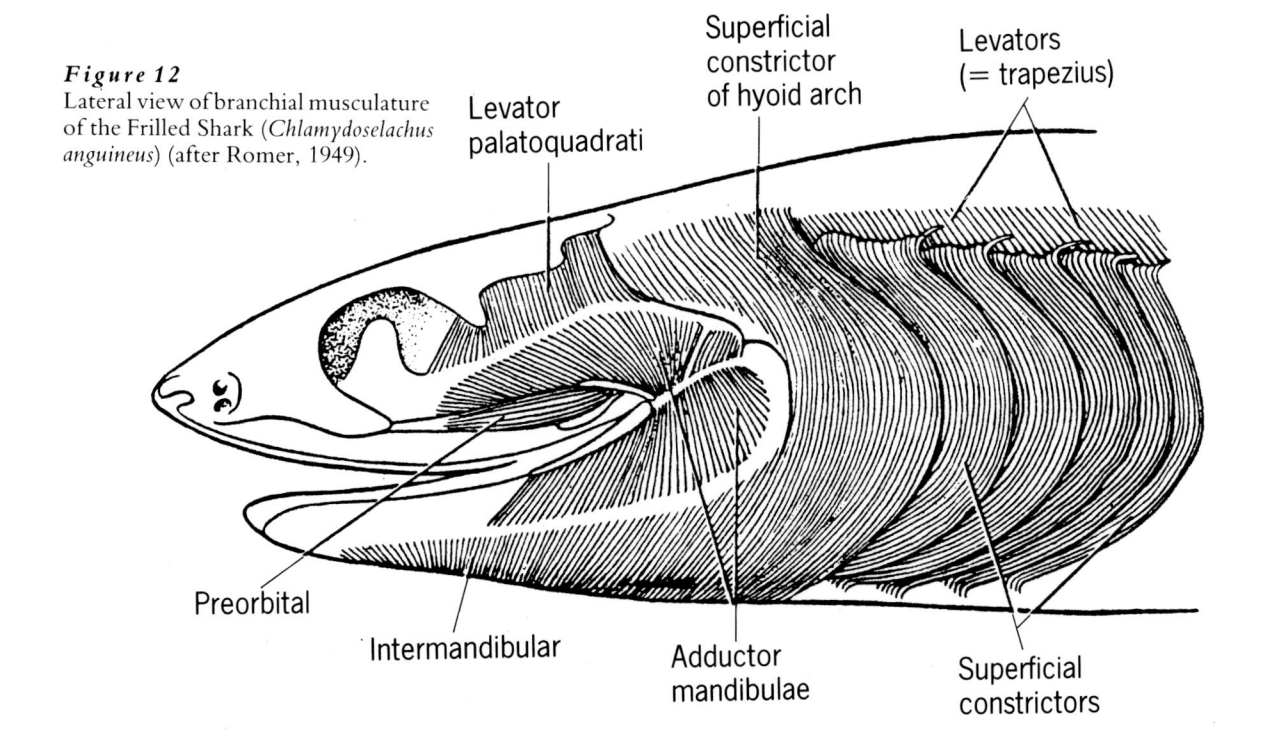

Figure 12
Lateral view of branchial musculature of the Frilled Shark (*Chlamydoselachus anguineus*) (after Romer, 1949).

Nervous System

The spinal cord of sharks extends from the brain nearly to the tip of the tail. As mentioned in the discussion of the skeletal system, it is protected by the cartilage of the neural arch of each vertebra. It is oval in cross-section and readily differentiated into an internal grey and an external white part. The grey has a finely branched double bilobed shape in cross-section; the two upper lobes are called the dorsal horns (or columns, as these run the length of the cord) and the larger, more lateral, lower lobes the ventral horns (or columns); the very small central canal passes through the middle of the juncture of the two ventral horns. The grey part consists of innumerable cell bodies of neurons and the white the myelinated fibers of neurons. The dorsal horns contain the cell bodies of interneurons (more cells which link sensory and motor neurons), and the ventral horns the cell bodies of motor neurons. Each body segment has a pair of spinal nerves; these emerge between the neural arches of adjacent vertebrae. The ventral rami of the spinal nerves are found in the myosepta. In the region of the paired fins they form plexi: the cervicobranchial plexus for the pectoral fin and the lumbrosacral plexus for the pelvic fin.

If the dorsal part of the chondrocranium is dissected away, the brain of the shark will be exposed (Figure 13). It is covered by a membrane, the primitive meninx (plural, meninges), which contains blood vessels. There is a noticeable gap between the brain and chondrocranium in elasmobranchs. The brain is

Figure 13
Brain and cranial nerves (Roman numerals) of the Spiny Dogfish (*Squalus acanthias*) (after Storer and Usinger, 1965).

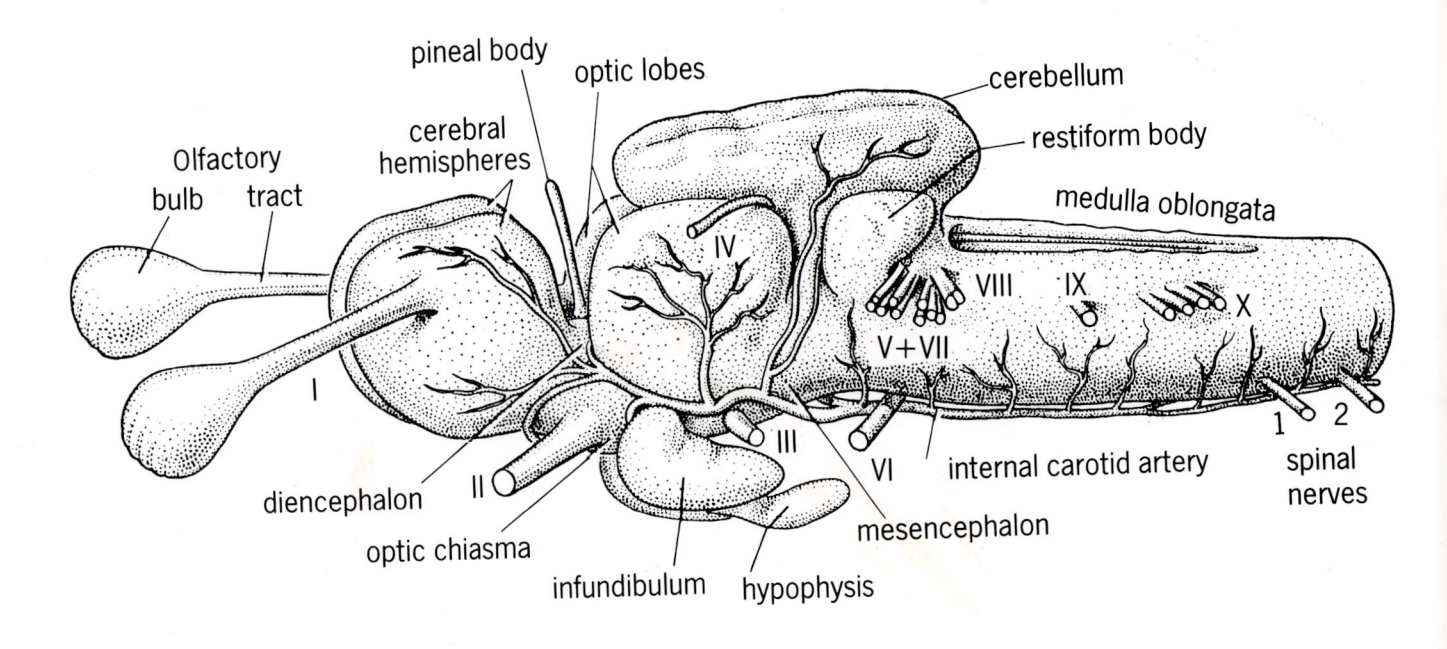

divisible into five main parts from anterior to posterior: the telencephalon, diencephalon, mesencephalon, metencephalon, and myelencephalon. The telencephalon consists of the pair of olfactory bulbs which are in contact with the dorsal wall of the olfactory sac (containing the olfactory epithelium), the narrow olfactory tracts, and the cerebral hemispheres. The fibers of the olfactory nerve (cranial nerve I) originate from the sensory cells in the olfactory epithelium and pass the short distance to the olfactory bulbs. The anterior part of each cerebral hemisphere to which the olfactory tract connects is the olfactory lobe. The diencephalon is a short, low part of the brain which is mainly a relay center for the cerebral hemispheres; it is divisible into three parts: the epithalamus, thalamus, and hypothalamus. It has a central cavity, the third ventricle, the thin highly vascular roof of which is called the tela choroidea; it has ventral projections, the choroid plexi. The optic nerve (cranial nerve II) enters the brain ventrally and crosses at the optic chiasma in the diencephalon (actually the optic nerves are not nerves but tracts of the brain). The pineal body (epiphysis) on its slender stalk extends dorsally from the diencephalon; the infundibulum projects ventrally, ending in the hypophysis (pituitary body). The mesencephalon (midbrain of the embryo) contains the pair of large rounded optic lobes. The oculomotor nerve (cranial nerve III) emerges from the ventral part, and the trochlear (cranial nerve IV) from the upper posterior part of the mesencephalon. Both of these nerves innervate muscles of the eyeball. The principal part of the metencephalon is the cerebellum which is large in active animals like sharks. It is concerned with the coordination of movements with the senses. It is located dorsally and partially overhangs the optic lobes anteriorly and the medulla posteriorly. The floor of the metencephalon shows little differentiation from the medulla. The myelencephalon is the medulla oblongata, the posterior part of which is much like the contiguous spinal cord, with a very small central canal. In the medulla proper this expands into the fourth ventricle, the roof of which, like the third ventricle, is thin and vascular, forming the tela choroidea, parts of which descend into the ventricle as choroid plexi. The fifth to tenth cranial nerves arise from the walls of the medulla: the trigeminus (V) is a large nerve which serves the jaws (originally the 'first' gill arch) and other parts of the head, including a somatic sensory branch to the eye region; the abducens (VI) is a motor nerve to the eyeball; the facial (VII) is the nerve of the second or hyoid gill arch (thus serving the musculature around the spiracle) and is concerned in part with the lateralis system and taste; the auditory nerve (VIII), a sensory nerve to the inner ear, is involved mainly with equilibrium; the glossopharyngeal (IX) is the nerve to the primitive third gill opening (the functional first in contemporary sharks); thus it serves the muscles derived from the third gill arch; it also has sensory components involved with taste more posteriorly in the mouth and of the lateralis system; the vagus (X) is a large nerve which innervates the remaining gill arches and most of the viscera; also the large lateral line nerve, devoted to the lateralis system, is part of the vagus. For a more comprehensive survey of shark brain morphology, the reader is referred to Northcutt in Hodgson and Mathewson (1978).

Until recently sharks have been regarded by many as having simple brains and being little more than a 'swimming nose'. Part of the basis for this has been the belief that these fishes are very primitive because of their cartilaginous skeleton and our knowledge of their ancient fossil record. Part has also been from early morphological work being done mainly on rather primitive living species such as *Squalus acanthias*.

Quiring (1941) noted that elasmobranch fishes have a very large brain, but this did little to dispel their alleged primitive nature. Aronson in Gilbert (1963) pointed out that shark brains have greatly expanded ventricular spaces which make them larger on a volume basis. He stated that although the cerebellum and olfactory part of the shark brain is large compared to bony fishes, certain bony fishes with smaller relative size of these brain parts appear to have as complex movements and as keen an olfactory sense as sharks. He reported the structure of the brain of elasmobranchs to be relatively uniform compared to the highly variable brains of teleosts which he correlated with the more diverse habits of bony fishes. He also noted that the behavioural repertoire of sharks is limited compared to bony fishes and that there seems to be less correlation between the senses.

On the other hand, Northcutt in Hodgson and Mathewson (1978) wrote that not only do sharks possess relatively larger brains on a brain-to-body weight ratio than teleost fishes, but the relative development of the major brain divisions closely parallels that of birds and mammals (Bauchot et al., 1976). He added that simple learning experiments with sharks have shown that they learn at a rate comparable to that of teleosts, birds, and mammals.

Contrary to Aronson, Northcutt stated that there is a great variation in the size and complexity of the central nervous system of elasmobranchs. Clearly more comparative studies are needed on the more advanced species such as the carcharhinids and sphyrnids. These two families of sharks are viviparous with a long gestation period, giving birth to well-developed young of relatively large size. They have the most complex neural organization and the highest brain-to-body weight ratios of the sharks. These are the families that occur on coral reefs, the most complex community in the sea. To be successful there, they must compete with and prey upon many of the most advanced of teleost fishes. Also of significance for the shark family Lamnidae is the discovery that these species maintain a level of body temperature well above that of the ambient environment (Carey and Teal, 1969) thus enabling them to prey upon the fast-swimming fishes of the pelagic realm. Detailed study of the lamnid brain might also reveal a high level of neural development.

Sharks, particularly the larger ones like carcharhinids and sphyrnids, are very difficult subjects for behavioural studies. If we could learn as much about their habits as we know of the other vertebrate groups we might find more complexity in behaviour patterns than has been believed existed. The most detailed behavioural study to date on any species of these families is that of Myrberg and Gruber (1974) on the Bonnethead Shark (*Sphyrna tiburo*). They documented 17 separate behavioural units, of which eight occurred in a social context. They did not investigate courtship, mating or feeding, thus more behavioural patterns remain to be elucidated in this species. For three species of sharks, presumed examples of cooperative predation by two or more individuals have been observed: *Alopias* (Budker, 1947); *Odontaspis taurus* (Coles, 1915); and *Carcharhinus melanopterus* (Masse and Baliyok, MS). Such behaviour clearly indicates a high level of social interaction. Northcutt ended his discussion on this subject with: "Future studies may well reveal that advanced sharks and batoids possess many behaviors thought to be characteristic of only birds and mammals."

SHARKS OF ARABIA

Whitetip Reef Shark
Triaenodon obesus
Photo by J. Randall

EVOLUTIONARY HISTORY

The earliest fish-like vertebrates were the ostracoderms. These originated in Ordovician time (about 435 million years ago) and flourished in the Silurian (Figure 14). Ostracoderm means 'shell-skin', in reference to the bony plates which covered the bodies of the majority we have found as fossils. These ancient vertebrates lacked jaws. Most had a broad head, large gill chamber, and a single median nostril. They probably fed by filtering small organisms through their gill system. The ostracoderms disappeared from the fossil record in the late Devonian (the Devonian period began nearly 400 million years ago and lasted million years), but a few specialized degenerate living forms, the hagfishes and lampreys (the cyclostomes), appear to have been

Figure 14
Distribution of the Agnatha, Acanthodii, Placodermi and cartilaginous fishes through geologic time (modified from Romer, 1945).

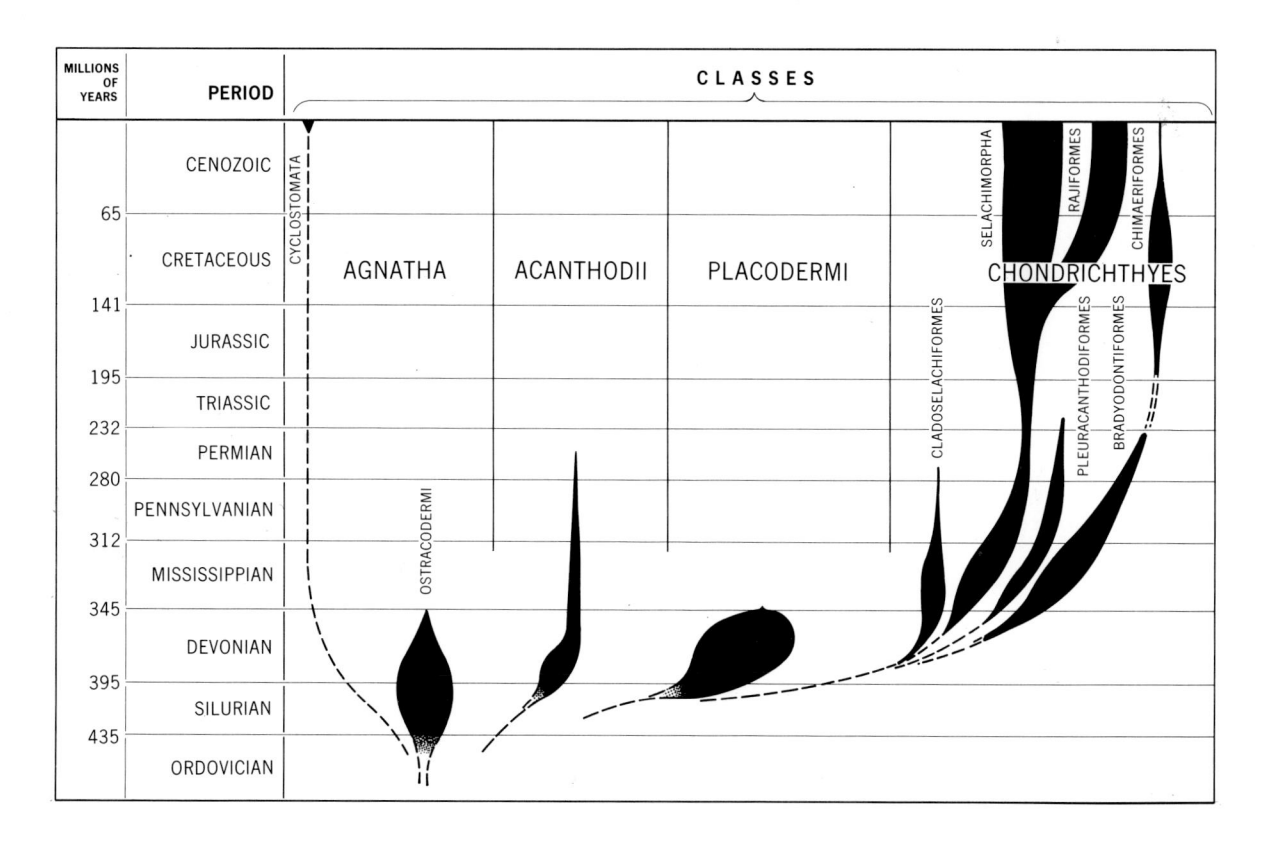

43

derived from them. The ostracoderms and cylostomes are placed together in the Class Agnatha (meaning 'without jaws').

The first fishes to develop jaws (probably the most significant evolutionary step of the lower vertebrates) were the acanthodians. These have been called 'spiny sharks', though they were not sharks. They had stout spines anteriorly in all the fins except the caudal which was tilted upward as in sharks. They had paired fins of a variable number, and their bodies were covered by diamond-shaped bony scales much like the ganoid scales found in bony fishes such as the gars. There has been much controversy where to place these ancient fishes in our system of classification. Some favour treating them as placoderms, some as intermediate to sharks and bony fishes, and some as ancestral to one or the other of the two last-mentioned groups. They are probably best placed in their own class, the Acanthodii. They appeared in the Upper Silurian (hence over 400 million years ago) and became extinct by the end of the Permian (about 230 million years ago).

The Placodermi were also very ancient jawed fishes; they appeared in the Silurian and were extinct by the end of the Devonian except for one genus which persisted into the Carboniferous (divisible into the Pennsylvanian and the older Mississippian). Eight orders are recognized by Nelson (1984). The best known are the arthrodires or jointed-necked fishes, the fossils of which are the most common vertebrate remains of the Devonian, and the antiarchs, odd fishes with a prominent head shield and long, jointed pectoral fins. Many of the placoderms had depressed bodies, and some were ray-like in appearance.

The sharks, rays and related chimaeras belong to the Class Chondrichthyes, meaning cartilaginous fishes. The sharks and rays are grouped as the Subclass Elasmobranchii and the chimaeras as the Subclass Holocephali. The internal skeleton of the Chondrichthyes consists entirely of cartilage. This disintegrates rapidly after an animal dies and is thus rarely preserved in fossil form. The cartilage of higher sharks may be calcified and therefore somewhat hardened. Calcified vertebrae and braincases are sometimes found as fossils, but these are rare compared to teeth and fin spines (for those species that possessed such spines). The first fossils of sharks, only teeth and some spines (classified as the Cladodontiformes), were found in middle Devonian strata (about 370 million years ago), thus the last of the major classes of fishes to appear in the fossil record. These teeth consist of a flat disc-like base, a large conical central cusp and two or more small lateral cusps. The group of sharks that bore these teeth are called cladodonts. It is very difficult to determine from ancient teeth alone what these animals were like and very difficult to link them to ancestral forms. Because of

EVOLUTIONARY HISTORY

their cartilaginous skeletons, sharks were first thought to be the most primitive of fishes. We now believe that they are derived from early jawed fishes with bone, perhaps the placoderms or forms ancestral to placoderms. The hypothesized replacement of bone by cartilage would therefore not be a primitive condition but a degenerative one (in the same sense that the lampreys and hagfishes may have had ancestors like the ostracoderms with bone and subsequently lost it).

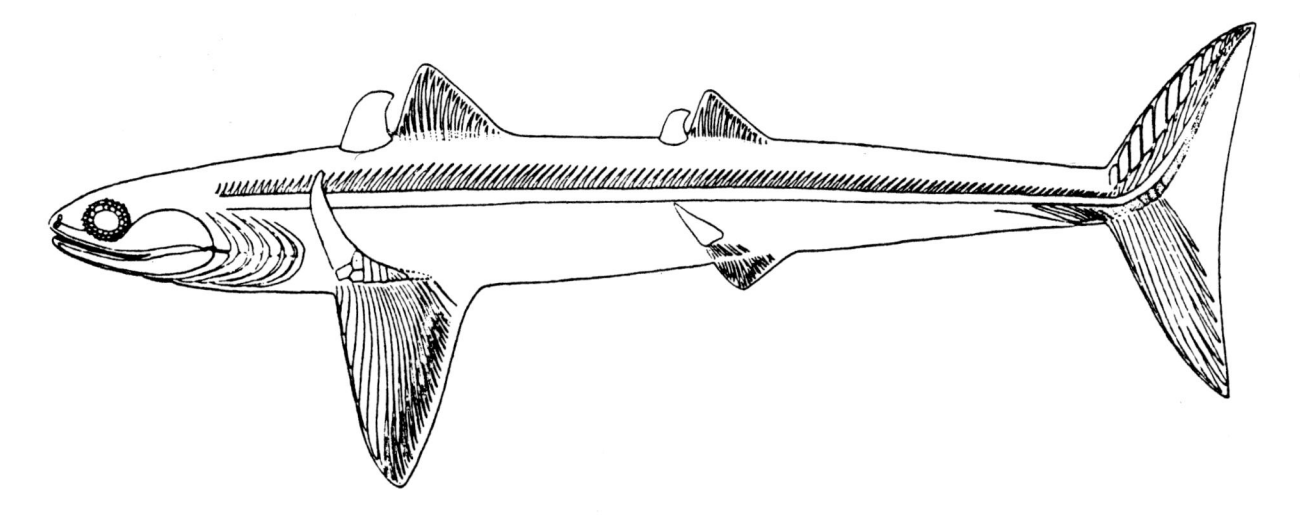

Figure 15
Restoration of skeleton of *Cladoselache* (after Dean, from Schaeffer in Gilbert, Mathewson, and Rall, 1967).

In the late Devonian in the black shale rock at the southern shore of Lake Erie (called the Cleveland shales) a number of exceptional complete fossils have been found of a primitive shark which was named *Cladoselache* (Figure 15), the best known of the Order Cladoselachiformes. The teeth were of the cladodont type. The dorsal and paired fins were broad-based, supported by basal and radial rods of cartilage and preceded by large broad spines; the pectoral fins were much larger than the pelvic fins; there were no claspers or anal fin; the caudal fin was symmetrical, with erect upper and lower lobes, but the vertebral column extended into the upper lobe, thus the fin is of the heterocercal type typical of sharks. The palatoquadrate cartilage (main supporting element of the upper jaw of sharks) was suspended from the chondrocranium (braincase) by ligaments to the postorbital and otic processes of the palatoquadrate; in addition there was some support to the jaws by way of attachment of the hyomandibular cartilage from the chondrocranium to the mandibular cartilage (lower jaw). This type of jaw suspension is called amphystylic, in contrast to the autostylic type as in placoderms where the upper jaw articulates directly to the braincase. The jaws of the early vertebrates were derived from the gill arches; the upper part of an anterior arch (some refer to it as the first, but one or two arches in front of it may have disappeared to provide for more gape to the mouth) became the palatoquadrate cartilage, and the lower part the mandibular cartilage. The upper part of the next (or hyoid) arch became the hyomandibular cartilage. The gill opening anterior to the hyoid arch was modified to the spiracle of elasmobranchs.

The cladoselachiforms became extinct in the Permian. The majority of animals found as fossils are side branches from the main evolutionary trunk. *Cladoselache* and its allies, however, appear to be close to the base of the stock leading to the higher forms of cartilaginous fishes.

The Pleuracanthiformes was an evolutionary side branch of the Chondrichthyes which was contemporary with the cladoselachiforms, first appearing in the late Devonian, flourishing in the Carboniferous, but dying out completely in the early Triassic. Unlike most shark fossils, these were found in freshwater deposits. *Pleuracanthus* was elongate with a long dorsal fin, two small anal fins, a secondarily symmetrical caudal fin and a long spine projecting dorsoposteriorly from the back of the head.

The next level in shark evolution was the Hybodontiformes, which first appeared in the late Devonian. These were intermediate to the cladoselachiforms and the higher sharks. The paired fins were narrow-based, hence more movable. Claspers appeared in males. The primitive amphystylic jaw suspension, however, was retained. In general, the teeth were sharp-bladed anteriorly in the jaws, but blunt or even molariform posteriorly (hybodont means 'hump tooth'). Many taxa in this group are known only from teeth. The best known genus is *Hybodus* of the Mesozoic Era (Figure 16) which was especially common in the Jurassic (135 to 140 million years ago). The hybodonts were largely extinct by the end of the Cretaceous (65 million years ago).

Figure 16
Hybodus hauffianus, a Mesozoic shark, about 2.3 m (after Smith Woodward, from Romer, 1945).

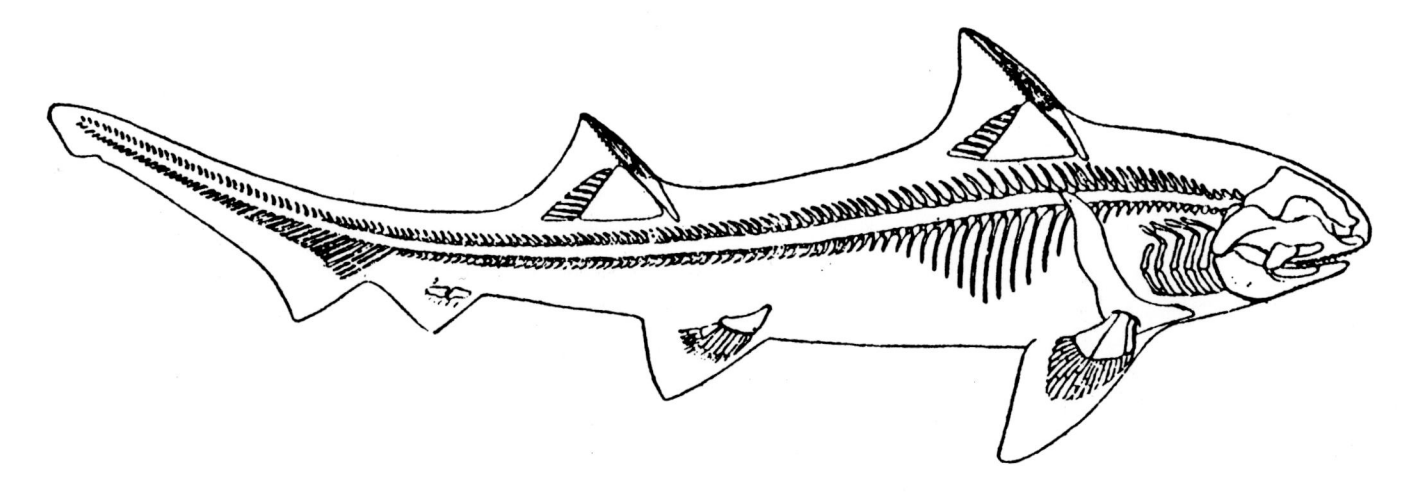

Heterodontus (Heterodontiformes) generally regarded as an offshoot from the hybodontiform line first appeared in the Jurassic. Sharks of this genus retained the stout spine anteriorly in each dorsal fin and have large molariform teeth posteriorly in the jaws; they feed on benthic invertebrates. Eight species survive today, one of which is recorded from Oman (see p. 67).

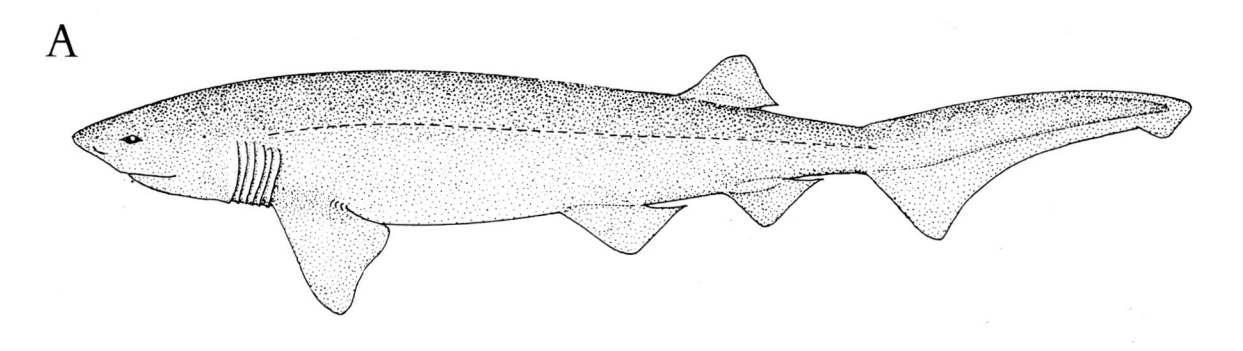

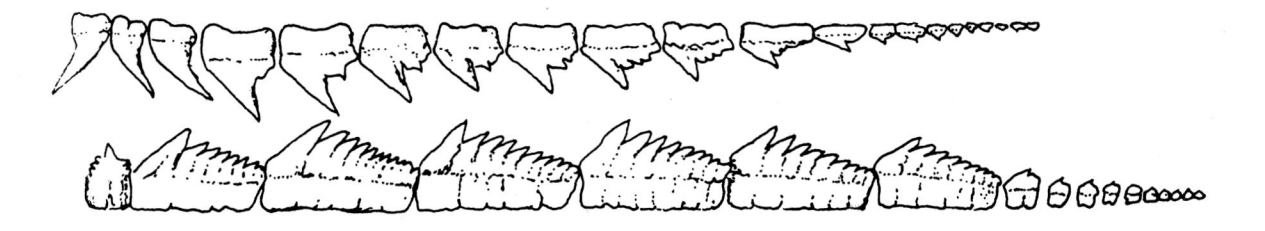

Figure 17
A. *Hexanchus griseus* B. Teeth of *H. griseus* (after Compagno, 1984a).

Another primitive group with survivors to the present is the Hexanchiformes. This includes the Six-Gill Sharks (*Hexanchus*) (Figure 17A), which first appeared in the Middle Jurassic, the Seven-Gill Sharks (*Heptranchias* and *Notorynchus*) and the Frilled Shark (*Chlamydoselachus*) (classified in its own family – the other three genera in Hexanchidae). They are characterized by having six or seven pairs of large gill openings, a single dorsal fin without a spine, an anal fin, and very distinctive teeth (those of *Chlamydoselachus* with three long slender sharp cusps and a short basal cusp between the central and each lateral cusp; those of the other genera with the lower teeth bearing many sharp cusps – often referred to as comb-like but more like a coarse saw) (Figure 17B). The jaw suspension is variable. It is typically amphystylic in *Hexanchus*, nearly so in *Chlamydoselachus* (the postorbital process of the palatoquadrate does not quite make contact with the chondrocranium), but is like the higher sharks in *Heptranchias*. Four members of this order of sharks are found today, but none are recorded from Arabian waters. They are primarily deepwater species.

The major advance of the so-called modern sharks has been the development of hyostylic jaw suspension. The connection from the palatoquadrate to the chondrocranium has been lost and the postorbital process has shortened. The jaws are suspended by the hyomandibular to the otic region of the chondrocranium. In the amphistylic form of jaw suspension, with articulation via the postorbital process to the braincase, the jaws are essentially in a fixed position. With the freeing of the palatoquadrate, protrusion of the jaws became possible. Also, the jaws shortened, thus providing for a more powerful bite. Most of the higher sharks have teeth modified for shearing or sawing pieces from their prey. Another important development in modern sharks was the replacement of a continuous notochord by calcified vertebral centra which strengthened the axial skeleton and provided better support for muscle attachment.

The modern sharks are divided into six orders: Squaliformes, Pristiophoriformes, Squatiniformes, Orectolobiformes, Lamniformes, and Carcharhiniformes.

The Squaliformes have living representatives in three families: the Echinorhinidae (Bramble Sharks) with two species, the Oxynotidae (Rough Sharks) with four species, and the Squalidae (Dogfish Sharks) with 66 species. *Squalus* was the first found fossil in the Upper Cretaceous. These sharks have five gill slits, all in front of the pectoral fins, spiracles, no anal fin, and two dorsal fins (the squalids often with a stout spine at the front of each). Most reside in deep water. The family includes the smallest shark in the world, *Squaliolus laticaudus* (24.3 cm) and some of the largest (*Somniosus* to 7 m). The oldest known modern shark is the long-extinct *Paleospinax* which was found in the Lower Jurassic of England. It had a fully hyostylic jaw suspension, and it is the first shark found with calcified vertebrae. Most authors have regarded this shark as in the evolutionary line leading to the Squalidae.

The Pristiophoriformes, or Sawsharks, consist of a single family of two genera and a total of five living species. They have a long, tapering, flat snout armed on each side by sharp, lateral-projecting teeth and a pair of long barbels extending ventrally, one from each side of the rostral saw; like the squaliforms, they lack an anal fin. They should not be confused with Sawfishes which have a similar blade-like rostrum with lateral teeth and lack an anal fin. Sawfishes are rays; their gill openings are ventral (rather than lateral) and medial to the pectoral fin bases (rather than anterior to the pectorals as on the Sawsharks). The extinct *Propristiophorus* first appeared in the Upper Cretaceous; and *Pristiophorus* in the Miocene.

The Squatiniformes, or Angelsharks, have 13 living representatives in the genus *Squatina* of the monotypic family

Squatinidae. They are strongly depressed and resemble rays more than sharks, but the broadly expanded pectoral fins are not fused with the head; the five pairs of gill openings are lateral in front of the pectoral fin bases, but continue ventrally; the pelvic fins are also broadly expanded; there are two dorsal fins, no anal fin, and the lower lobe of the caudal fin is larger than the upper. *Squatina* has been found fossil from the Upper Jurassic of Europe.

The Orectolobiformes consists of seven Recent families: Parascyllidae (Collared Carpet Sharks) with seven living species, Brachaeluridae (Blind Sharks) with two species, Orectolobidae (Wobbegongs) with five species, Hemiscyllidae (Bamboo Sharks) with 12 species, the monotypic Stegostomatidae (Variegated Shark family), Ginglymostomatidae (Nurse Sharks) with three species, and the monotypic Rhincodontidae (Whale Shark family). This order is characterized by five pairs of gill openings, the fourth and fifth over pectoral fin bases, spiracles present, nostrils connected to the mouth by a deep groove (except *Rhincodon*), nasal barbels present, and two dorsal fins on the posterior half of body, the second nearly as large as first (except *Rhincodon*). *Orectolobus* dates back to the Upper Jurassic, *Ginglymostoma* to the Upper Cretaceous, and *Chiloscyllium* to the Miocene.

The Lamniformes also includes seven Recent families of sharks: the Odontaspididae (Sand Tiger Sharks) with four species, the monotypic Mitsukurinidae (Goblin Shark family), the monotypic Pseudocarcharhinidae (Crocodile Shark family), the monotypic Megaschasmidae (Megamouth Shark family), the Alopiidae (Thresher Sharks) with three species, the monotypic Cetorhinidae (Basking Shark family), and the Lamnidae (Mackerel Sharks) with five species. Sharks of this order have five gill slits, no oronasal grooves or nasal barbels, no nictitating lower eyelids, have two dorsal fins without spines, the origin of the first over the space between the pectoral and pelvic fins or over the pectoral fin bases, and the intestinal valve of the ring type. *Odontaspis* and *Isurus* have been found fossil back to the Lower Cretaceous, *Carcharodon* to the Upper Cretaceous and *Alopias* to the Eocene. *Carcharodon carcharias*, the Great White Shark, is the largest living predaceous fish, reliably reported to 6.4 m but probably attaining a maximum of nearly 8 m (Randall, 1973a). Seventy nominal fossil species and varieties of have been named, based primarily on teeth. The largest tooth, from *C. megalodon* in the Miocene, has an enamel height of 117.5 mm. A *Carcharodon* with teeth this size is estimated to have had an awesome length of 13 m.

The final order of modern sharks, the Carcharhiniformes, is the largest, with eight Recent families: Scyliorhinidae (Catsharks) with 86 species, the monotypic Pseudotriakidae

SHARKS OF ARABIA

(False Catshark family), the Proscyllidae (Finback Catsharks) with six species, the monotypic Leptochariidae (Barbeled Houndshark family), the Triakidae (Houndsharks) with 54 species, the Hemigaleidae (Weasel Sharks) with five species, the Carcharhinidae (Requiem Sharks) with 47 species, and the Sphyrnidae (Hammerhead Sharks) with eight species. They have five gill slits, the last one to three over the pectoral fin bases, usually no oronasal grooves or barbels, nictitating lower eyelids present, two dorsal fins without spines, caudal fin with a long upper lobe, the lower lobe notably shorter or absent, and the intestinal valve of the spiral type. *Galeus* dates back to the Upper Jurassic, *Mustelus* to the Oligocene, *Hemipristis* to the Upper Cretaceous, *Carcharhinus* to the Eocene, *Galeocerdo* to the Upper Cretaceous, and *Sphyrna* to the Upper Cretaceous.

As mentioned, the first sharks appeared in the Devonian, which has been called the Age of Fishes because fishes became the dominant animals in the sea in that period. At that time the early sharks were much less numerous than the ostracoderms, acanthodians, and placoderms. Most were small and were probably preyed upon by the larger acanthodians and placoderms. With the dying out of these older groups by the end of the Devonian, the sharks (cladoselachians and hybodonts), along with bradyodonts (forerunners of the chimaeras), dominated the seas. Commencing in the Triassic, the bony fishes (Osteichthyes) began to increase in numbers and diversity while the cartilaginous fishes declined, such that today there are about 30,000 species of bony fishes and only about 780 sharks, skates, rays, and chimaeras.

Compared to bony fishes, which have radiated into an unbelievable variety of forms, the sharks are much more homogeneous in general morphology (notable exceptions being the Sawsharks, Angelsharks, and Bullhead Sharks). Also, Recent genera of sharks, as indicated in the above summaries of modern shark orders, generally extend further back in geologic time. It is indeed remarkable that some shark genera we recognise today are identifiable as fossils from the Cretaceous and even the Jurassic periods.

Hammerhead Shark
probably *Sphyrna lewini*
Photo by F.J. Jackson

MAN AND SHARKS

MAN AND SHARKS

The average person thinks of sharks in negative terms: they attack and sometimes kill people in the sea; they reduce the populations of food and game fishes, sea turtles, and marine mammals; they take fishes from fishermen's lines and damage their nets and traps. Let us examine these negative aspects.

Grey Reef Shark
Carcharhinus amblyrhynchos
Photo by J. Randall

Shark Attacks

As a number of authors have pointed out, shark attack as a cause of serious injury or death is negligible compared to some other kinds of accidents, in particular the carnage by the automobile on the highways. Even being struck by lightning takes a greater toll of human life than sharks. Of course, it has to be admitted that far more people are exposed to injury or death from automobile accidents or by bolts of lightning than face possible attack by sharks. Nevertheless, of the millions of people who bathe or dive in the sea every year, the chance of any one of them being bitten by a shark is infinitesimally small.

With the establishment of the Shark Research Panel in 1958 and its operation for 10 years (with support of the Office of Naval Research and the American Institute of Biological Sciences), a concerted effort was made to document all the known shark attacks that have occurred in the world (Gilbert, 1963 and Schultz and Malin in Gilbert, 1963). A shark attack file was established at the National Museum of Natural History in Washington, D.C. It was later moved to the Mote Marine Laboratory at Sarasota, Florida.

In a report to the Office of Naval Research on shark attacks, Baldridge (1973) examined the data on 1165 cases. 730 of these occurred in the 28-year period from 1941 through 1968; 29% were fatal. Thus there were only 435 attacks for all the preceding years (in Schultz and Malin's list of records, only two were recorded before the year 1803). Obviously, the further back in time, the less the chance of obtaining authentic records of attacks. Nevertheless, it is clear that the number of attacks have increased over the years, particularly in recent decades. Even within the period 1941 to 1959 there was an average increase of 1.2 cases per year.

Randall in Gilbert (1963) has pointed out the apparent reasons for the increase in the number of shark attacks. The most important is the greater number of persons bathing or diving in the sea. This is a function of the increase of human population in the world, greater tourist visitation to seaside resorts, and the phenomenal development of various aquatic sports. Also the shark populations have increased in many areas as a result of the decline in commercial fishing for sharks. Still another factor is the greater likelihood of such incidents being reported in the news media in recent years compared to decades ago.

It has been stated in the literature that about 100 shark attacks occur in the world every year. The average for the period 1941 to 1968, however, was 26, with the highest number, 56, occurring in 1959. Certainly many attacks go unreported, particularly those resulting in minor injuries. Undoubtedly some swimmers who have disappeared at sea were victims of shark attacks. Nevertheless, it seems unlikely that the number of attacks would reach 100 in any year, with the possible exception of the aftermath of a major air or sea disaster in an area where dangerous sharks are abundant.

Persons who spend a great deal of time in the sea such as spearfishermen, aquarium fish collectors or ichthyologists have, of course, reason to be more concerned about the shark hazard than the occasional weekend bather. During the course of his field work, the author has met 21 persons who have been bitten by sharks or had something they were wearing bitten; two of these attacks were fatal.

Captain Baldridge has made a computer analysis of the 1165 cases of shark attacks, relating them with many factors such as sea temperature, time of day, and water depth; he has also analyzed the attacks themselves from various standpoints. The more interesting of his findings are reported below.

There have been 65% more shark attacks on weekends than working days of the week, reflecting the greater use of the sea by people on Saturdays and Sundays.

Other comparisons such as time of day, clear days vs. cloudy, and stormy days vs. calm also correlate with the number of persons entering the sea. 91.8% of the attacks took place during daylight hours, 1.3% near dawn, 3.8% at dusk, and 3.1% at night. Actually these figures indicate a greater risk at night, for certainly less than 3.1% of swimming and diving in the sea occurs at night.

Baldridge compared the occurrence of shark attacks with latitude, finding, as one might expect, that there is a decided preponderance in the middle latitudes where the bulk of the world population resides. He did not make an analysis by countries. Schultz in Gilbert (1963: Figs. 1-4, Table 1) has done this by major areas. Australia heads the list, and when the relatively small human population is considered, this is all the more striking. On a per capita basis South Africa also stands out as a country with a major shark hazard. In reference to tropical and subtropical regions, Coppleson in Gilbert (1963) wrote, "The places with the worst reputation for attacks are the Persian Gulf and Red Sea. Since classical times, much has been related about the ferocity of sharks in the Red Sea. Stories of attacks in the Persian Gulf are enough to scare most swimmers." He added that information concerning attacks in these areas has been difficult to obtain.

Comparison of the incidence of shark attacks in clear water and murky water revealed a surprising 51.5% in clear water. Again, there is a factor of preference, certainly for divers, to enter clear water instead of turbid. On the other hand, there are two considerations which favor fewer attacks in clear water. There would be more chance of mistaken identity by a shark (as of a black-suited diver for a seal) in murky water, and in clear water a person is more apt to detect the presence of a shark and be able to avoid an attack by leaving the sea or by defensive action.

Coppleson (1958) and Coppleson in Gilbert (1963) has indicated that shark attack below a 'critical' sea temperature of 20° to 21°C is highly unlikely. Schultz in Gilbert (1963) and Baldridge contend that this lower limit in temperature is related more to the reluctance of swimmers to enter the sea at colder temperatures.

Every species of shark has its own range of temperature tolerance, and narrower than this is the range at which it will feed. Relating sea temperature to shark attacks has to be carried out species by species. Rarely is a positive identification made of an attacking shark, and data on water temperature are often not available. For three species, however, there are limited data on sea temperature at the time of attacks. Thirty-two attacks have

The author feeding a young Whitetip Reef Shark by hand in the lagoon of Kwajalein, Marshall Islands (Nathan A. Bartlett).

been attributed to the Great White Shark (*Carcharodon carcharias*); for 18 of these, water temperatures were recorded; they ranged from 10.5° to 26.5°C. Six of twenty-seven attacks by Tiger Sharks (*Galeocerdo cuvier*) had a sea temperature range of 15.5° to 31.5° C. Ten attacks by Bull Sharks (*Carcharhinus leucas*) at known temperatures ranged from 18.3° to 27.5°C. Such data were also given by Baldridge for Hammerhead Sharks (*Sphyrna* spp.); nine of 12 attacks ranged from 17.5° to 29.5°C. But these could have been from any of nine species of Hammerheads. Similarly there are data for sharks called Makos (*Isurus* spp.). Not only are there two species in the genus *Isurus*, but some attacks attributed to Makos have been due to the Great White Shark (Randall and Levy, 1976).

Data on the depth of water was available for 470 shark attack cases. Of these, 62% occurred in water 1.5 m deep or less, and 16% in water knee-deep or less. Again, this is not an indication of a greater likelihood of shark attack in shallow water but of the greater number of bathers in the sea at inshore depths. In reality, the farther a swimmer is from shore and the deeper the water, the greater are his chances of attack.

It is generally believed that swimmers at the surface are more apt to be attacked than SCUBA divers below the surface. Data from the 881 cases for which the depth of attack was known would seem to support this; 90% of the victims were either at the surface or within 1.5 meters of it. More attacks occurred on individuals who were actively swimming than all other surface activities combined. Of the 1165 cases of shark attacks, 244 (hence 21%) were on divers (whether skindivers or SCUBA divers and whether at the surface or not).

Analysis of the race or age of shark attack victims seems to show no preference on the part of the shark. The percentages in these different categories approximate what one would expect from the numbers of people in these groupings that enter the sea. More whites and more young people have been bitten.

For sex, however, there is a divergence. 93.1% of the attack victims have been males, but on bathing beaches there is only a slight preponderance of males over females entering the water. However, men venture farther from shore and are more active in the water, thus their movements constitute a greater stimulus to sharks. Also there are many more male divers than female.

From data available on colour of bathing suits and wetsuits, more attacks have been on individuals who wore dark colours. However, most bathing suits and a very high percentage of wet-suits are dark-coloured. Baldridge wrote, "... in the absence of control data [meaning knowledge of the colour of suits worn by persons in the water at the same time and place who were not attacked], it is not possible to draw meaningful correlations between incidence of shark attack and colors reportedly worn by victims." However, he pointed out that tests involving survival gear of different colours have shown that sharks have a predilection for attacking objects that have a bright, contrasting and/or reflective appearance. A yellow life vest worn by a child dummy was repeatedly attacked by Blue Sharks (*Prionace glauca*), whereas strikes on a red vest were few and on black there were only two. The Shortfin Mako Shark (*Isurus oxyrinchus*) struck only the yellow-vested dummy. Tests on the least attractive colours to sharks for a large floating plastic bag for a person awaiting rescue in the sea revealed dark blue and black the least attractive to sharks, and white and silver the most.

It is popularly believed that the presence of dolphins or porpoises makes shark attack on humans unlikely. Supposedly a dolphin can ram into a vulnerable soft part of a shark such as the gill region and incapacitate or kill it. Baldridge casts doubt on this porpoise-induced immunity to shark attack by citing the studies under controlled conditions of Mathewson and Gilbert (1967), Wood, Caldwell, and Caldwell (1970), Gilbert, Irvine, and Martini (1971), Gilbert (1972), and Irvine, Wells, and Gilbert (1973) which failed to demonstrate any high-level animosity between sharks and dolphins. Also pieces of porpoises or dolphins have on occasion been found in the stomachs of sharks (though it is not known if the sharks ate these mammals when they may have been old, sick, or even dead).

Schultz (1967) determined from 275 cases of shark attack that 31% of the victims had no companion within 31 m at the time of attack. Baldridge analyzed 637 cases on this basis and found that 34% of the victims were essentially alone. Schultz reported 44% of the attack victims to have had a companion within 3 m of them. Thus the presence of a companion would not seem to be any major deterrent to a marauding shark.

The presence of blood in the water, as from an injured person in the sea, has long been regarded as a strong motivator for attack by sharks. Yet in only 19 of the cases reviewed by Baldridge were the victims believed to have been bleeding to a significant degree before the attack. Blood from other persons may have been a factor in 12 other cases. Baldridge also noted that sharks often bite a victim only once. Even though the wound may be massive with much loss of blood to the sea, no second attack may follow. In fact, twice as many persons are bitten a single time compared to ones with multiple bites. Tricas and McCosker (1984) have explained this for attacks by the Great White Shark as a strategy for feeding on marine mammals. The prey is strongly bitten, then released to die or be greatly weakened by its wound, at which time the shark returns for an easier time of feeding. A human bitten once may succeed in getting out of the water before

RIGHT:

The author preparing the head of a Shortfin Mako Shark for the photograph of figure 34. This shark was responsible for a near-fatal attack on a woman swimming at the northern end of the Gulf of Aqaba. Photo by Ofer Gom.

a second bite ensues.

Spearfishing has long been known to be a dangerous pastime in that it may result in shark attack. In 191 cases the victim was a person engaged in spearfishing, and in another 107 cases spearfishing was taking place nearby. The low frequency vibration transmitted by a fish frantically struggling on a spear can bring sharks unerringly to the scene of the spearing where blood and other body fluids can further excite them. Spearfishermen who foolishly tie their catch to their waist or hold it in a bag are exposing themselves further to attack. Some wounds which have been inflicted by sharks on such persons are believed to have resulted from the shark's attempt to take a speared fish.

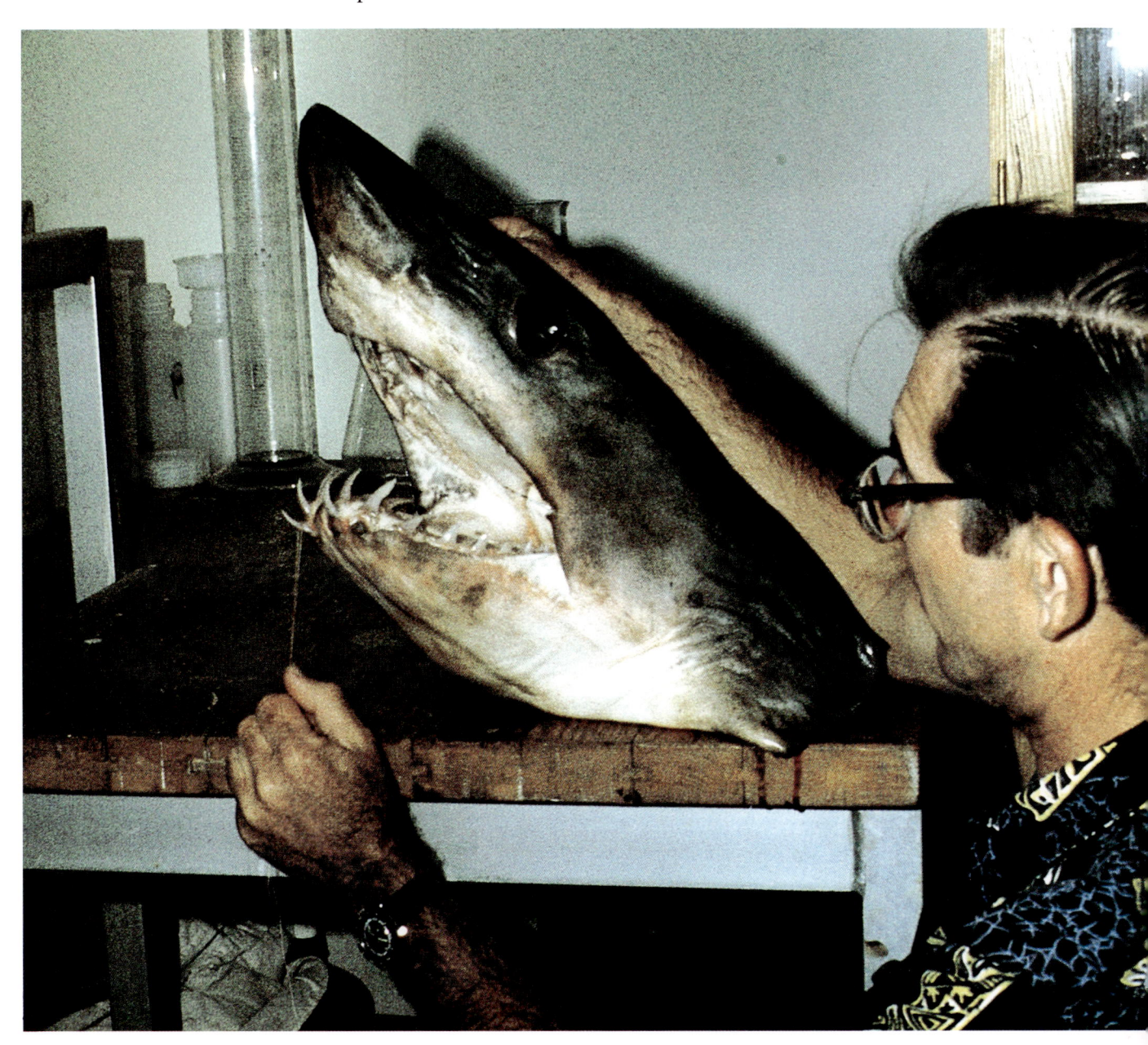

In 530 cases it was possible for the victim or a companion to report whether the shark was seen or not before the attack. Of these victims, 63% were not aware of the shark before they were bitten. Of the remaining 161 victims who saw the shark, 41% noted that it came directly for them. In only 21% of the cases did it circle the victim before attacking. 94% of the attacks were considered to have been executed by a single shark.

In 296 cases it was possible to determine the direction of the original attack on the victim: from the front in 33% of the cases, from behind in 31%, from the side in 17%, from below in 16%, and from above in 3%. Of 409 cases, the initial contact of the shark with the victim was sudden and violent. In 119 cases the shark made one or more close passes before striking the victim.

In 835 cases the location of the wounds was documented (in 31 the wounds were so extreme that localization was not possible). 77.9% occurred on the appendages: 22.5% to the calves or knees; 18.3% to the thighs; 13% to the arms; 9.9% to the feet; 8.5% to the hands; and 5.7% to the fingers and toes. Only 1.3% of the wounds were to the head. The high percentage to the legs is in part explained by the many attacks on persons who were merely wading.

Information was available on rescue of victims of shark attacks in 586 cases. Of these, victims were aided by a single rescuer in 132 instances and by more than one in 138, all in conditions where there was a distinct possibility of injury to rescuers by the shark or sharks. When a single rescuer was involved, only one person was killed and only six were injured by a shark or sharks. There were two fatalities among rescuers when there was more than one helping the victim and three others were injured.

Gilbert (1963) and Baldridge (1973) have summarized recommendations for persons who enter waters where dangerous sharks might occur. This advice includes such measures as swimming or diving with a companion, not venturing far from shore or near deep channels, not entering water with an open wound, and not swimming at night (especially without a light) or in turbid water. Among other recommendations: do not spear a shark, grab its tail, or provoke it in any way, no matter how small it may be; remove a speared fish from the water as soon as possible; avoid wearing brightly coloured swimwear and bright metallic objects such as chrome-plated depth gauges; carry some kind of device to ward off a shark (an explosive powerhead is the best); keep constantly alert, particularly toward the open sea, for an approaching shark; leave the water as soon as possible if a shark of reasonable size is sighted, but not with rapid movements (the swimming movements should be steady and rhythmic). Gilbert suggests deliberately charging the shark and hitting it on the snout with a club or 'shark billy' if it comes close. This may work for some sharks, but it is the worst thing to do for the Grey Reef Shark (*Carcharhinus amblyrhynchos*) and probably others, especially if it is exhibiting its threat behaviour (Johnson and Nelson, 1973). An overt movement toward a shark of this species is apt to trigger an attack.

Other Negative Aspects

Some persons contend that sharks reduce the populations of food and game fishes. The larger predaceous sharks are at the top of the food chain. They are an important part of the balance of nature in the sea. When man upsets that balance, deliberately or otherwise, the result is often to his disadvantage in some unexpected way. To combat the very real shark hazard in South African waters, the authorities at Durban commenced the 'meshing' of the beaches in 1952. This consisted of setting large-mesh gill nets 450 feet (137 m) long parallel to the beaches about 1500 feet (460 m) offshore. These nets do not just divert sharks elsewhere as barrier nets do, but they often capture the large sharks by entangling them in the mesh. Meshing has successfully reduced the populations of the large sharks, and the number of shark attacks in recent years has decreased significantly. The same is true of Australia. With the reduction of the numbers of large sharks in South African waters, however, the populations of small sharks has greatly increased (large sharks often prey upon small sharks). It is believed that these small sharks are making serious inroads into the populations of some of the important gamefishes of the area, such as the Bluefish (*Pomatomus saltator*), which is called Elf in South Africa.

Grey Reef Shark
Caraharhinus amblyrhynchos
Photo J. Randall.

The predation on sea turtle by large sharks such as the Tiger Shark was not a problem until man began to over exploit the turtles, take their eggs, and destroy or alter their nesting sites. In areas where turtle populations are greatly reduced by man, the predation pressure by sharks could be significant. The same may be true of the endangered monk seal (*Monachus schauinslandi*) in the Hawaiian Islands. In special cases such as this it might be advisable to reduce shark populations temporarily (and instigate conservation measures to reduce the depredations by *Homo sapiens*) until the turtle and seal populations can recover. In Arabian waters investigations should be made of the impact of both man and the shark on the dugong (*Dugong dugong*), the population of which is alarmingly low in much of its range.

The damage by sharks to fishermen's catch and their gear is unfortunate, but it is what might be expected from generalized opportunistic carnivores. In equatorial waters of the Pacific there is an average 20% loss of the longline tuna catch due to the Oceanic Whitetip Shark (*Carcharhinus longimanus*) and the Silky Shark (*C. falciformis*) (Murphy and Shomura, 1955; Iversen and Yoshida, 1956).

Commercial Value

What can we say about sharks that is positive, apart from their important role as predators to help maintain the delicate balance of nature in the various marine communities of which they are a part? The main answer is that sharks have a real commercial value for a number of uses, though some are not fully realized. One is as live animals in large aquariums and oceanariums. A tank with live sharks is always among the most popular exhibits at such entertainment centers.

Some sharks are officially recognised as gamefishes by the International Gamefish Association. The most sporting, because of their fighting ability and sensational leaps, are the two Makos (*Isurus* spp.); records are kept for them only at the generic level. The same is true of the Hammerhead Sharks (even though there are nine species in the genus *Sphyrna*), and the Thresher (*Alopias* spp.) where three species are lumped. Perhaps one day the Association will refine their catch records to the species level. The four remaining game sharks are recorded as single species: the Blue, Tiger, Great White, and Porbeagle (*Lamna nasus*). A minor use of small sharks, especially the Dogfish Shark (*Squalus acanthias*), is for dissection in zoological laboratories.

As a fishery resource sharks offer a surprisingly varied series of products: the meat as food, fins as a thickener for soup, shark liver oil for squalene, the hide for leather, the jaws and teeth as curios, and the residue as shark meal (Kreuzer and Ahmed, 1978). Each will be discussed separately below.

In many places in the world there are small fisheries for incidental landings of sharks for food. These are mainly in developing nations. The author has obtained sharks as specimens in local fish markets in Trinidad, Hawaii, Japan, Taiwan, Hong Kong, Philippines, Indonesia, Sri Lanka, India, Oman, Bahrain, Qatar, Saudi Arabia, and Sudan. Among the developed nations only a few such as Japan (which has the largest landings), the United Kingdom, Australia, Federal Republic of Germany, and Italy utilize shark meat in significant amounts as food. Some minced shark meat is processed into fish meat balls in Singapore, Hong Kong, and Thailand. In recent years the market for shark meat has been expanding in the Soviet Union and the United

States as the consumer prejudice against eating shark slowly breaks down and the realisation emerges that shark meat can be tasty when fresh and properly prepared. Hawaii provides an example of the bias against eating shark. Shark was successfully sold for years as a reasonably priced produce labelled fish cake. When it was decreed that it had to be labelled shark, sales dropped dramatically and the small local shark fishery collapsed (shark meat, however, is beginning to reappear in Hawaiian markets.) There is another reason why shark meat is not popular food. As mentioned in the previous chapter, sharks have solved their osmotic problem in the sea by retaining a high percentage of urea in their blood and body fluids. Urea is colorless and odorless, but it is broken down quickly by bacterial action after a shark dies; one of the by-products is ammonia. This is largely responsible for the pungent odor and objectionable taste of shark which is not fresh. To prepare shark meat for human consumption, the shark should be bled immediately after being caught (as by cutting off the caudal fin). The second step is washing the meat in freshwater, salt brine or an acid solution. Then it must be chilled or frozen. Importers of shark to European countries pay a higher price for meat that is frozen at sea rather than when landed at shore. The smaller species of sharks are the most valuable as food. In Europe the most popular are the Spiny Dogfish (*Squalus acanthias*) (in the United Kingdom it is preferred that it not be referred to as shark), Porbeagle (*Lamna nasus*), Mako (*Isurus oxyrinchus*), and triakids of the genus *Mustelus*. In Japan the Mako, Salmon Shark (*Lamna ditropis*), and the Blue Shark (*Prionace glauca*) are the preferred species for the production of kamaboko. The Scalloped Hammerhead (*Sphyrna lewini*), Great White Shark (*Carcharodon carcharias*), and the Spiny Dogfish are the favorite species for shark eaten in steak form. In Australia the consumption of shark rose steadily from the early fifties until by 1970 it represented the greatest tonnage landed. Most, as in the United Kingdom, was used as the fish in fish-and-chips. The principal species was the School Shark (*Galeorhinus australis*). In 1972 the Government of Australia placed a ban on School Sharks over 41 inches (slightly more than 1 meter) in length due to the high mercury content of larger individuals of this species. Increased fishing for other sharks such as *Mustelus antarcticus* has not overcome the setback to the shark fishery from the ban. Most governments have issued regulations stipulating the maximum level of mercury that can be permitted in fish or fish products. The larger predaceous species, which includes many of the larger sharks, are the ones most apt to accumulate dangerous levels of mercury.

The fins are the most valuable part of sharks because of their use in Chinese cookery. Those generally used are the first dorsal, pectorals, and lower lobe of the caudal fin, but others may be taken from large sharks. The fins of nearly all sharks over 1.5 m have some value, an exception being the Nurse Sharks (Ginglymostomatidae). The species with the most highly prized fins are the Hammerheads, the Blue Shark, and most of the larger carcharhinids. The fins are cut from sharks in a concave curve into the base (except the lower lobe of the caudal which is cut straight). Further preparation involves skinning, cleaning, and drying. In a restaurant the fins are soaked overnight in vinegar and water, then steamed or boiled for two or three hours until the rays (ceratotrichia) begin to separate into gelatinous noodle-like strands. The strands are then steamed again with chicken broth or other flavorsome substances since they have no flavor of their own. Japan is the major exporter of shark fins and Hong Kong the major importer, accounting for about 70% of all exports. More than 3000 tons of dried shark fins are used in Hong Kong in a year. Singapore is the next most important buyer, with over 20% of the total exports. Both Hong Kong and Singapore also export shark fins.

Beginning in the forties, a large market developed for shark liver oil because of its high vitamin A content. Major shark fisheries for the livers were established in the United States and Australia. When it became more economical to synthesize vitamin A, the fishing for sharks in the U.S. essentially ceased. In Australia, however, it continued, the emphasis shifting to use of the meat as food. Today the value of shark liver oil is low unless it has a high content of squalene ($C_{30}H_{62}$), a non-saponifiable substance. The livers of about ten species of Squalidae have a level of squalene of 80% or more. These are small sharks generally found at depths of 600 to 1000 m (*Squalus acanthias* is not one of them). Livers of species high in squalene tend to have a low vitamin A content. Processing of liver for squalene should begin within about 15 minutes after capture. The principal market for squalene is in Japan where it is used mainly in the cosmetic industry. Norway is second in the utilization of this special shark liver product. Small quantities of shark liver oil are used in the textile and tanning industries, and a little as lubricating oil because of its heat-resisting quality.

Hides can be prepared of sharks about 1.5 m or longer. Those from large females often cannot be used because of the wounds and scars inflicted by males. Curiously, the hides of Nurse Sharks, the fins of which are worthless, are the most highly prized. Among the other sharks with valuable hides are the Tiger Shark (*Galeocerdo cuvier*), Lemon Sharks (*Negaprion* spp.), Sand Tiger Sharks (*Odontaspis* spp.), Mackerel Sharks (*Lamna* spp., *Isurus* spp.), the Great Hammerhead (*Sphyrna mokarran*), the Blue Shark (*Prionace glauca*), and several of the larger Requiem Sharks

(*Carcharhinus* spp.). Sharks for hide preparation should not be iced or frozen. If not chilled or frozen, the highest quality meat cannot be obtained, so a decision has to be made at sea whether a particular shark is destined for hide production (species, size, and condition of skin being factors) or meat for consumption. Skinning a large shark takes about 20 to 30 minutes, even by the most skilled. The dermal denticles of the skin of sharks quickly dull knives. Some shark skin used to be processed into "shagreen" for its sandpaper-like property, but this has given way to other commercial abrasives. An American industrial chemist discovered an economically feasible process whereby the denticles of shark skin can be removed, a necessary first-step in leather production. This has somewhat revitalized the shark leather industry. Leather from shark skin is durable and scuff-proof, yet supple so it can be made into many things such as shoes, wallets, purses, and belts. These products sell at high prices because of the recognised quality of shark skin. However, the high cost of labour in developed countries for skinning and preparation of hides and the difficulty of achieving a supply on a regular basis have prevented more widespread use.

Some pharmaceutical substances in addition to vitamins A and D are obtained from sharks. An example is chondroitine, obtained from elasmobranch cartilage.

A small market exists in various parts of the world for the jaws of sharks and the teeth as curios. Sharks teeth, particularly those of the Tiger Shark, Makos, and the Great White Shark, are sometimes used in jewellery.

If full utilisation of the shark resource is to be made, the residue after the removal of the hides, the better parts for food, and the liver oil should be processed into fish meal. This is best done in major shark processing plants.

With the reduced stocks of many species of commercial fishes in the world from the effects of overfishing and pollution, and the restriction imposed on the major fishing nations by the adoption of the 200-mile offshore exclusive zone for all maritime countries, a greater utilisation of sharks has begun. As pointed out by Holden (1974), sharks are not good subjects for intensive fisheries because of the small number of young produced by individual females, the long gestation period, and slow growth to adult size. Fishery pressure on resident populations of sharks soon causes a sharp drop in numbers from which recovery is slow. Shark fisheries established in areas visited by large numbers of migrating sharks fare better, but these too have been shown to suffer soon from a decline in catch per unit of effort. Clearly, the development of shark fisheries should be accompanied by careful management measures.

Arabian Shark Families

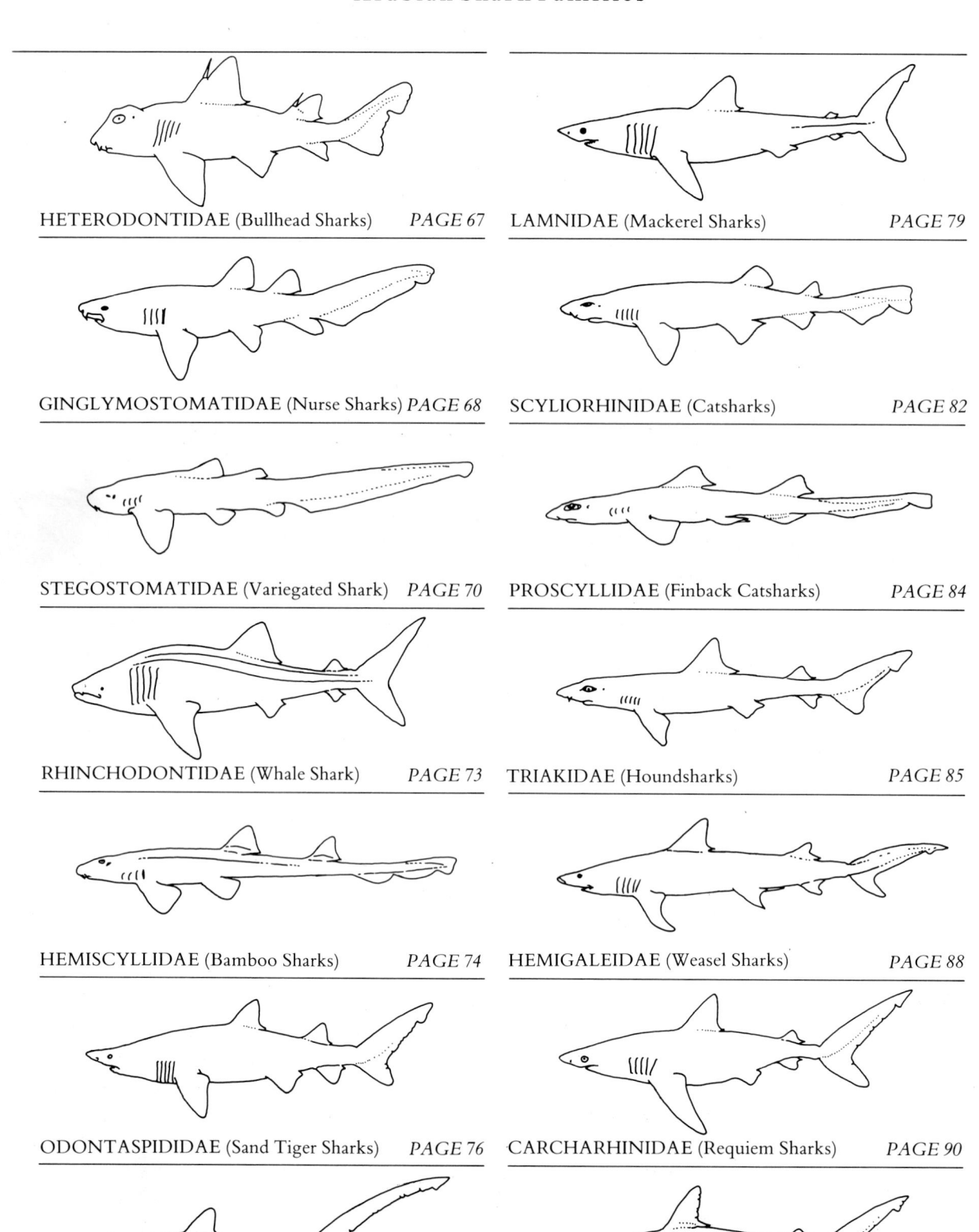

HETERODONTIDAE (Bullhead Sharks) PAGE 67	LAMNIDAE (Mackerel Sharks) PAGE 79
GINGLYMOSTOMATIDAE (Nurse Sharks) PAGE 68	SCYLIORHINIDAE (Catsharks) PAGE 82
STEGOSTOMATIDAE (Variegated Shark) PAGE 70	PROSCYLLIDAE (Finback Catsharks) PAGE 84
RHINCHODONTIDAE (Whale Shark) PAGE 73	TRIAKIDAE (Houndsharks) PAGE 85
HEMISCYLLIDAE (Bamboo Sharks) PAGE 74	HEMIGALEIDAE (Weasel Sharks) PAGE 88
ODONTASPIDIDAE (Sand Tiger Sharks) PAGE 76	CARCHARHINIDAE (Requiem Sharks) PAGE 90
ALOPIIDAE (Thresher Sharks) PAGE 78	SPHYRNIDAE (Hammerhead Sharks) PAGE 125

CLASSIFICATION

ORDER HETERODONTIFORMES

FAMILY HETERODONTIDAE (BULLHEAD SHARKS)

Diagnosis
Body cylindrical; head slightly elevated; snout short; five gill slits on each side, the posterior three above pectoral base; eyes high on head; no nictitating lower eyelid; spiracles present, ventroposterior to eye; nostrils without a barbel but with a well-developed nasal flap which reaches posteriorly to mouth; mouth moderate; teeth small and cuspidate anteriorly, large and molariform posteriorly; two dorsal fins, each preceded by a stout spine; anal fin present; caudal fin with a dorsal and ventral lobe (the latter broadly triangular), without precaudal pits.

Remarks
Oviparous, bottom-dwelling, sluggish and nocturnal; feeds mainly on benthic invertebrates such as sea urchins, crustaceans and molluscs. One genus, *Heterodontus*, with eight species (Taylor, 1972; Compagno, 1984a). Figure 9 shows the skeleton. Sometimes called Horn Sharks.

Whitespotted Bullhead Shark
Heterodontus ramalheira (Smith, 1949)

Diagnosis
Supraorbital ridge moderately elevated; first dorsal fin nearly twice as large as second, its origin over middle of pectoral base; spine at front of dorsal fins about half height of these fins; anal fin moderately pointed, its apex nearly reaching origin of ventral lobe of caudal fin; dark reddish brown with numerous small white spots. Maximum total length 83 cm for females, about 64 cm for males.

Remarks
A rare species known to date only from southern Mozambique (type locality, Inhambane) and the southeastern shore of the Arabian Peninsula (coast of Oman outside the Gulf of Oman) in the depth range of 108-275 m. Crabs have been reported from the stomachs of two individuals.

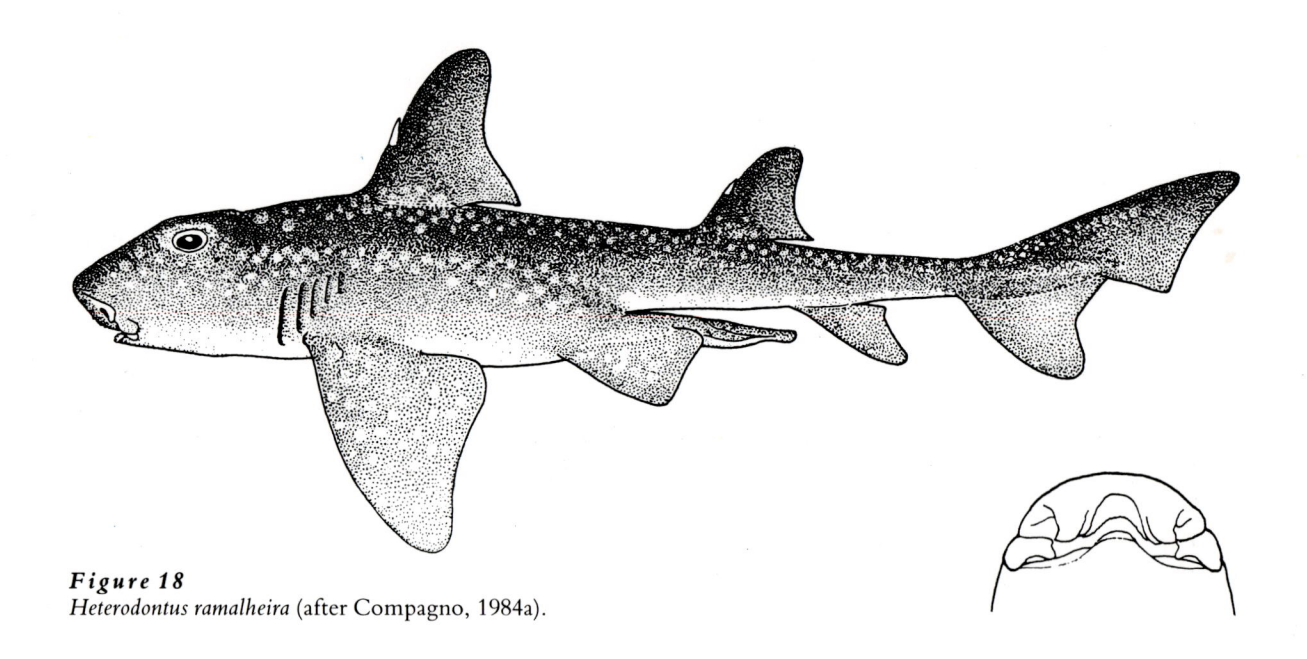

Figure 18
Heterodontus ramalheira (after Compagno, 1984a).

ORDER ORECTOLOBIFORMES

FAMILY GINGLYMOSTOMATIDAE (NURSE SHARKS)

Diagnosis
Body cylindrical to slightly depressed, without ridges; head broad and depressed, without cutaneous flaps; snout short and broadly rounded; five gill slits on each side, the fourth and fifth close together above pectoral base; eyes small, dorsolateral on head; spiracles small, each behind lower part of eye; nostrils with a barbel; mouth moderate; teeth small, in two to four functional rows, with a large central and small lateral cusps; two close-set dorsal fins posteriorly on body; anal fin as large or nearly as large as second dorsal fin, its origin below anterior half of base of second dorsal fin; no precaudal pits; caudal fin with upper lobe one-fourth to one-third total length, angling only slightly upward, without a well-developed lower lobe.

Remarks
Ovoviviparous, bottom-dwelling sharks of shallow tropical and subtropical seas. Two genera, *Nebrius* and *Ginglymostoma*. Some authors have regarded *Nebrius* as a subgenus of *Ginglymostoma*, but most shark authorities accord full generic status to *Nebrius*.

Figure 19
Nebrius concolor, dorsal view, 67.5 cm, Gilbert Islands (photo by J. Randall)

Tawny Nurse Shark
Nebrius concolor Ruppell, 1837

Diagnosis

Characteristics of the family (see above); teeth in numerous rows, the first three or four rows functional; teeth with a large central cusp and four to six smaller cusps on each side; distal ends of dorsal and anal fins distinctly angular; second dorsal fin nearly as large as first; origin of first dorsal fin slightly anterior to a vertical at origin of pelvic fins; anal fin origin below middle of base of second dorsal fin; caudal fin about 30% total length; pectoral fins falcate; vertebrae of one specimen 189, of which 95 are precaudal; greyish to yellowish brown, paler ventrally; attains at least 320 cm.

Remarks

This shark, the only member of the genus *Nebrius*, is wide-ranging in the Indo-Pacific region from the Red Sea (type locality) and coast of East Africa to the Marshall Islands in the Northern Hemisphere and the Society Islands in the Southern. It occurs at depths of less than 1 to at least 70 m. Feeds at night on a wide variety of benthic animals such as reef fishes, spiny lobsters, crabs, and octopuses. It is reported to suck in prey that may be out of reach of its teeth with its large powerful pharynx. Shelters in caves or beneath ledges by day, sometimes in close association with other individuals of its species. Although contact by humans is usually without incident, there are a few records of bites on divers when this shark is provoked. Development ovoviviparous, with as many as four egg cases per uterus; young about 40 cm long at birth. The name *Nebrius ferrugineus* (Lesson, 1830) has been used by some authors (such as Compagno, 1984a) for this species, but Dingerkus (1984) regards it as a *nomen nudum* because of the inadequate description and the lack of a type specimen.

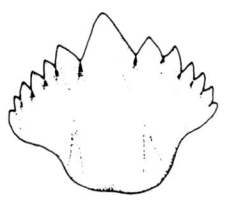

Figure 20
Lower tooth of *Nebrius concolor* (after Compagno, 1984a).

Figure 21
Nebrius concolor, 118 cm (after Bass, D'Aubrey and Kistnasamy, 1975a).

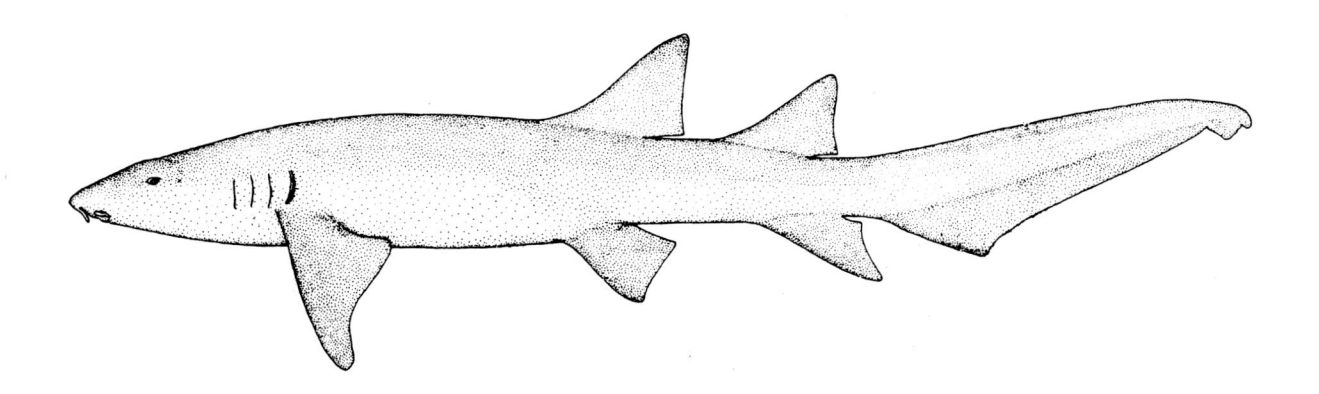

FAMILY STEGOSTOMATIDAE (VARIEGATED SHARK FAMILY)

For Diagnosis see account of the single species of the family.

Variegated Shark
Stegostoma varium (Seba, 1758)

Diagnosis

Body cylindrical with a prominent median dorsal and two longitudinal ridges on each side (lower ridge lacking in small juveniles); head broad and slightly depressed, without cutaneous flaps; snout short, broadly rounded; five gill slits on each side, the last three above pectoral base, the fourth and fifth very close together; eyes small, lateral on head; spiracles as large or larger than eye, each directly behind eye; nostrils with a short barbel; mouth moderate; teeth in several close-set functional rows, tricuspid, the cusps strongly pointed, the central one much the largest; first dorsal fin about twice as large as second, its origin in about middle of body (but origin difficult to determine, as it grades into middorsal ridge); origin of pelvic fins slightly anterior to a vertical at rear base of first dorsal fin; anal fin origin below rear base of second dorsal fin; caudal fin very long (about half total length), without a lower lobe; pectoral fins broadly rounded; total number of vertebrae 217 to 234; juveniles with alternating black and pale yellowish bars, white below; adults brownish yellow, shading to white ventrally, with numerous black spots of variable size (most the size of spiracle or smaller). The 58-cm specimen of Figure 24 is just beginning to show the breakdown of the dark bars and formation of the dark spots. Reaches 280 cm (one unconfirmed record of 354 cm).

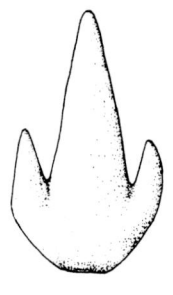

Remarks

Not only does this species show dramatic change in colour from young to adult, but the body and fin proportions also alter with growth (see Bass et al., 1975a: table 17). *S. varium* from the Red Sea (type locality) south to Cape Saint Francis, South Africa (34° 20' S) and east to the western Pacific where it is found from southern Japan to New South Wales; in the South Pacific it extends east to the Samoa Islands (Wass, 1984) and in the North Pacific to the Caroline Islands (BPBM 8887, 1635 mm, 18.5 kg, speared at Ulithi by author). Despite its broad distribution, this shark is not very common at any locality. It occurs from the shallows to depths of about 30 m, often on or near coral reefs; it is generally encountered during the day at rest on the bottom. It is not aggressive to man. It feeds mainly on molluscs and crustaceans, occasionally on fishes. Individuals in oceanariums readily take fish from a diver's hand. Sexual maturity is attained at about 150 cm for males and 170 cm for females. Oviparous, the egg cases about 20 cm long (Masuda et al., 1975: fig. 5 C) with a tuft of adhesive filaments on either side for attachment to the bottom. The young hatch at a length of 20 to 30 cm (van der Elst, 1981). Some authors (such as Compagno, 1984a) use the name *Stegostoma fasciatum* (Hermann) for this species in the belief that Seba's *varium* is not valid because many Seba names are nonbinomial; however, this one (as *Squalus varius*) is. Klausewitz (1960) described and illustrated the 105-cm lectotype of *varium*. *Stegostoma tigrinum* (Gmelin) is another synonym occasionally in use.

Figure 22
Lower tooth of *Stegostoma varium* (after Compagno, 1984a).

Figure 23
Adult of *Stegostoma varium*, Natal (J. Randall).

Figure 24
Juvenile of *Stegostoma varium*, 58 cm, Bahrain (J. Randall).

SHARKS OF ARABIA

FAMILY RHINCODONTIDAE (WHALE SHARK FAMILY)

For Diagnosis see account of the single species of the family.

Whale Shark
Rhincodon typus Smith, 1829

Diagnosis

Body ovate in cross-section, the head strongly flattened with a truncate snout; a median dorsal and three prominent longitudinal ridges on each side commencing above gill openings, the lowermost ending in a well-developed keel on side of caudal peduncle; mouth very large, nearly terminal; teeth minute, in over 300 rows (of which 10 to 15 are functional), each tooth with a single, sharp, backward-curved cusp; five large gill slits high on side, their internal openings with branchial filters; eyes small; spiracles about as large as eyes, each behind and slightly above an eye; a barbel overlapping upper-lip on each side; first dorsal fin much larger than second, its origin in about middle of fork length; pelvic fins below posterior half of first dorsal fin; anal fin below second dorsal fin; caudal fin with a strongly elevated narrow upper lobe, without a subterminal notch; no upper precaudal pit; lower caudal lobe about half length of upper; pectoral fins long and falcate; one count of 153 vertebrae, of which 81 are precaudal; dark above with narrow vertical whitish lines and rows of whitish spots, becoming whitish ventrally. The largest fish in the world; attains 13.7 m (unauthenticated reports to 18 m).

Remarks

The Whale Shark is a surface-dwelling, pelagic species of tropical, subtropical, and warm temperate seas. It feeds mainly on zooplankton and small nekton such as fishes and squids. It is often observed in association with schools of tuna, and for good reason. When tunas have concentrated small fishes at the surface, the Whale Shark can rise vertically from below to ingest the fishes. Occasionally the tunas themselves are eaten. Its ability to feed on the more active prey animals is a result of powerful suction as well as forward motion (Compagno, 1984a). Harmless to man; divers have at times hitched rides on these huge sharks by holding onto a fin or the ridges on the back. Not infrequently Whale Sharks have been rammed by steamers (Gudger, 1940). Reproduction probably ovoviviparous (Compagno, 1984a). The smallest free-living Whale Sharks with an 'umbilical' scar measure 55 to 56 cm in total length. The first description of the Whale Shark was made by Dr. Andrew Smith, an army surgeon, from a specimen harpooned in Table Bay, South Africa; its skin was deposited in the Museum National d'Histoire Naturelle in Paris. The description appeared in a newspaper in 1828 (Penrith, 1972); the generic name used then was *Rhiniodon*. In the more formal description in 1829 Smith spelled the name *Rhincodon*; still later he used *Rhinodon*. Some authors have amended the spelling to *Rhineodon*. Strong arguments have been put forth for acceptance of both *Rhiniodon* and *Rhincodon*. The author agrees with that of Wheeler (1982) in support of *Rhincodon*. A decision has just been made by the International Commission on Zoological Nomenclature (Opinion No. 1278) to recognise *Rhincodon* as the valid generic name for the Whale Shark. *R. typus* shares a number of characteristics with the Nurse Shark and the Variegated Shark. Dingerkus (1984) favors its classification in the same family with these other orectolobiforms, hence the Ginglymostomatidae. The extreme specialisations of *Rhincodon*, however, would seem to justify its placement in a separate family.

Figure 25
Rhincodon typus, Hawaii (Tomoko Kimura).

SHARKS OF ARABIA

Figure 26
Chiloscyllium arabicum, Bahrain
(J. Randall).

Figure 27
Chiloscyllium arabicum Bahrain
(J. Randall).

FAMILY HEMISCYLLIDAE (BAMBOO SHARKS)

Diagnosis
Elongate, slender sharks with a cylindrical to slightly depressed body, sometimes with a longitudinal ridge on upper side; head not greatly depressed, without cutaneous flaps; snout varying from slightly pointed to broadly rounded; eyes dorsolateral on head; supraorbital crest present on cranium (though not pronounced); five gill slits, the posterior three above pectoral fin base, the last two very close together; spiracles large, each below and posterior to centre of eye; a prominent barbel present medial to nasal opening; mouth small, usually near front of snout; teeth small, in 12 to 17 rows on each side of jaws, with a single cusp (*Hemiscyllium*) or with a large central cusp and a small cusp on each side (*Chiloscyllium*); two dorsal fins of nearly equal size, the origin of first near centre of body; anal fin very posterior, ending at lower origin of caudal fin; no precaudal pits; caudal fin less than one-fourth total length, only slightly elevated above level of body, with a subterminal notch but no ventral lobe; colour uniform or with spots or bars; species small, not exceeding 100 cm.

Remarks
Inshore, bottom-dwelling sharks, harmless to man. Western Pacific to Arabian Gulf (except one species confined to Madagascar). Reproduction oviparous (for those in which development is known). Two genera, *Hemiscyllium* with five species and *Chiloscyllium* with seven (Dingerkus and DeFino, 1983).

Arabian Bamboo Shark
Chiloscyllium arabicum
Gubanov, 1980

Diagnosis
Orbit diameter 1.4 to 1.8% total length; spiracle of adults larger than orbit; teeth in jaws in 9 to 10 rows (anterior to posterior), about the first three or four functional; 12 to 15 teeth in first row on each side of jaws; first dorsal fin slightly larger than second, but base of second dorsal fin longer than that of first (or rarely equally long); first dorsal fin slightly larger than pelvic fins; origin of first dorsal fin anterior to rear base of pelvic fins; posterior margins of dorsal fins straight; a prominent middorsal ridge on back (absent posterior to second dorsal); caudal fin length (measured ventrally to rear base of anal fin) 17 to 21% total length; vertebrae 143 to 171; tan, becoming whitish ventrally; edges of fins (especially the paired fins) sometimes orangish; juveniles coloured like adults; largest recorded, 78 cm.

Remarks
Unaware of the description of *C. arabicum* Gubanov in Gubanov and Shleib (eds.), 1980, Dingerkus and DeFino (1983) named this species *C. confusum* and described it much more thoroughly. They gave the distribution as Arabian Gulf (the type locality, where it is common) to the southern tip of India. The depth range was given by Gubanov as 3 to 100 m. Oviparous. Feeds mainly on molluscs and crustaceans, occasionally on squids and fishes. Dingerkus and DeFino figure an x-ray of a subadult with a snake eel in its stomach. This species has been confused in the past with *C. griseum*; it is distinguished by its longer second dorsal fin base (in *griseum* the base of the first dorsal fin is longest) and by its larger spiracle. Also the juveniles and subadults of *griseum* have large saddle-like dark bars which are lacking in *arabicum*.

Grey Bamboo Shark
Chiloscyllium griseum
Müller and Henle, 1838

Diagnosis
Orbit diameter 1.34 to 2.2% total length; spiracle diameter smaller than greatest orbit diameter; teeth in about 10 rows, the anterior three or four functional; about 14 teeth on each side of front row of jaws; first dorsal fin slightly larger than second, its base longer than base of second fin; first dorsal fin and pelvic fins about equal in size; origin of first dorsal fin over rear base of pelvic fins; posterior margins of dorsal fins straight; a middorsal ridge on back; interdorsal space only slightly greater than length of first dorsal fin base, 8.7 to 11.5% total length; caudal fin length (measured ventrally to rear base of anal fin) 16 to 22% total length; vertebrae 157 to 169; adults light yellowish brown, paler ventrally; juveniles and subadults with broad dark bars and saddle-like blotches; largest recorded, 77 cm.

Remarks
This species is known only from the Arabian Gulf (Gubanov, 1980), Pakistan, and both coasts of India (type locality, the Malabar coast of SW India). Oviparous, depositing its small egg cases on the bottom. Food habits not reported, but probably similar to that of *C. arabicum*. Some authors have failed to distinguish this species from the Indo-Malayan *C. hasselti* Bleeker. The latter has a shorter interdorsal space (less than 9.3% total length of adults) and shorter dorsal fins (height of first dorsal less than 6.6% total length); the dark bars of juvenile *hasselti* are outlined in black.

Figure 28
Chiloscyllium griseum, 64 cm, Cebu (J. Randall)

ORDER LAMNIFORMES
FAMILY ODONTASPIDIDAE (SAND TIGER SHARKS)

Diagnosis
Body moderately stout, cylindrical to slightly compressed; head short, the snout slightly depressed and pointed; eyes small to large, in front of corner of mouth; no nictitating eyelid; gill openings moderately large, though not extending onto dorsal half of head, all anterior to pectoral fins; spiracle small; mouth large; anterior teeth long and prong-like, smooth-edged, with one to three sharp cusplets on each side; roots of teeth highly arched; posterior teeth progressively smaller; first dorsal fin moderately large; upper precaudal pit present; caudal fin with a long upper lobe (as much as 30% total length) and short lower lobe; colour uniform or with dark spotting; largest, 370 cm.

Remarks
This family consists of a single genus with three or four living species. Compagno (1984a), however, prefers to recognise a second genus, *Eugomphodus* Gill, for the Sand Tiger Shark and the doubtful species *E. tricuspidatus* (Day). Initially these three (or four) sharks were classified in the genus *Carcharias* Rafinesque 1810a. The International Commission on Zoological Nomenclature suppressed the name *Carcharias* in favor of *Odontaspis* Agassiz 1838, which was based chiefly on fossils, on the grounds that the latter had greater usage (Opinion 723.5a, which might be questioned). All of these species attain large size. They are found from tropical to cold temperate waters, but their distributions are disjunct. They occur from shallow to deep water (to perhaps 1600 m). They feed mainly on fishes but also on crustaceans and pelecypods. Development is ovoviviparous; uterine cannibalism is normal; typically only one surviving pup per uterus.

Figure 29
Odontaspis taurus (after Compagno, 1984a).

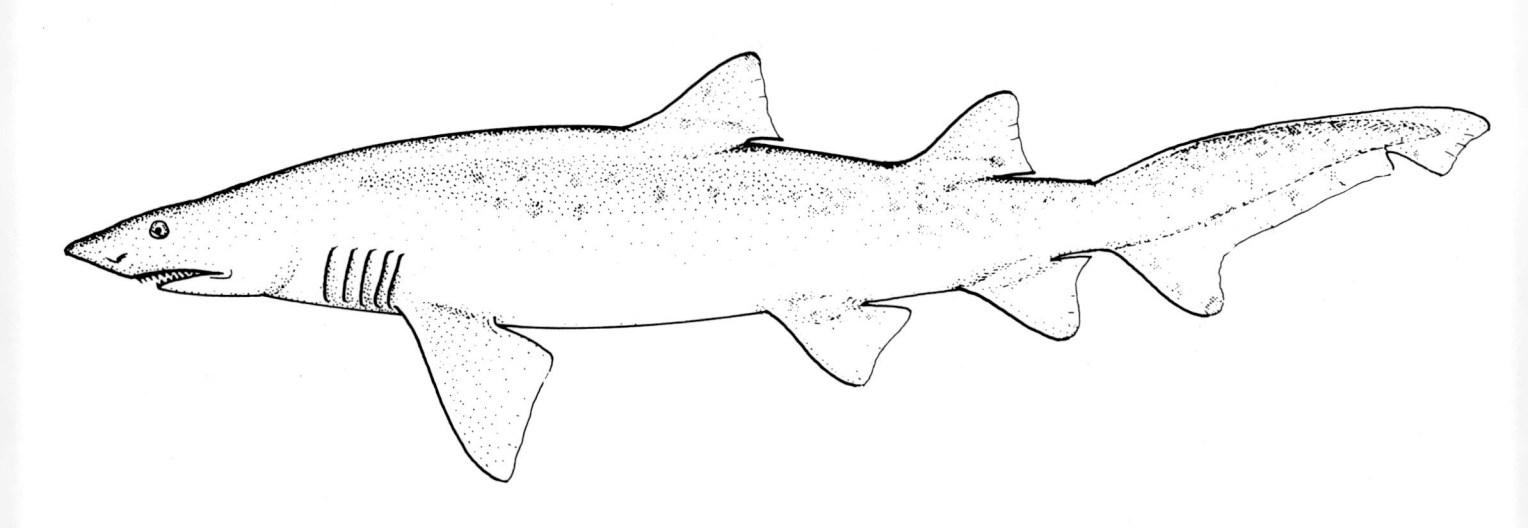

Sand Tiger Shark
Odontaspis taurus (Rafinesque, 1810)

Diagnosis

Characters of the family; snout short, the preoral length about 5% total length; eyes small, about 1% total length; 28 to 38 teeth in outer row on each side of upper jaw and 26 to 37 in lower jaw, the anterior teeth large (except two small ones lateral to the three median teeth on each side of upper jaw), with a long, slender, smooth-edged central cusp and a small sharp cusplet on each side at base (these teeth are slightly incurved basally, with slight reverse curvature distally, and they protrude from the jaws); both dorsal fins, anal fin, and pelvic fins subequal; origin of first dorsal fin slightly closer to pelvic fin bases than pectoral fin bases; origin of anal fin below midbase of second dorsal fin; upper lobe of caudal fin about 27% total length, the lower lobe about 11%; brown with scattered dark spots on body and caudal fin (often disappearing with age); vertebrae 170 to 186, of which 91 to 97 are precaudal (counts of 42 South African specimens from Bass et al., 1975a), (counts of nine eastern United States specimens, 156 to 170, from Springer and Garrick, 1964); maximum length about 320 cm.

Remarks

Odontaspis taurus has a curious distribution: eastern seaboard of the United States, Mediterranean (Sicily is the type locality (to equatorial Africa, southeastern South America, southeastern Africa, the Red Sea (where it known only from one record – Tortonese, 1935-36), coast of Australia (except the northern central part), and Viet Nam to China and Japan. It is a littoral species, though has been taken in depths to 191 m. In some areas it is migratory, penetrating higher latitudes in warm months. Often found in aggregations; has been observed to feed cooperatively on schooling fishes. Preys on a great variety of fishes; also on crustaceans and cephalopods. In South Africa where this shark is called the Ragged Tooth and in Australia where it is known as the Grey Nurse, it has an undeserved sinister reputation due to reports of attack on humans, many of which have been fatal. In all probability these attacks are due mainly to carcharhinids, especially the Bull Shark (*Carcharhinus leucas*). The few authenticated attacks by *O. taurus* on man are primarily the result of provocation or attraction to speared fish. *O. tricuspidatus* (Day), described from India, is a possible second species. The holotype (a dried skin) is lost. Compagno (1984a) stated that this nominal species may be a synonym of *taurus*.

Figure 30
Teeth of *Odontaspis taurus* (after Compagno, 1984a).

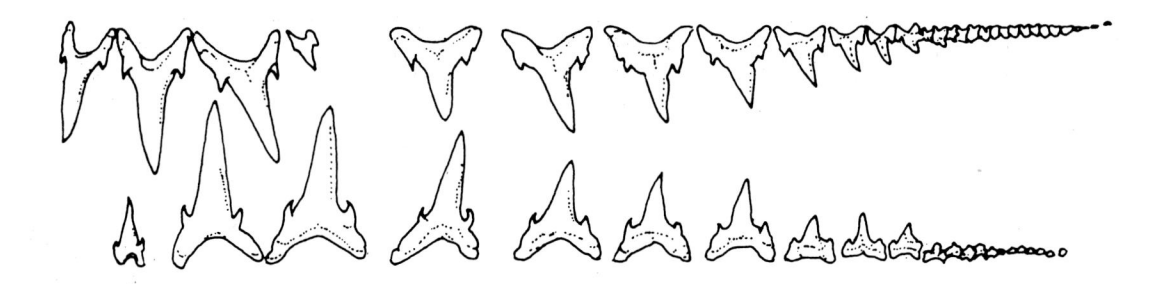

Figure 31
Alopias pelagicus, 99 cm, 9 kg, Hawaii (J. Randall).

Pelagic Thresher
Alopias pelagicus Nakamura, 1935

Diagnosis

Interorbital space strongly convex; head narrow, its width at first gill opening about 1.6 in head depth; snout moderately long; eyes lateral, moderate in size, 1.3 to 1.9% total length; no labial furrows; teeth small, 21 to 23 on each side of upper jaw and 21 on each side of lower jaw, the main cusp strongly oblique laterally, most with one or two small basal cusps on posterolateral edge; origin of first dorsal fin near centre of precaudal length, the fin moderately large (height about 5.6% total length); upper lobe of caudal fin thin, about as long as precaudal length, with a tiny terminal lobe; vertebrae of one specimen 472, of which 126 are precaudal (highest count reported for any shark); grey, becoming white ventrally below level of base of pectoral fins; attains at least 330 cm.

Remarks

This shark was not described until 1935 when Nakamura named it from an adult female and a 96-cm embryo from Taiwan. It has often been misidentified as *A. vulpinus* which differs in having a broader head and shorter snout, the origin of the second dorsal fin distinctly posterior to hind tip of pelvic fins (over hind end of pelvics on *pelagicus*), and the pale ventral part of the body as high as level of dorsal end of gill slits. *A. pelagicus* is primarily an epipelagic warm-water species, but it has been taken near shore. The illustrated specimen was caught in 146 m off Hawaii. This species is reliably reported from a number of isolated localities in the Indo-Pacific, including Taiwan (type locality), Japan, New Caledonia, Tahiti, Red Sea, off Pakistan, off Somalia, and in the eastern Pacific. Ovoviviparous, most often with two pups, one per uterus; the embryos are oophagus (Otake and Mizue, 1981). Sometimes called the Smalltooth Thresher.

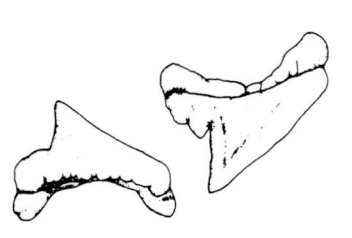

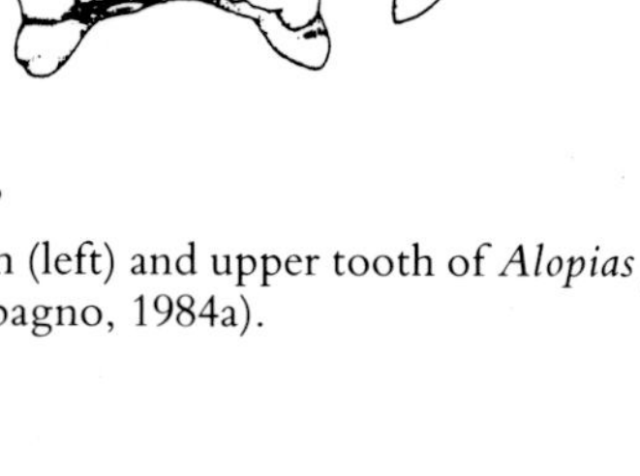

Figure 32
Lower tooth (left) and upper tooth of *Alopias pelagicus* (after Compagno, 1984a).

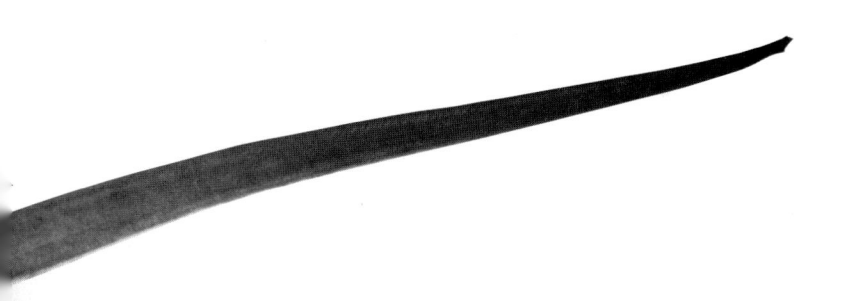

FAMILY ALOPIIDAE (THRESHER SHARKS)

Diagnosis
Body moderately stout and cylindrical; head short, but snout moderately long and conical; eyes moderate to large; spiracles small; mouth small and strongly curved; teeth compressed with sharp edges, in two rows in jaws; five short gill slits, not extending onto dorsal half of head, the last two above pectoral base; first dorsal fin large, erect, in middle of body; second dorsal and anal fins very small; upper lobe of caudal fin as long or nearly as long as body; precaudal pits present; pectoral fins very long and narrow, the posterior margin concave.

Remarks
There are three species of thresher sharks, all in the genus *Alopias*, for which the most obvious character is the extremely long caudal fin. All three are broadly distributed (two circumglobal), but their exact ranges are not known due to difficulty in identification. All are primarily epipelagic, though they may be encountered in coastal waters. The Bigeye Thresher (*A. superciliosus*) penetrates deeper water (to at least 500 m). Threshers feed mainly on small fishes; they are known to circle and concentrate their prey with the aid of their long caudal fins. Also they are reported to stun fishes by lashing with their tail (they are sometimes caught by their caudal fin on tuna longlines as a result of striking the bait with this fin). The meat of thresher sharks is of high quality and the fins of value for shark-fin soup.

FAMILY LAMNIDAE (MACKEREL SHARKS)

Diagnosis
Body spindle-shaped with pointed snout and narrow caudal peduncle bearing a well-developed keel (*Lamna* with a lower secondary keel); five large gill slits extending above midlateral line, the fifth at leading edge of pectoral fins; eyes moderate, lateral in position; spiracles minute or absent; mouth large, ventral, semicircular in outline; teeth large, those anteriorly either long and prong-like with smooth edges (with a small basal cusp on each side in *Lamna*), or triangular and blade-like with coarsely serrate edges (*Carcharodon*); first dorsal fin moderately large and erect, its origin slightly anterior to middle of precaudal length; second dorsal and anal fin very small; precaudal pits present; caudal fin lunate, the upper lobe only slightly larger than lower; pectoral fins long, narrow, and falcate; pelvic fins distinctly smaller than first dorsal fin; species of moderate to large size.

Remarks
These swift sharks swim in tuna-like fashion by lateral strokes of the tail rather than sinuous movement of the entire body as is typical of other sharks. Epipelagic, occasionally inshore. Partially warm-blooded, thus permitting a high level of activity. Tropical to cold temperate. Ovoviviparous. The family includes five species; the Great White Shark (*Carcharodon carcharias*); two Mako Sharks, the Shortfin (*Isurus oxyrinchus*) and the Longfin (*I. paucus*); the Salmon Shark (*Lamna ditropis*); and the Porbeagle (*L. nasus*). The last two mentioned are temperate species. The flesh of lamnids is of high quality for food.

SHARKS OF ARABIA

Figure 33
Isurus oxyrinchus, 233 cm, Red Sea (J. Randall).

Figure 34
Head of *Isurus oxyrinchus* of Figure 33 (J. Randall).

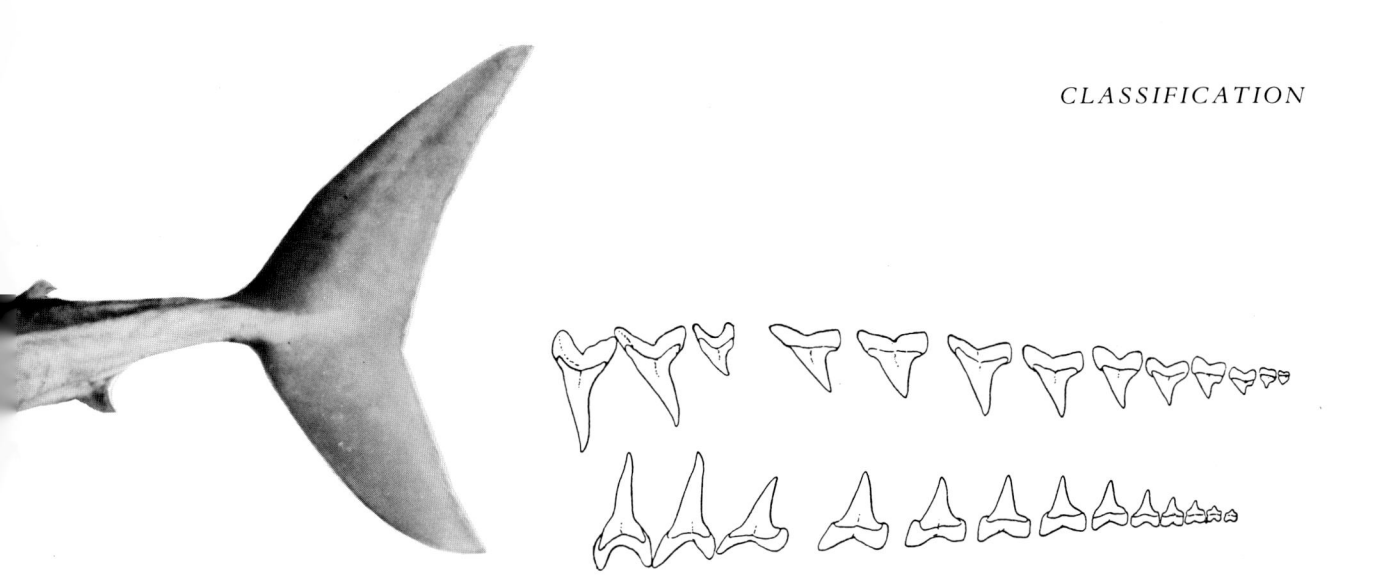

Figure 35
Teeth of *Isurus oxyrinchus* (after Compagno, 1984a).

Shortfin Mako
Isurus oxyrinchus Rafinesque, 1810

Diagnosis
Body slender, the depth about 15% total length; snout moderately long, conical, and distinctly pointed, its length about 6.5% total length; 12 or 13 teeth on each side of front row in jaws, the anterior teeth slender with sharp, nonserrate edges, and incurved except tips which have a slight reverse curvature; posterior teeth progressively smaller and more triangular; origin of first dorsal fin slightly posterior to a vertical at inner posterior corner of pectoral fins; pectoral fins distinctly shorter than head length (measured to last gill slit); origin of anal fin beneath midbase of second dorsal fin; vertebrae 183 to 194, of which 107 to 112 are precaudal; dark blue on back in life, fading to grey after death, white below; reported to 394 cm.

Remarks
The Shortfin Mako is among the most broadly distributed of marine animals, occurring circumglobally in tropical to temperate seas (not yet reported from the Arabian Gulf, however). The type-locality is Sicily. The lower limit in sea temperature for this shark is about 16°C. Migration to higher latitudes takes place during summer as a result of following warm currents on the east side of continents. Probably the fastest of all sharks and certainly one of the swiftest swimming of all fishes. A highly esteemed gamefish (all-tackle world record, 490 kg), famous for its spectacular leaps when hooked. Feeds mainly on small fishes, since its slender raptorial teeth are not well-suited for rendering large prey into pieces. Nevertheless, large adults have been found with chunks of swordfish and porpoise in their stomachs. There are many reports of Makos biting boats (particularly after being hooked), but few authenticated attacks on humans are recorded. Randall and Levy (1976) documented a near-fatal attack on a swimmer in the Gulf of Aqaba, Red Sea. One litter of 10 embryos (largest 69.8 cm) reported. Males mature at about 195 cm, females at about 280 cm. *Isurus glaucus* (Müller and Henle) is a synonym. The Longfin Mako, *I. paucus* Guitart Manday, was not named until 1966; its exact distribution is not known due to confusion with *I. oxyrinchus*. Its pectoral fins are as long or longer than its head, its snout is shorter, its front teeth lack the reverse curvature near the tips, and the origin of its anal fin is below the rear base of the second dorsal fin.

ORDER CARCHARHINIFORMES
FAMILY SCYLIORHINIDAE (CATSHARKS)

Diagnosis
Slender-bodied sharks, the head somewhat depressed without cutaneous flaps; eyes moderate to large and horizontally elongate; spiracles moderately large, behind eyes; five short gill slits, the last one or two above pectoral fin base; nasal apertures usually not connected by a groove to mouth; no nasal barbel (except the genus *Poroderma*); teeth small and numerous, multicuspid (cusps acute, the central one largest), in alternating rows, several of which are functional; two dorsal fins (except one species), the first over or behind pelvic fin bases, the second usually nearly as large as first (larger in a few species); no precaudal pits; caudal fin not long, the upper lobe angling only slightly above the horizontal, if at all, the ventral lobe absent or small; pectoral fins short and broad; colour varying from uniform to strongly marked; maximum length about 1.5 m.

Remarks
The most speciose of all families of sharks. S. Springer (1979) reviewed the family, recognizing 86 species. Undoubtedly more remain to be discovered. Scyliorhinids are found from tropical to arctic seas and from the shallows to depths greater than 2000 m. Most live on or near the bottom. They are weak swimmers and probably do not undertake any significant migrations. The distributions of many are very localized. Little is known of the biology of most species. They appear to feed mainly on benthic invertebrates and small fishes. Most appear to be oviparous (the egg cases distinctive in being large, strong, broader at the posterior end, with tendrils at the corners), but some are known to be ovoviviparous. Catsharks have little commercial importance, in general, and are harmless to man.

The Swell Shark, *Cephaloscyllium sufflans* (Regan), known from Mozambique and the Natal Coast of South Africa has been recorded once from the Gulf of Aden by Norman (1939), but Compagno (1984a) considers this record doubtful.

Halaelurus alcocki Garman (1913) was named from a single specimen taken in deep water in the Arabian Sea which Alcock (1899) had misidentified as *Scyllium canescens* Günther. The specimen was never illustrated and apparently is no longer extant. Springer (1979) noted that the description fits that of no known scyliorhinid, and he prefers not to recognise the species. Compagno (1984a) listed it, but with a question mark.

Smallbelly Catshark
Apristurus indicus (Brauer, 1906)

Diagnosis
Body elongate; snout long (9 to 10% total length), broad, distinctive in dorsal outline (rounded with a slight concavity before each nasal aperture); horizontal diameter of eye 2.4 to 2.8% total length; origin of first dorsal fin over middle of pelvic fin base; second dorsal fin distinctly larger than first; anal fin very long, its base 16 to 20% total length, angular, and elevated; caudal fin about one-third total length; paired fins moderately large, the space between the bases short; teeth numerous, most with five cusps, in 60 to 62 rows in upper jaw; colour dark brown to black; maximum size not known; immatures to 34 cm.

Remarks
This shark was described from three specimens from off the coast of Somalia (the type locality by virtue of lectotype designation) and the Gulf of Aden at depths of 1289 to 1840 m. Also reported from Oman.

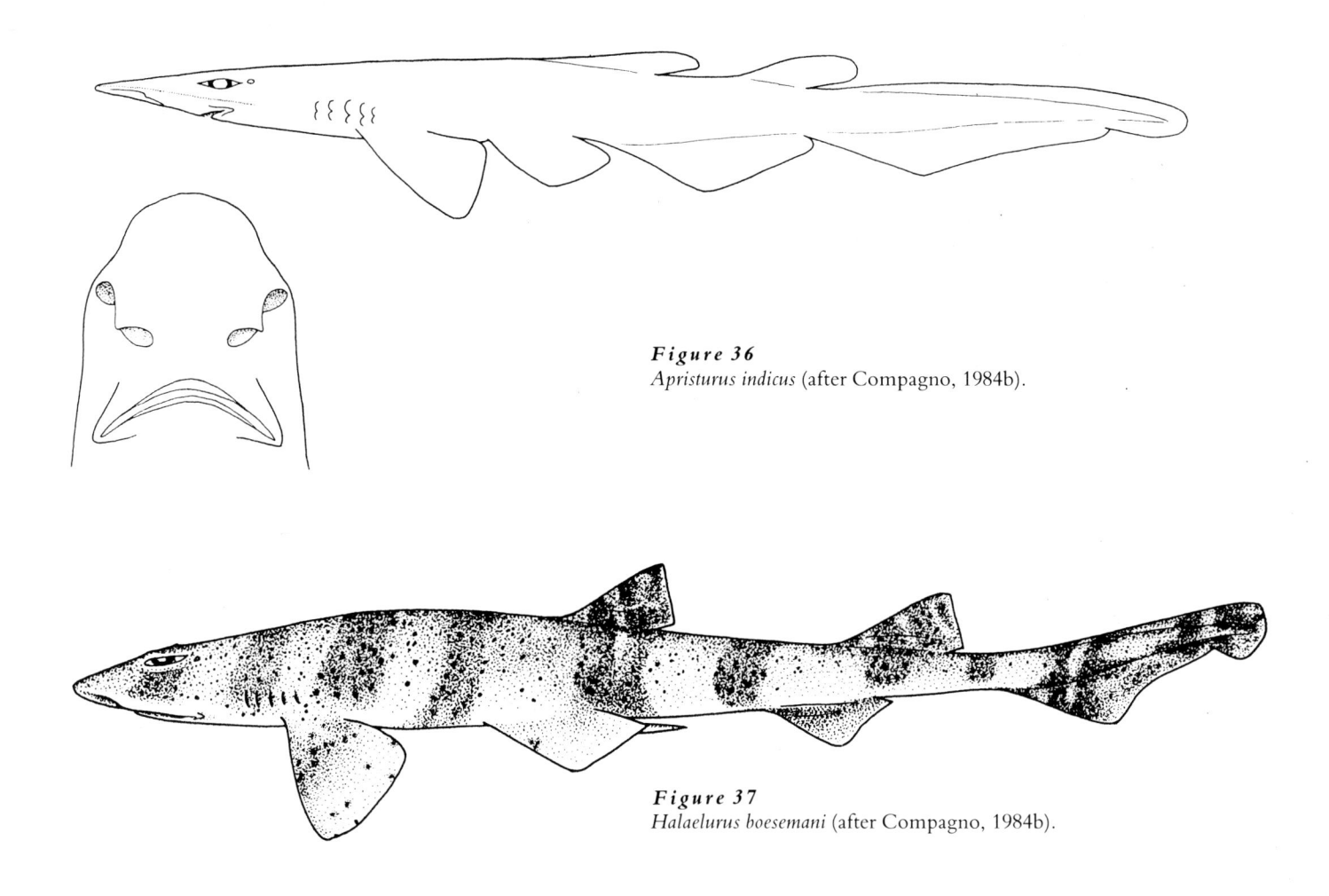

Figure 36
Apristurus indicus (after Compagno, 1984b).

Figure 37
Halaelurus boesemani (after Compagno, 1984b).

Speckled Catshark
Halaelurus boesemani Springer and D'Aubrey, 1972

Diagnosis
Body elongate, the maximum depth about 9% total length; head moderately depressed; snout somewhat pointed but short, its preoral length about 4% total length; small labial furrows present; dorsal fins about equal in size, the origin of the first over last third of pelvic fin bases, and the origin of the second over last third of anal fin base; caudal fin short, about one-fifth total length; teeth small (largest about 1 mm high) and numerous, with a pointed central cusp and one or two small and poorly defined cusps on each side; vertebrae 135 to 139; broad dusky bars and saddles on head, body, and caudal fin, this pattern overlaid by numerous small black spots (most the size of spiracle or smaller), these spots sometimes in clusters; large dark blotches on dorsal fins; length to 48 cm.

Remarks
This species was not distinguished from *H. buergeri* (Müller and Henle) until 1972 when Springer and D'Aubrey described it from specimens taken off the coast of Somalia. It is known from the Philippines, Viet Nam, Indonesia, Western Australia, and the Gulf of Aden. It occurs at depths of 37 to 91 m. As many as four egg capsules have been found in an oviduct. In some, the embryos may be in an advanced stage of development; however, it is not known if the eggs are laid before hatching takes place.

FAMILY PROSCYLLIDAE (FINBACK CATSHARKS)

Diagnosis
Body elongate; head broad and depressed; eyes horizontally elongate, the length more than twice as long as height; nictitating eyelid present but rudimentary; spiracles moderately large; no nasal barbels or oronasal grooves; labial furrows absent or very short; teeth small, in numerous rows, with a narrow central cusp and often with small lateral cusps; two dorsal fins, the first well in advance of the pelvic fin bases, the second nearly as large as the first; anal fin smaller than second dorsal fin, its origin beneath or slightly posterior to second dorsal fin origin; no precaudal pits; upper lobe of caudal fin on same axis as body or angling only slightly upward; no ventral caudal lobe or a weakly developed one; colour uniform or with dark markings; maximum length 1.2 m.

Remarks
The Proscyllidae is a small family of four genera, of which three are monotypic and the fourth, *Eridacnis*, contains only three known species. All live in moderately deep water (50 to 713 m) in tropical to warm temperature waters of the Atlantic and Indo-Pacific. They are ovoviviparous except for *Proscyllium habereri* which is oviparous. They feed on small fishes and invertebrates. Commercial importance negligible.

Pygmy Ribbontail Catshark
Eridacnis radcliffei Smith, 1913

Diagnosis
Body elongate, the depth about 9% of total length; head depressed; snout short and broadly rounded; eye large, its length about 4.5% total length; five short gill slits, the fourth and fifth above pectoral base; mouth subtriangular; posterior teeth comb-like; leading edges of dorsal, anal, and paired fins strongly oblique; origin of first dorsal fin slightly posterior to rear bases of pelvic fins; anal fin below second dorsal fin; caudal fin relatively long (about 28% total length) and narrow; brown with two bars across caudal fin and two large dark markings on dorsal fins; maximum length about 24 cm.

Remarks
This species is unusual in its small size; of all the sharks in the world, only one squaloid, *Squaliolus laticaudus*, appears to be smaller. Wide-ranging in the Indo-Pacific, with records from Tanzania, Gulf of Aden, Gulf of Mannar, Andaman Islands, Viet Nam, and the Philippines (type locality). It has been taken in the depth range of 71 to 766 m, usually on mud bottoms. Feeds mainly on small fishes and crustaceans. Ovoviviparous, with only one or two young per litter which are 10.1 to 10.7 cm long at birth. Surprisingly, females are mature at only about 15 cm.

Figure 38
Eridacnis radcliffei (after Compagno, 1984b).

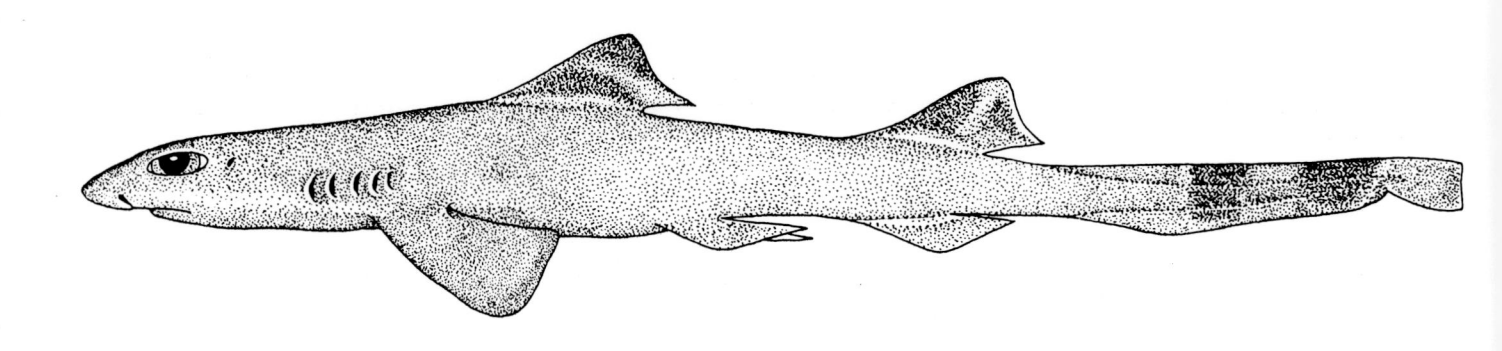

FAMILY TRIAKIDAE (HOUNDSHARKS)

Diagnosis
Moderately slender-bodied; head depressed; snout moderately long, rounded to somewhat pointed; eyes horizontally elongate, the length 1.5 to 2.5 times longer than the height; supraorbital crest present; spiracles present, varying from small to moderately large; nictitating eyelids present (external, transitional or internal); labial furrows moderately to very long; teeth varying from cuspidate (though not blade-like) to thickened and molariform; two well-separated dorsal fins, the first large, its base well in advance of pelvic fin bases; no precaudal pits; caudal fin without a well-developed ventral lobe; radials of pectoral fins confined to base; colour usually uniform, but may be strongly marked; a few species attain 2 m in length.

Remarks
A family of nine genera and 34 species (as recognised by Compagno, 1984a) which are found in tropical to temperate seas from inshore to depths as great as 2000 m. Most live on or near the bottom. Some feed mainly on fishes, others on crustaceans, and a few on squids. Ovoviviparous or viviparous. Some species such as the Soupfin Shark (*Galeorhinus galeus*) are of considerable commercial importance.

Blacktip Houndshark
Hypogaleus hyugaensis (Miyosi, 1939)

Diagnosis
Body slender, the depth about 10% of total length; snout moderately long (preoral length about 6.5% total length) and slightly pointed; eyes large, horizontally oval, their length about 3% total length; spiracles about one-sixth eye diameter; internal nictitating lower eyelid present; gill slits about 1.6 times longer than eye except the last (over pectoral fin base) which is shorter; anterior nasal flaps vestigial; lateral labial furrow moderately long, about twice as long as medial; teeth small, 23 to 25 in front row on each side of upper jaw and 22 to 23 on lower, blade-like, the cusp oblique on teeth laterally in jaws, with three to five large cusplets along lateroposterior edge; dorsal fins broadly separated, the origin of the first slightly posterior to inner posterior corner of pectoral fins; second dorsal fin about two-thirds as large as first dorsal; anal fin distinctly smaller than second dorsal fin, its origin slightly anterior to midbase of second dorsal; outer posterior margins of fins concave; upper lobe of caudal fin an average of 23% total length; terminal and ventral lobes of caudal fin well-developed, subequal, about 10% total length; vertebrae 154 to 160, of which 93 to 97 are precaudal; grey, paler ventrally, the tips of the dorsal fins and upper lobe of caudal fin dusky to blackish; largest recorded, 127 cm.

Remarks
Described in 1939 from Kyushu, Japan; now known from Taiwan, Arabian Gulf, and coast of East Africa south to Natal. It is not known if further collecting will fill in the gaps in this disjunct distribution. Depth of capture has varied from 40 to 230 m. Limited data on food habits indicate this species is piscivorous. Viviparous; litters of 10 to 11 have been reported; length at birth 33 to 35 cm. *H. hyugaensis* is the only species of the genus. *H. zanzibariensis* Smith (1957) from Tanzania is a synonym. The shark illustrated on p.70 of Randall et al. (1978) (Fig. 39 herein) is not *Hypogaleus balfouri*, as labelled, but *H. hyugaensis*. It was collected off Bahrain and represents the first record of the species from the Arabian Gulf.

Figure 39
Hypogaleus hyugaensis, 62 cm, 0.8 kg, Bahrain (J. Randall).

Bigeye Houndshark
Iago omanensis (Norman, 1939)

Diagnosis
Body deepest at origin of first dorsal fin, tapering posteriorly; head depressed, the dorsal profile from snout to nape concave; snout broad, obtusely pointed; eyes large, about twice as long as high; spiracles slit-like, behind eyes; nictitating membrane transitional, its edge nearly horizontal; five short gill openings, not extending onto dorsal half of head, the last two above pectoral base; no oronasal grooves; no nasal barbels; labial furrows curve around corners of mouth; mouth subtriangular; teeth small, in numerous alternating rows (two or three of which are functional), 23 to 28 on each side at front of upper jaw and 18 to 23 in lower, each tooth blade-like, low, and oblique with a deep notch posterolaterally; first dorsal fin large and very anterior in position (its origin anterior to axilla of pectoral fins); outer posterior margins of dorsal and anal fins concave; second dorsal fin about 70% height of first dorsal fin; anal fin smaller than second dorsal, its origin slightly posterior to that of second dorsal; caudal fin 20 to 22% total length, the ventral lobe better developed in juveniles than adults; vertebrae 129 to 147; brownish to greyish above, paler ventrally, with no markings; largest male, 36.5 cm; largest female, 58.2 cm.

Remarks
Iago omanensis is known from the Red Sea, Arabian Sea, Gulf of Oman (type locality), and Pakistan to southwest India from depths of about 100 to at least 1000 m (possibly over 2000 m in the Red Sea). Feeds on fishes (particularly lanternfishes), squids, crustaceans, pelecypods, and gastropods. Viviparous, the litter size varying from two to ten.

Figure 40
Iago omanensis, Red Sea (Avi Baranes).

Figure 41
Mustelus mosis, 66 cm, Red Sea (J. Randall).

Arabian Houndshark
Mustelus mosis Hemprich and Ehrenberg, 1899

Diagnosis
Body moderately slender; head short, 17 to 22% total length; preoral snout 5.5 to 5.6% total length, the tip expanded in adults; eyes large, the length 2.5 to 3.3% total length; lateral labial furrows about equal to medial, 1.3 to 2.0% total length; teeth molariform with a low cusp, in close-set regular alternating rows, giving a cobblestone-like appearance; first dorsal fin large, its origin slightly in advance of inner posterior corner of pectoral fins, well separated from second dorsal fin; height of second dorsal fin about 0.6 height of first dorsal; anal fin about half as large as second dorsal fin, its origin below middle of second dorsal fin base; outer posterior margins of dorsal and anal fins strongly concave; upper lobe of caudal fin about 20% total length, its terminal lobe and the ventral lobe about equal in size; grey, shading to whitish ventrally; reaches 150 cm.

Remarks
Known from the Red Sea (type locality), Arabian Gulf, Pakistan, India, Sri Lanka, and the Natal coast of South Africa. There is evidence that there are isolated populations in the Red Sea and off Natal. Individuals from off South Africa have white-tipped first dorsal fins and black-tipped second dorsal and caudal fins. Occurs from near shore (even on coral reefs) to moderately deep water. Common in some areas, as off India and Pakistan where it is taken commercially. Feeds on small benthic fishes, crustaceans, and molluscs. Viviparous, with 6 to 10 pups per litter. Males mature between 63 and 67 cm, and females around 82 cm.

FAMILY HEMIGALEIDAE (WEASEL SHARKS)

Diagnosis

Body moderately elongate; snout not very long, rounded to slightly pointed; eyes horizontally oval; internal nictitating eyelids; spiracles small; five gill slits, the last one or two over pectoral fin base; no oronasal grooves or barbels; labial furrows moderately long; teeth varying from small to moderately large, blade-like in upper jaw, cuspidate but not compressed in lower; first dorsal fin moderately large, distinctly anterior to pelvic fins; second dorsal fin moderate in size, well posterior to pelvic fins; outer posterior margins of fins concave; precaudal pits present; upper lobe of caudal fin angling upward, with a well-developed terminal lobe; lower lobe of caudal fin large; colour usually uniform grey or brownish, but may have stripes; most species small, but *Hemipristis elongatus* attains 2.4 m.

Remarks

This family consists of only four genera and a total of five species, two of which occur in Arabian waters. Most authors have classified these sharks in the Carcharhinidae; Compagno (1979; 1984a) is followed here in treating them in the family Hemigaleidae. They occur in tropical seas from a few to at least 100 m, feeding on fishes, cephalopods, crustaceans, and echinoderms. *Hemipristis elongatus* is primarily a fish feeder in contrast to *Hemigaleus microstoma* which eats mainly cephalopods. Development viviparous.

Figure 42
Chaenogaleus macrostoma (after Bleeker).

Hooktooth Shark
Chaenogaleus macrostoma (Bleeker, 1852)

Diagnosis
Body moderately elongate, the depth about 12% total length; snout fairly long and pointed in both dorsal and lateral views; its length about 7% total length; eyes large, slightly oval, the horizontal diameter about 2% total length; each spiracle a small horizontal slit two-thirds eye diameter behind eye; gill openings twice as long as eye diameter, the first four subequal, the last, above pectoral base, a little shorter; lateral labial furrow twice as long as medial; 14 teeth in outer row on each side of jaws, the most medial tooth small; upper teeth obliquely triangular with a broad angular notch on posterolateral side, the lower half of which bears sharp cusplets (usually four); lower teeth with a long, slender, smooth-edged, incurved cusp, those at front of jaw protruding; first dorsal fin moderately large, its origin slightly anterior to inner posterior corner of pectoral fins; interdorsal space long with a narrow median ridge; second dorsal fin about two-thirds as high as first dorsal; anal fin slightly smaller than second dorsal, its origin slightly posterior; upper lobe of caudal fin about 23% total length; pectoral fins about 17% total length; greyish brown, the second dorsal broadly tipped with black. Attains about 100 cm.

Remarks
Described from Java, this species ranges from the Arabian Gulf to southern Japan. A littoral shark with one depth record to 59 m. Food habits not reported, but its dentition would suggest that it feeds primarily on fishes. Viviparous, with four embryos per litter. Common off Pakistan, India, and Sri Lanka where it is used as food. *Hemigaleus balfouri* Day is a synonym.

Snaggletooth Shark
Hemipristis elongatus (Klunzinger, 1871)

Diagnosis
Body moderately elongate, the depth about 14% total length; head depressed; snout moderately long and broadly rounded anteriorly, its preoral length 5 to 6% total length (longer in young than adults); eye large, about 1.5 to 2% total length; each spiracle a small horizontal slit nearly an eye length behind eye; 13 or 14 teeth on each side at front of upper jaw and 18 in lower; upper two medial teeth on each side slender and prong-like; more lateral teeth compressed, triangular with oblique cusps, and strongly serrate; teeth at front of lower jaw fang-like, slightly incurved, smooth-edged, with a basal cusp on each side (except medial two teeth); more lateral lower teeth progressively more triangular and oblique with two to six sharp cusplets basally on the posterior edge; first dorsal fin large, apically pointed, the origin slightly posterior to inner posterior corner of pectoral fins; second dorsal fin about half as large as first, distinctly posterior to pelvic fins; anal fin slightly smaller than second dorsal fin, its origin below about middle of base of second dorsal; upper lobe of caudal fin about one-fourth total length, 2.5 times longer than lower lobe; vertebral counts of three specimens 190 to 194, of which 103 or 104 are precaudal; grey, shading to whitish ventrally, without markings; reaches 2.4 m.

Remarks
This shark was first named *Dirrhizodon elongatus* by Klunzinger (1871) from the Red Sea. Later its teeth were shown to be the same as fossil teeth described in *Hemipristis* by Agassiz in 1843. Though wide-ranging, this species is not common. It is reported from the coast of East Africa south to Margate, South Africa (30° 52' S), Madagascar, Gulf of Oman, Pakistan, India, Thailand, Viet Nam, Philippines, China, and the east and west coasts of Australia. It is not known from any oceanic islands. It occurs from depths of 1 to 30 m. As its slender raptorial teeth would indicate, it is a fish feeder. Six to eight pups per litter; length at birth about 45 cm. Not implicated in any attacks on man but would seem to have the potentiality from its size and dentition.

Figure 43
Hemipristis elongatus, 185.5 cm, 27.3 kg, Gulf of Oman (J. Randall).

Figure 44
Teeth of *Hemipristis elongatus* (after Smith, 1957).

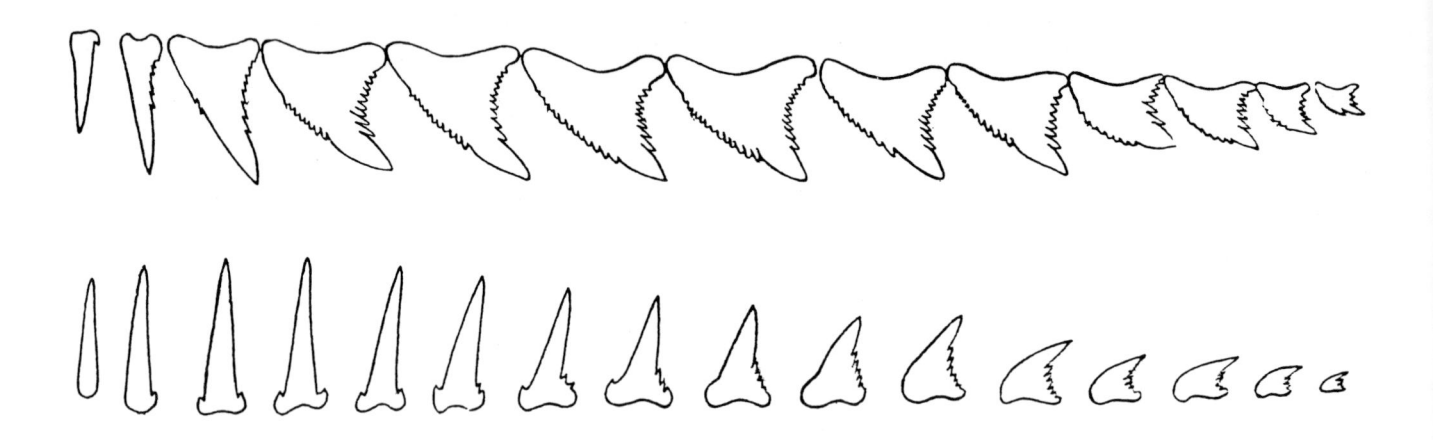

FAMILY CARCHARHINIDAE (REQUIEM SHARKS)

Diagnosis

Body varying from robust to moderately elongate; eyes circular to subcircular; no supraorbital crest on neurocranium; internal nictitating eyelid present; spiracles usually absent; no nasal barbels or oronasal grooves; labial furrows varying from short (may not be visible when mouth closed) to long; five gill slits, the last one or two above pectoral fin base; mouth large; teeth small to large with a sharp cusp that varies from narrow to broad, smooth-edged to serrate, with or without basal cusplets; first dorsal fin moderate to large, its base entirely anterior to pelvic fin bases (usually closer to pectoral fin bases); second dorsal fin less than half height of first dorsal (except *Glyphis, Lamniopsis, Negaprion,* and *Triaenodon*); anal fin slightly smaller to approximately the same size as the second dorsal (anal fin larger in *Rhizoprionodon* and *Scoliodon*); precaudal pits present; no keels on caudal peduncle (except *Galeocerdo* with a well-developed one and *Prionace* with a small one); caudal fin less than 30% total length, the upper lobe angling dorsally, with a distinct terminal lobe, and more than twice length of the well-developed lower lobe; colour variable; usually without a distinctive pattern; most of moderate to large size (*Galeocerdo* to at least 6 m).

Remarks

A large family of 12 genera and 47 species, mainly of tropical seas. The most important family of sharks from the standpoint of general abundance, impact on marine communities and commercial importance. The majority of Requiem Sharks are found in coastal or insular environments, but a few are pelagic, such as the extremely wide-ranging Blue Shark (*Prionace glauca*), the Oceanic Whitetip Shark (*Carcharhinus longimanus*), and the Silky Shark (*C. falciformis*). The great majority of species are purely marine, but the Bull Shark (*C. leucas*) and the two species of *Glyphis* can live in freshwater for long periods. The largest genus of the family (and of all sharks as well) is *Carcharhinus* which was ably revised by Garrick, 1982. Compagno (1984b) recognised 29 species in the genus (he and Castro, 1983, place the species of *Hypoprion* in *Carcharhinus*), but cast doubt on the validity of *C. wheeleri* Garrick (see account of *C. amblyrhynchos* below). Carcharhinids are voracious predators which feed on a great variety of animal life, but mainly fishes, cephalopods, and the larger crustaceans. Large sharks of this group tend to have a more varied diet and include among their prey other sharks, rays, sea turtles, sea birds, and marine mammals. The serrations of the teeth of most of these large sharks aid them in dismembering large animals. After the jaws are engaged, the entire body of the shark is shaken, bringing shearing forces to bear on the teeth which virtually saw pieces from the prey. Several of these sharks are among the most dangerous to divers and bathers, in particular the Tiger Shark (*Galeocerdo cuvier*) and the Bull Shark. With the exception of the Tiger Shark, which is ovoviviparous, all carcharhinids are viviparous. The original family spelling was Carcharinidae. Following Garman (1913), the International Commission on Zoological Nomenclature (1965: Opinion 723.7b) amended the name to Carcharhinidae. Opinion 723.2c (1965) established *Carcharias melanopterus* Quoy and Gaimard (1824) as the type species of the genus *Carcharhinus*. *Eulamia* and *Pterolamiops* are among the 18 generic synonyms of *Carcharhinus*.

Silvertip Shark
Carcharhinus albimarginatus (Rüppell, 1837)

Diagnosis

Snout moderately long and broadly rounded, the preoral length 6.8 to 9.2% total length; eyes 1.8 to 3.0% total length; gill slits short, the third 2.5 to 3.8% total length; lateral labial furrows short; 12 to 14 teeth on each side of jaws (usually 13 upper and 12 lower, discounting one or two small symphyseal teeth); upper teeth broadly triangular, serrate (serrations larger basally), with a broad angular notch on each edge (laterally in jaws the cusp is progressively more oblique, the notch becoming more pronounced on the posterolateral side and less so on the anteromedial edge); lower teeth with a narrow, erect, finely serrate cusp (becoming notably oblique only posteriorly); interdorsal ridge present; first dorsal fin moderately large, its height 7.1 to 10.6% total length, the apex somewhat pointed, the origin over inner posterior corner of pectoral fins; height of second dorsal fin 1.5 to 2.3% total length; anal fin slightly larger than second dorsal fin, its origin below or slightly anterior to second dorsal; pectoral fins large, slightly falcate, their length (anterior margin) 16.2 to 22.0% total length; vertebrae 216 to 231, of which 115 to 125 are precaudal; dark grey dorsally, shading to white ventrally, with a horizontal grey zone on midside invading the white of upper abdomen from anteriorly; first dorsal fin, caudal fin lobes, and pectoral fins conspicuously tipped with white, the outer posterior margins of these and other fins narrowly white (more so on smaller than larger individuals); outer part of second dorsal fin broadly dusky; reaches about 300 cm.

Remarks

Wide-ranging in the Indo-Pacific region and tropical eastern Pacific. In the western Indian Ocean it occurs from the Red Sea (type locality) south to northern Natal and Madagascar; apparently absent from the Arabian Gulf and Gulf of Oman. In the western Pacific it is found in Taiwan, the Philippines, and Indonesia. Although not yet reported in Australia, it definitely occurs there. The author was closely approached by one of about 200 cm on a drop-off on the seaward side of Yonge Reef, Great Barrier Reef at a depth of 35 m in December, 1982. In Oceania it ranges to French Polynesia, but is absent from the Hawaiian Islands. This shark is most common in clear water, outer-reef areas of islands and banks, particularly on steep slopes, generally at depths greater than 30 m (maximum depth at least 600 m); it may be encountered in shallow reef or lagoon environments, however. Feeds on a variety of fishes, including tunas and reef fishes (Fourmanoir, 1961; Bass et al., 1973). Randall (1980) reported a 61.6-cm Grey Reef Shark (*Carcharhinus amblyrhynchos*) in the stomach of a 165-cm *C. albimarginatus*, along with parrotfish remains. A dangerous species which has been implicated in attacks on man (Jones, 1971; Read, 1971). Cousteau and Cousteau (1970) included an underwater photograph of a Silvertip in the process of removing a leg from a baited dummy dressed as a SCUBA diver. Litters vary from 1 to 11, most often 5 or 6; gestation period about one year; size at birth 55 to 80 cm. Males mature between 160 and 180 cm, and females at about 200 to 210 cm. *C. platyrhynchus* (Gilbert, 1892) from the Revillagigedo Islands is a synonym by virtue of lectotype designation (Rosenblatt and Baldwin, 1958). See Remarks for *C. longimanus* for comparison of *C. albimarginatus* with two other white-tipped carcharhinid sharks.

CLASSIFICATION

Figure 45
Carcharhinus albimarginatus, 120 cm, 12 kg, Marshall Islands (J. Randall).

Figure 46
Teeth of *Carcharinus albimarginatus* (after Garrick, 1982).

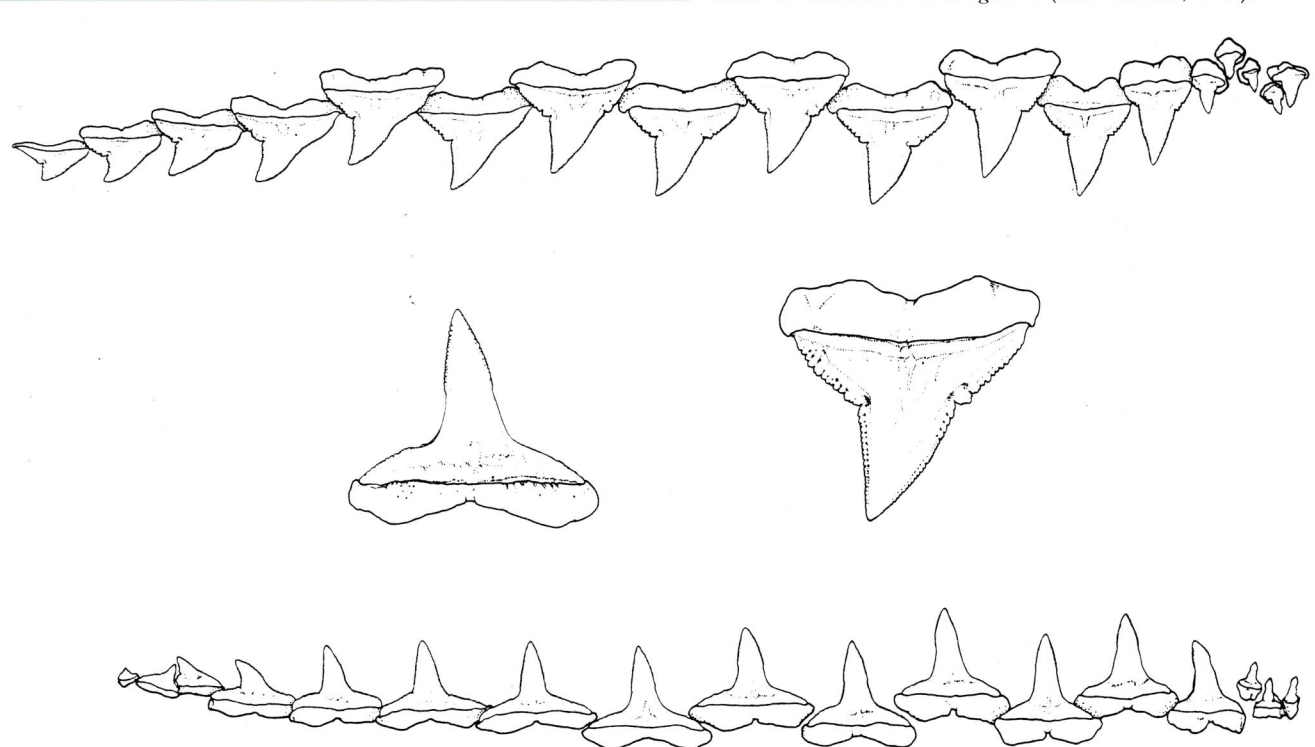

93

Bignose Shark
Carcharhinus altimus (Springer, 1950)

Diagnosis
Snout long and slightly pointed, its preoral length 7.5 to 10% total length; eyes 1.3 to 2.3% total length; gill openings moderate, the third 3.1 to 4.5% total length; nasal lobes prominent; lateral labial furrows short; 14 to 16 (usually 15) teeth on each side of upper jaw (not counting small symphyseals) and 14 or 15 in lower; upper teeth large, broadly triangular, moderately serrate, with a slight indentation on posterolateral margin (more so posteriorly in jaw as a result of the cusp becoming more oblique); lower teeth with a narrow, erect, finely serrate cusp; interdorsal ridge prominent; first dorsal fin moderately large, its height 8.3 to 11.9% total length, its apex bluntly pointed, its origin over or slightly posterior to axil of pectoral fins; second dorsal fin moderate for the genus, its height 2.8 to 3.4% total length; anal fin slightly larger than second dorsal fin, its origin a little posterior to that of second dorsal; pectoral fins moderately long, the posterior margin only slightly concave, the length of anterior margin 19.6 to 24.0% total length; vertebrae 194 to 206, of which 101 to 110 are precaudal; grey, becoming whitish below; distal ends of all fins except pelvics dusky (pigment on tips of pectorals darker on underside of fins); attains about 300 cm.

Figure 47
Carcharhinus altimus, 134 cm, 14 kg, Red Sea (J. Randall).

Figure 48
Teeth of *Carcharhinus altimus* (after Garrick, 1982).

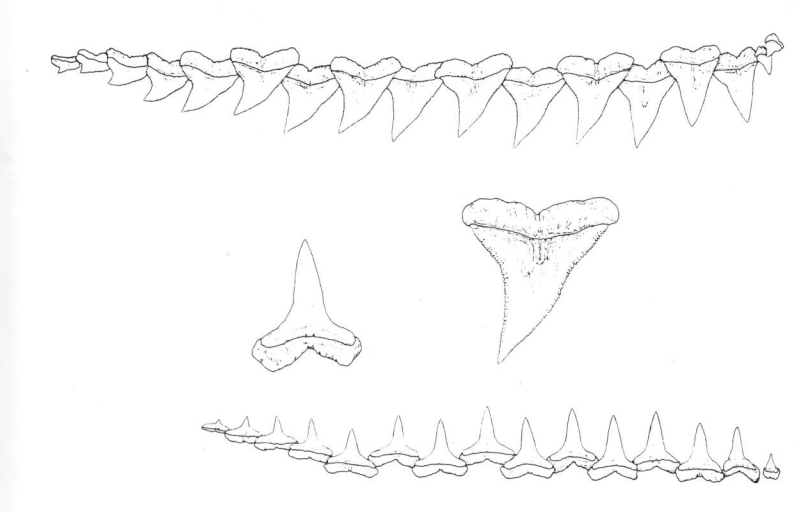

Remarks
This shark was not recognised until 1950 when S. Springer described it from a small specimen from the Florida Keys. It has since been recorded from the Bahamas, Caribbean Sea, West Africa, South Africa, Madagascar, Red Sea, India, Hawaiian Islands, and the eastern Pacific from the Gulf of California to Ecuador. Moreno and Hoyos (1983) reported it from the Mediterranean Sea. It usually occurs at depths of 90 m (the young may be found shallower) to at least 430 m. Feeds on many different kinds of fishes, including sharks and rays, and cephalopods. Because of its occurrence in deeper than usual diving depths, it is not regarded as a threat to man in the sea. The number of young per litter varies from 3 to 11; size at birth about 65 to 80 cm. Males mature at about 215 cm and females at about 225 cm. *C. radamae* Fourmanoir (1961) from Madagascar is a synonym.

Figure 49
Carcharhinus amblyrhynchoides, 155 cm, Gulf of Thailand (after Garrick, 1982).

Figure 50
Teeth of *Carcharhinus amblyrhynchoides* (after Garrick, 1982).

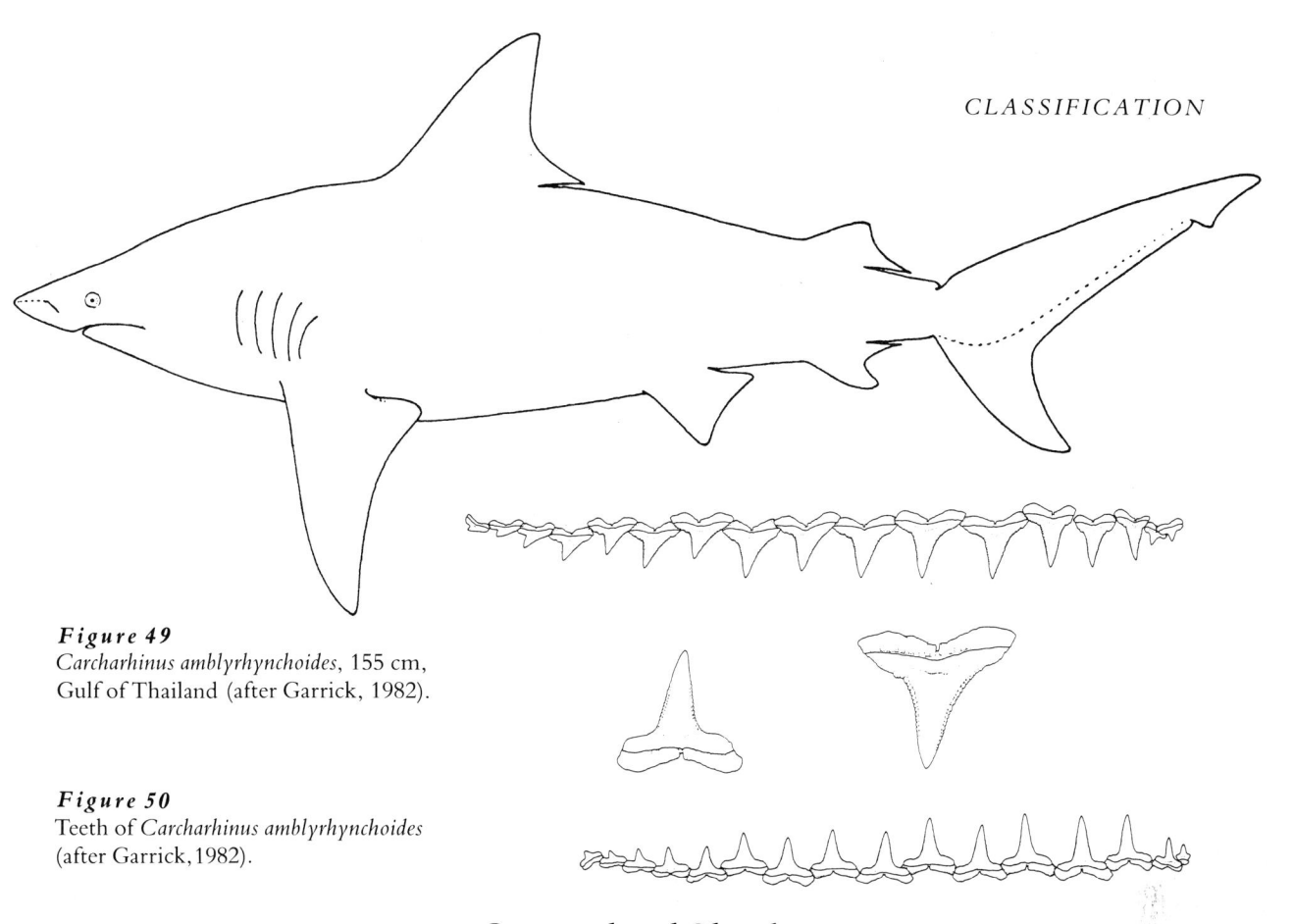

Queensland Shark
Carcharhinus amblyrhynchoides (Whitley, 1934)

Diagnosis

Heavy-bodied; snout short, wedge-shaped, the preoral length 5.3 to 6.9% total length; eyes 1.2 to 2.0% total length; gill slits moderately long, the third 4.0 to 5.6% total length; lateral labial furrows short; 15 teeth on each side of upper jaw and 14 or 15 on lower (disregarding small symphyseal teeth); upper teeth moderately serrate with cusps nearly as narrow as the lowers (except posteriorly where obliquely triangular), the anteromedial margin concave and the posterolateral broadly notched; cusp of lower teeth erect and finely serrate; no interdorsal ridge; first dorsal fin moderately large, its height 8.6 to 12.6% total length, the apex somewhat pointed, its origin over or slightly posterior to axil of pectoral fins; height of second dorsal fin 3.1 to 3.7% total length; anal fin about equal in size to second dorsal fin, its origin below that of second dorsal or slightly posterior to it; pectoral fins not long, the posterior margin slightly concave, the leading edge 16.3 to 19.7% total length; vertebrae 168 to 193, of which 78 to 96 are precaudal; coppery, becoming white below; tips of pectoral fins (especially the underside), tips of both dorsals, and tip of lower caudal lobe black; pelvic fins also dark-tipped but not as strongly; upper lobe of caudal often with a blackish margin; maximum size reported, 167 cm, but probably attains a greater length.

Remarks

This is a poorly known shark which has been confused with other species such as *C. limbatus*. It differs from *limbatus* in having a shorter snout (preoral snout length of *limbatus* 6.3 to 9.0% total length) and higher second dorsal fin. Described from Queensland; also reported from Indonesia, Gulf of Thailand, Philippines, and the Gulf of Aden. Size at birth about 55 cm. No data on food habits, etc. Marshall (1964) wrote that the species is common in the waters of North Queensland. He listed the common name as Graceful Shark which he probably derived from a comment in Whitley's original description (1934: 190), 'gracefully fusiform'. Such a stocky shark would not be expected to be more 'graceful' than other species of the genus, the majority of which are more slender. The common name Queensland Shark is here proposed for this species, in reference to the type locality and its abundance there. The shark illustrated by Grant (1982: col. pl. 16) as *C. amblyrhynchoides* is *C. amblyrhynchos*.

Grey Reef Shark
Carcharhinus amblyrhynchos (Bleeker, 1856)

Diagnosis

Snout rounded, moderate to short in length, the preoral length 6.4 to 8.7% total length; eyes 1.8 to 3.0% total length; gill openings moderately long, the third 2.5 to 4.2% total length; lateral labial furrows short; 13 or 14 teeth (usually 14) on each side of upper jaw (disregarding small symphyseals) and 12 to 14 (usually 13) on lower; upper teeth serrate with a fairly narrow cusp which is erect on medial two teeth, but then progressively more oblique posteriorly in jaw, the posterolateral edge with a broad angular notch, the serrae on basal part of this notch coarse; lower teeth finely serrate with a narrow, slightly oblique cusp; no interdorsal ridge; first dorsal fin moderate, its height 8.6 to 11.3% total length, the apex slightly pointed, the origin above or slightly anterior to inner posterior corner of pectoral fins; height of second dorsal fin 2.7 to 4.1% total length; anal fin about equal in size to and directly beneath or slightly posterior to second dorsal fin; pectoral fins narrow and falcate, the length of the anterior edge 17.9 to 21.4% total length; vertebrae 210 to 227, of which 110 to 119 are precaudal; colour of Red Sea specimens greyish brown (may be bronze when first caught), shading to white ventrally, often with a broad zone of light brown on lower middle side extending slightly diagonally downward and posteriorly into the whitish of the upper abdomen; upper half of trailing edge of first dorsal fin narrowly whitish, this margin broader distally; second dorsal and anal fins broadly dark brown distally; trailing edge of caudal fin with a broad blackish band which becomes very wide as it passes ventrally on the lower lobe, covering the full width of the distal part of the lobe; paired fins dark brown on upper surfaces, the pectorals white below, grading to blackish at tips; maximum length about 180 cm.

Remarks

The type locality of *C. amblyrhynchos* is the Java Sea. Garrick (1982) described *Carcharhinus wheeleri* from specimens from the Red Sea, Gulf of Aden, Kenya, and Réunion which he differentiated from *C. amblyrhynchos* 'in having a white-tipped first dorsal fin, shorter prenarial and preoral lengths, and usually in having one less tooth on each side of the upper jaw. None of these characters is exclusive. Prenarial and preoral proportions overlap'. With the exception of one juvenile from Madagascar identified as *amblyrhynchos* by Bass et al. (1973), the distributions of the two 'species' do not overlap, that of *wheeleri* being western Indian Ocean and that of *amblyrhynchos* eastern Indian Ocean and western and central Pacific. Garrick was also influenced by a report of *wheeleri* being less aggressive than

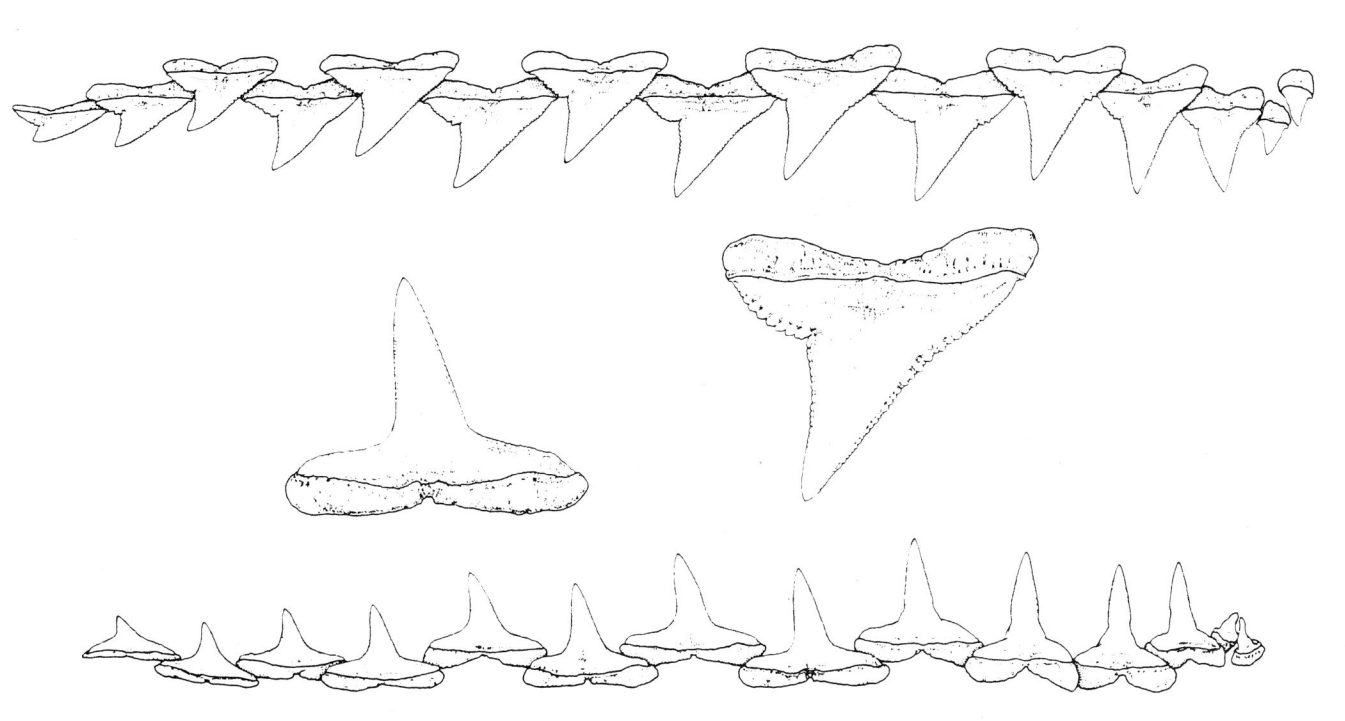

Figure 51
Carcharhinus amblyrhynchos, 134.5 cm, 13 kg, Red Sea (J. Randall).

Figure 52
Teeth of *Carcharhinus amblyrhynchos* (after Garrick, 1982).

amblyrhynchos. He added, however, that his evidence 'does not lend unequivocal support' to the recognition of *wheeleri* as a separate species. Compagno (1984b) listed *wheeleri* but commented that it may not prove to be distinct from *amblyrhynchos*. A. Baranes (pers. comm. from PhD thesis on Red Sea sharks) has concluded that *wheeleri* should be regarded as a synonym of *amblyrhynchos*, and he is followed here. It seems clear, however, that Garrick has differentiated two populations of *amblyrhynchos* even though not divergent enough to warrant nomenclatorial recognition at the species level. Schultz in Schultz and collaborators (1953) and others have used the name *C. menisorrah* (Valenciennes) for the Grey Reef Shark, but Garrick has shown that this name has been misapplied perhaps more than any other in the genus. By lectotype designation he has made *menisorrah* a junior synonym of *C. falciformis*. Similarly, Bass et al. (1973) used *C. spallanzani* (Peron and Lesueur) for the *wheeleri* form of *amblyrhynchos*. Garrick has rejected this name (see Remarks for *C. sorrah* below). The Grey Reef Shark is one of the three most common species of sharks found on Indo-Pacific reefs (the other two being *C. melanopterus* and *Triaenodon obesus*). It prefers relatively clear water so is not apt to be found in turbid inshore areas of continental shelves or high islands. Although it may be encountered in shallow water, it tends to occur in deeper zones, leaving the shallow reefs to *C. melanopterus*. It has been observed from a research submarine to depths of 274 m off Johnston Island (Randall et al., in press) where, incidentally, the first dorsal fin usually has a whitish margin. This shark is a small species, and any lengths in excess of 180 cm (such as 255 cm reported from the literature by Compagno, 1984b) are probable misidentifications. The largest of 74 specimens collected by the author at Pacific localities measured 163 cm (Randall, 1980); the largest of 180 specimens examined by Wass (1971) from Pacific islands (except Hawaii) was 161 cm. The species appears to reach a larger size in the Hawaiian Islands; the largest of 28 mature Grey Reef Sharks measured there by Wass was 177 cm. *C. amblyrhynchos* feeds mainly on bony fishes, occasionally on cephalopods and crustaceans. It is more active at night than by day but will feed opportunistically by day. Sometimes seen in aggregations. In spite of its small size, it is to be respected. The author has met five different men who have been bitten by this species, one a diving companion (Randall, 1980), and has nearly been bitten himself on two occasions. The greatest hazard exists when spearfishing and when this shark exhibits its threat posture (Johnson and Nelson, 1973). This consists of highly exaggerated sinuous movement with slow progression forward, the head arched upward, the jaws opening and closing, and the pectoral fins depressed. Any overt movement toward the shark at this time could elicit an attack which can be incredibly rapid. Usually a single slashing bite results without any intention to feed. The number of young per litter varies from one to six; the gestation period is about one year.

Pigeye Shark
Carcharhinus amboinensis (Müller and Henle, 1839)

Diagnosis
A very heavy-bodied species, the depth as much as 20% total length; snout short and bluntly rounded, the preoral length 5.7 to 7.7% total length; internarial distance large, 6.6 to 7.3% total length; eyes small, 0.7 to 1.6% total length; gill slits moderate in size, the third 3.2 to 3.8% total length; lateral labial furrows short; 11 to 13 (usually 12) teeth on each side of upper jaw (omitting the small symphyseal teeth) and 10 to 12 (usually 11) in the lower; upper teeth broadly triangular, coarsely serrate, with only a slight emargination on the posterolateral edge except the more posterior teeth with a more oblique cusp; lower teeth with a narrower, moderately serrate cusp which is slightly oblique anteriorly in jaw, shorter and more oblique posteriorly; no interdorsal ridge; first dorsal fin large, the height 10.8 to 13.6% total length, the distal end pointed, the origin over or slightly posterior to inner posterior corner of pectoral fins; height of second dorsal fin 2.8 to 3.6% total length; anal fin about equal in size to second dorsal fin, its origin slightly posterior to origin of second dorsal; pectoral fins broad, somewhat falcate and long, the anterior edge 20.0 to 25.2% total length; vertebrae 185 to 195, of which 85 to 95 are precaudal; grey above, white below, with a horizontal band of grey on midside of body extending into the white of upper abdomen; fins dusky-tipped (more so on young than adults); a large species, attaining about 280 cm.

Remarks
As indicated by the specific name, this species was described from a specimen from Ambon, Indonesia in 1839. Many authors have confused this species with *C. leucas*, both being large, deep-bodied, short-snouted sharks without an interdorsal ridge, with similar dentition and colour pattern. D'Aubrey (1964) showed that *C. amboinensis* is distinct, having fewer precaudal vertebrae, usually one fewer teeth on each side of lower jaw, and a higher first dorsal fin relative to the second dorsal. In addition to Indonesia, it is reported from West Africa (off Nigeria), South Africa, Madagascar, Gulf of Aden, Pakistan, Sri Lanka, and eastern Australia. Undoubtedly more localities will be added in the future, now that its separation from *leucas* is documented. Feeds mainly on benthic fishes, including other sharks, crustaceans, and molluscs. The number of young per litter is not known. A free-swimming individual with a fresh umbilical scar measured 72 cm. An inshore species, but not reported to enter freshwater like *leucas* (though it is known from brackish water). Although not implicated in any attacks on man, it seems likely that it has done so and been misidentified as some other species such as *leucas*.

Figure 53
Carcharhinus amboinensis, 58 cm, Bahrain (J. Randall).

Spinner Shark
Carcharhinus brevipinna (Müller and Henle, 1839)

Diagnosis

Body slender, the depth about 13 to 14% total length; snout long, the preoral length 7.7 to 9.0% total length, and pointed; eyes small, 0.8 to 2.0% total length; gill openings moderately long, the third 3.6 to 5.5% total length; lateral labial furrows long (for the genus); 15 to 18 (usually 16) teeth on each side of upper jaw (symphyseals excepted) and 14 to 17 (usually 15 or 16) on lower; teeth in both jaws with a narrow cusp on a broad base, erect or nearly so anteriorly in jaw, becoming oblique posteriorly (more so on upper than lower jaw); edges of upper teeth finely serrate, of lowers smooth; no interdorsal ridge; first dorsal fin relatively small (height 6.0 to 10.2% total length), pointed at apex, its origin over or slightly posterior to inner posterior corner of pectoral fins; height of second dorsal fin 1.8 to 2.7% total length; anal fin a little larger than second dorsal fin, its origin slightly anterior to that of second dorsal; pectoral fins falcate and short, the length of the leading edge 13.4 to 18.0% total length; vertebrae 155 to 185, of which 76 to 91 are precaudal; grey, shading to white ventrally, sometimes with a faint white band on midside into the grey; fins of subadults and adults often dusky to black-tipped, especially the lower caudal lobe; margin of caudal fin narrowly blackish except leading edge of lower lobe; greatest length reported, 278 cm.

Remarks

Carcharhinus brevipinna was described from Java. It is wide-ranging in tropical to warm temperate seas; in the western Atlantic from North Carolina to southern Brazil; in the eastern Atlantic from the Mediterranean to Angola; in the western Indian Ocean from the Red Sea, Gulf of Oman and India to southern South Africa, including the Seychelles, Mauritius, and Madagascar; on all but the southern coasts of Australia through Indonesia to southern Japan. Garrick (1982) pointed out that a literature listing from the Philippines by name only needs substantiation. The author recently obtained a specimen in the Cebu market, Philippines. The species is absent from the islands of Oceania and the eastern Pacific. It is a migratory shark, moving into temperate waters during the warmer months; it may occur in schools. Feeds mainly on fishes, often on schooling species; it has been observed to attack a school of fishes rapidly from below, spinning as it moves into the school to feed, often ending with a spinning leap out of the water, hence its common name. Litter size varies from 2 to 15; gestation period 12 to 15 months; size at birth 46 to 80 cm. Males mature at 159 to 200 cm and females at 170 to 200 cm. A nonfatal attack on a bather off Florida has been attributed to this species (Bigelow and Schroeder, 1948), but it is not regarded as among the more dangerous species of sharks. *C. maculipinnis* (Poey) is a synonym.

Figure 54
Carcharhinus brevipinna, 80.5 cm, 2.5 kg, Lombok, Indonesia (J. Randall).

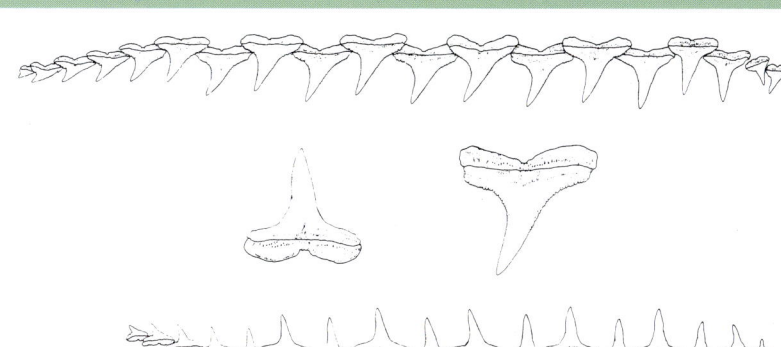

Figure 55
Teeth of *Carcharhinus brevipinna* (after Garrick, 1982).

Whitecheek Shark
Carcharhinus dussumieri (Valenciennes, 1839)

Diagnosis
Snout moderately long, and slightly pointed, its preoral length 5.8 to 7.9% total length; eyes 2.0 to 2.7% total length; third gill opening 2.4 to 3.5% total length; lateral labial furrows short; 12 to 14 (usuallly 13) teeth on side of upper jaw (discounting small teeth at symphysis) and 11 to 15 (usually 13 or 14) on lower; upper teeth with a strongly oblique, broad, serrate cusp and a deep notch on the posterolateral surface, the basal part of this notch with enlarged serrae; lower teeth with a narrow oblique finely serrate cusp on broad root, becoming rudimentary posteriorly in jaw; a low interdorsal ridge present; first dorsal fin moderately small, its height 8.0 to 10.7% total length, its tip somewhat pointed, its origin slightly anterior to inner posterior corner of pectoral fins; height of second dorsal fin 2.6 to 4.0% total length; anal fin slightly larger than second dorsal fin, its origin a little anterior to that of second dorsal; pectoral fins small, the posterior margin only slightly concave, the length of the anterior edge 14.5 to 17.2% total length; precaudal vertebrae 54 to 74; caudal vertebrae 53 to 79; total vertebrae 109 to 150; grey, white below, with a conspicuous large black spot covering the distal part of the second dorsal fin; other fins unmarked; maximum length slightly more than 100 cm.

Remarks
Carcharhinus dussumieri was described by Valenciennes in Müller and Henle, 1839; the type locality is Pondicherry, India. It ranges from the Arabian Gulf and India through Indonesia to China and southern Japan; it is a shallow-water species of the Asian continental shelf and of large Asian islands. Feeds mainly on small fishes, cuttlefish, and shrimps. Females generally produce two young at one time, exceptionally four; size at birth 38 to 39 cm. A small species; of 78 reported from the Arabian Gulf (as *Carcharias menisorrah*) by Blegvad (1944), few exceeded a meter in length. Blegvad concluded from a Danish trawl survey of the Gulf that *Carcharhinus dussumieri* is the most common shark. It is abundant in other parts of its range and often exploited for food. This species has often been confused with *C. sealei* (Pietschmann) (Randall et al., 1978, for example, identified a specimen of *dussumieri* from off Bahrain as *sealei*). The two species are very similar in external morphology and identical in colour (*sealei* also having as its single dark marking a broadly black-tipped second dorsal fin). Garrick (1982) separated the two in his key to the genus by *sealei* having a more falcate first dorsal fin, one fewer teeth on each side of the jaws, a narrower mouth, and 74 to 85 precaudal vertebrae. *C. sealei* has a broad distribution from the western Indian Ocean to southern Viet Nam (the record of Garrick, 1982 from Cochin, China is actually Viet Nam). The species is not known from the Arabian Peninsula.

Figure 56
Teeth of *Carcharhinus dussumieri* (after Garrick, 1982).

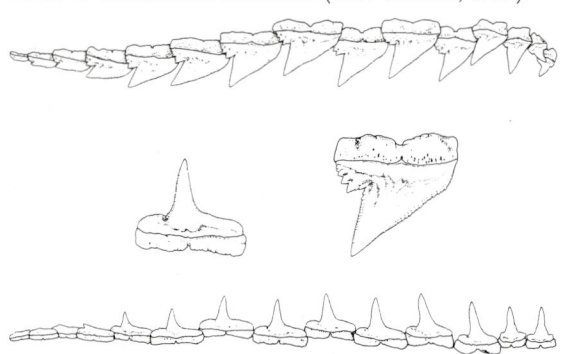

Figure 57
Carcharhinus dussumieri, 71.5 cm, 2.25 kg, Bahrain (J. Randall).

Figure 58
Carcharhinus falciformis, 111 cm, 7.5 kg, Taiwan
(J. Randall).

Silky Shark
Carcharhinus falciformis (Bibron, 1839)

Diagnosis

Slender-bodied, the body depth varying from about 11.5 to 17.5% total length; snout moderately long and slightly pointed, the preoral length 6.9 to 9.3% total length; eye diameter 1.0 to 2.7% total length; gill slits moderate in size, the length of the third 2.9 to 3.8% total length; lateral labial furrows short; 14 to 17 (usually 15) teeth on each side of upper jaw (disregarding the small ones at symphysis) and 14 to 17 (usually 15) on each side of lower jaw; upper teeth triangular with a slight indentation on the anteromedial edge and a deeper angular notch on the posterolateral edge (more pronounced on teeth posteriorly in jaw as the cusp becomes more oblique), the serrae coarse on basal part of these teeth; lower teeth with a narrow, erect, smooth-edged cusp on a broad root, not becoming oblique posteriorly in jaw (except slightly on the last few teeth); a narrow interdorsal ridge present; first dorsal fin small, its height 5.2 to 9.9% total length, very falcate, the apex narrowly rounded, the origin posterior to inner rear corner of pectoral fins; second dorsal fin very small, its height 1.4 to 2.2% total length, its free inner posterior margin long, 1.6 to 3 times longer than fin height; anal fin larger than second dorsal, its height 2.1 to 2.9% total length, its origin slightly in advance of second dorsal origin, its inner free posterior margin also long; pectoral fins large, narrow, and falcate, the anterior edge 14.2 to 22.0% total length (longer in adults than juveniles); vertebrae 199 to 215, of which 98 to 106 are precaudal; grey to dark grey dorsally, shading to white ventrally, sometimes with a faint band of white invading the grey on upper abdomen; first dorsal fin unmarked; second dorsal, anal, lower caudal lobe, and pectoral fins may have dusky tips; reported to 330 cm.

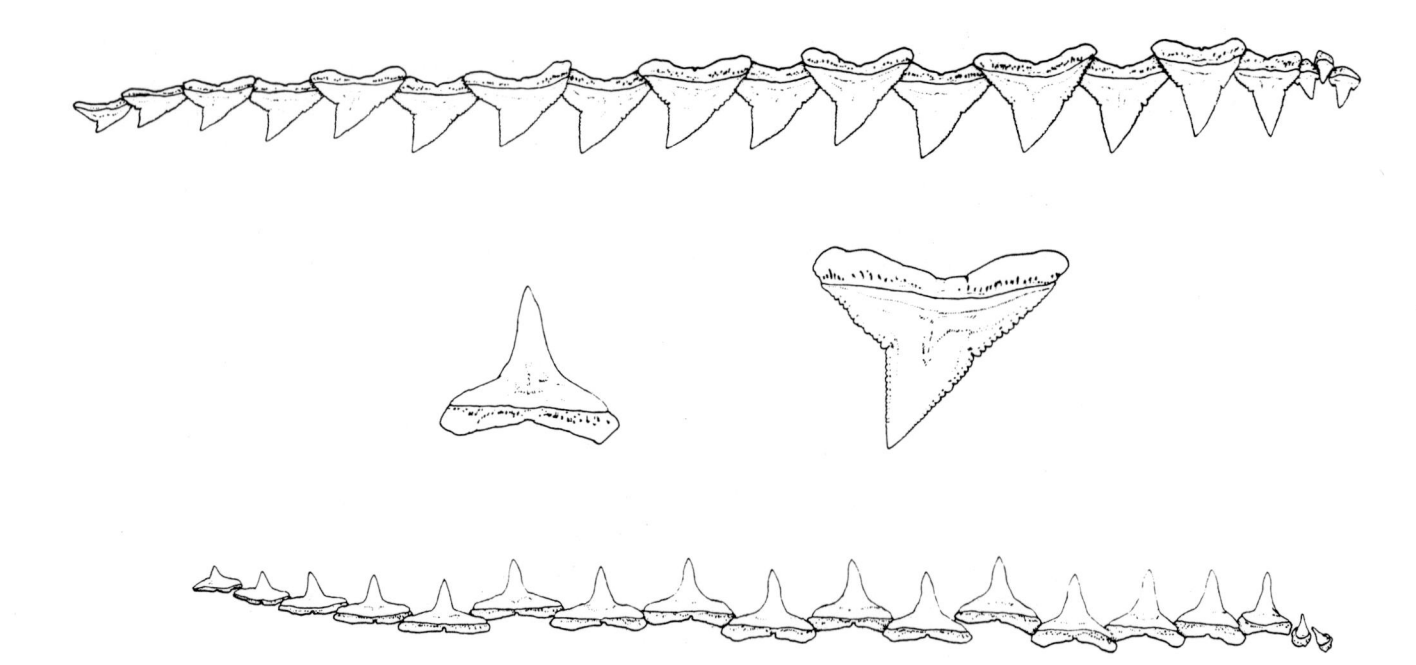

Remarks

Carcharhinus falciformis was described by Bibron in Müller and Henle (1839) from a female embryo from Cuba. This slim, swift-swimming shark is pelagic to semipelagic in all warm seas. Although it may be found far from land, it is usually associated with water masses within the influence of land and occasionally enters inshore waters where depths are as shallow as 18 m. Strasburg (1958) reported on the collection of 2176 specimens of the Silky Shark from the Central Pacific, finding them from 10°N and S of the equator but more abundant near land, in contrast to the Oceanic Whitetip and Blue Sharks. In offshore waters it occurs from the surface to at least 500 m. The southernmost record in the Indian Ocean is off southern Mozambique at 26° 35' S (Bass et al., 1973). This shark feeds mainly on fishes, especially pelagic species such as scombrids, but also on squids and pelagic crabs. Along with the Oceanic Whitetip, this shark causes much damage to longline tuna catches in tropical waters; also it is very destructive to purse seine nets and catches of tuna in the eastern Pacific. The number of embryos found in a single female have varied from 2 to 14; size at birth 70 to 87 cm. Males mature at 187 to 217 cm and females at 213 to 230 cm. *C. floridanus* Bigelow, Schroeder, and Springer was shown by Garrick et al. (1964) to be a synonym of *C. falciformis*. As mentioned in the Remarks for *C. amblyrhynchos*, *C. menisorrah* (Valenciennes) is also a synonym as a result of lectotype designation by Garrick.

Figure 59
Teeth of *Carcharhinus falciformis* (after Garrick, 1982).

BELOW RIGHT

Figure 60
Carcharhinus hemiodon (after Compagno, 1984b).

Figure 61
Teeth of *Carcharhinus hemiodon* (after Garrick, MS).

Pondicherry Shark
Carcharhinus hemiodon (Valenciennes, 1839)

Diagnosis
Body moderately stout; snout long and somewhat pointed, its preoral length 6.5 to 7.4% total length; eyes 2.1 to 2.4% total length; gill openings not large, the third 3.1 to 3.8% total length; nasal lobes short but slender; lateral labial furrows short; 14 or 15 (usually 14) teeth on each side of upper jaw (discounting symphyseals) and 12 to 14 in lower; upper teeth with a narrow, fairly oblique cusp which is smooth-edged or weakly serrate, the base on each side with about 4 prominent cusplets; lower teeth with cusp more erect and slender, smooth-edged, the base without cusplets; interdorsal ridge present; first dorsal fin of medium size with a narrowly rounded apex, its height 9.4 to 11.6% total length, its origin sightly posterior to axil of pectoral fins; second dorsal fin moderately large, its height 1.9 to 2.7% total length, its inner margin about 1.5 times fin height; anal fin slightly larger than second dorsal fin, its height 2.8 to 3.8% total length, its origin a little anterior to that of second dorsal; pectoral fins 16.3 to 19.2% total length, the posterior margin slightly concave; vertebrae 147 to 155, of which 69 to 71 are precaudal; grey dorsally and on sides, white ventrally, with a whitish band cutting into the grey on lower side from posteriorly; pectoral fins, lower lobe of caudal fin, and to a lesser extent second dorsal fin black-tipped; tip of first dorsal fin and dorsal edge and tip of upper caudal lobe dusky; maximum size unknown.

Remarks
Valenciennes described this shark in Müller and Henle (1839) from Pondicherry on the southeast coast of India. It ranges along the continental shelf of India and Pakistan to the Gulf of Oman. Records to the east of India are scattered: Viet Nam, Java, Borneo, Australia, and Philippines. According to Garrick (MS), *Hypoprion atripinna* Chu from China is a junior synonym. Reports that *C. hemiodon* has been taken in rivers are in need of confirmation. This shark has often been confused with other species. For example, Day (1878) recorded it as *Carcharias limbatus* in his *Fishes of India*. Because of the large basal cusplets of its upper teeth, it has often been placed in the genus *Hypoprion*, along wth *Carcharhinus macloti* and the Night Shark (*C. signatus*) from the western Atlantic. Immature specimens up to 60 cm have been taken; adults probably reach at least 100 cm.

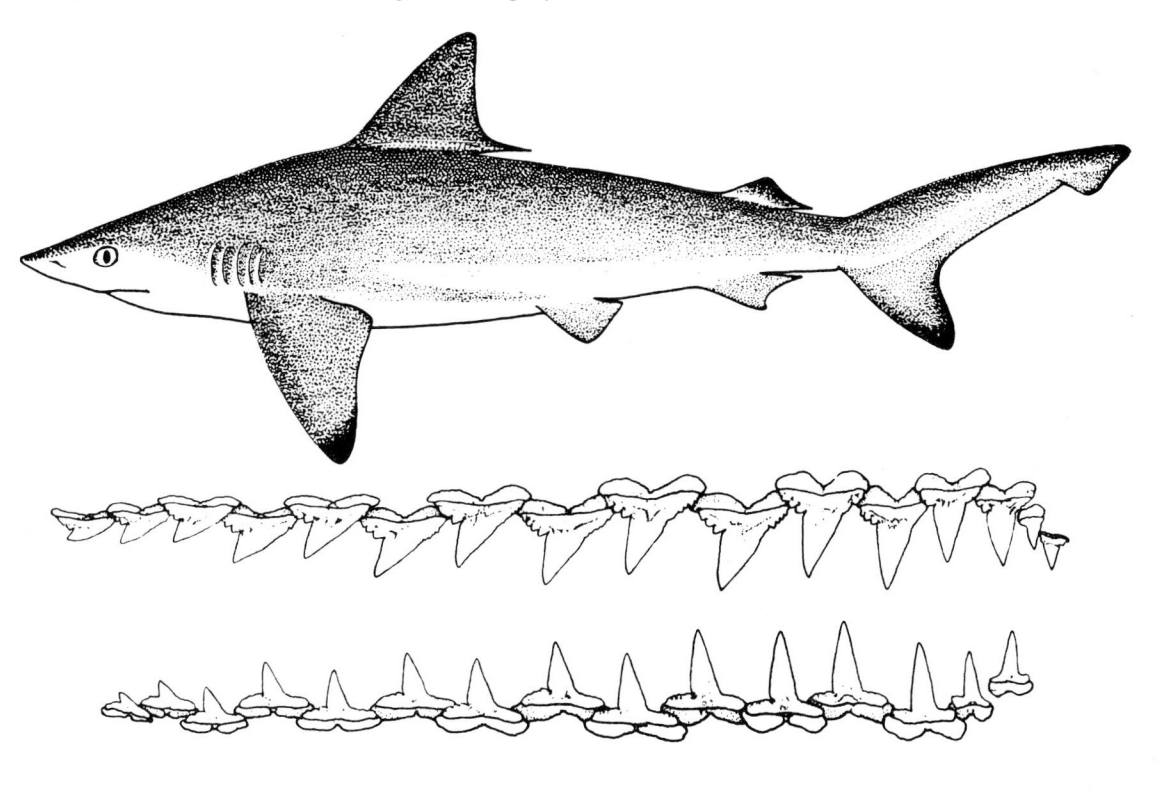

Bull Shark
Carcharhinus leucas (Valenciennes, 1839)

Diagnosis
Heavy-bodied; snout short and broadly rounded, the preoral length 4.6 to 6.7% total length; internarial distance 5.9 to 7.0% total length; eyes small, 0.8 to 1.8% total length; gill openings moderately large, the third 3.1 to 5.5% total length; lateral labial furrows short; 12 to 14 (usually 13) teeth on each side of upper jaw (disregarding small symphyseals), and 12 or 13 (usually 12) teeth on each side of lower jaw; upper teeth broadly triangular and strongly serrate, only slightly emarginate along posterolateral edge (more so posteriorly in jaw where the cusp is somewhat oblique); lower teeth with a narrower cusp, erect medially in jaw (but progressively more oblique laterally and posteriorly), and less strongly serrate than uppers (nevertheless, the lower teeth have a broader cusp and stronger serration than other species of the genus, in general); no interdorsal ridge; first dorsal fin moderately large, its height 7.0 to 11.3% total length, the apex fairly pointed, the origin over or slightly posterior to axil of pectoral fins; second dorsal fin moderately large, its height 3.2 to 4.5% total length; anal fin about equal in size to second dorsal, its origin distinctly posterior to that of second dorsal; pectoral fins large and falcate, the length along the anterior margin 17.6 to 22.2% total length (longer in larger individuals); vertebrae 198 to 227, of which 101 to 123 are precaudal; grey, becoming white ventrally, often with a faint pale grey horizontal band extending into the white of the upper abdomen; fins of small individuals tipped or edged with blackish (as in Figure 62); these markings become paler with growth until in large adults only the undersides of the paired fins have dusky tips and occasionally the distal ends of the anal fin and lower caudal lobe; largest recorded, 324 cm, but believed to attain about 340 cm.

Remarks
Valenciennes described *C. leucas* in Müller and Henle (1839) from four specimens from the Antilles. It is now known to be a very widespread species, occurring along continental shores of nearly all warm seas and in many insular localities, particularly the larger islands near continents such as those of Indonesia, the Philippines, and Melanesia. Exceptional is a record from the atoll of Rangiroa in the Tuamotu Archipelago (Johnson, 1978). It is unusual in its tolerance of both low and high salinities. It is often found in rivers and in freshwater lakes linked to the sea. That it is not yet recorded from the Red Sea may be related to the limited freshwater drainage to this body of water. It is known from the Tigris River and Shatt-el Arab in Iraq. Typically this shark is found in shallow water, often in estuarine areas, harbours, etc. where the water can be very turbid. It may also occur in hypersaline lagoons such as the St. Lucia lake system of Natal where it has been found in salinities as high as 53 ppm (though tends to move away from salinities this high). It has been taken at depths up to 152 m, however. The Bull Shark is very catholic in its food habits; stomach content analyses have revealed an unbelievable variety of prey, including bony fishes, sharks, rays, crustaceans, sea turtles, cephalopods and other molluscs, and marine mammals. It also takes terrestrial mammals, dead or alive, as the opportunity arises. Although it does not have quite the sinister reputation of the Great White Shark or Tiger Shark, its greater abundance and its predilection for inshore environments bring it into more frequent contact with humans. The attacks attributed to *Odontaspis taurus* in Australia (where it is known as the Grey Nurse Shark) are believed to be due mainly to the Bull Shark. The number of embryos per litter varies from 3 to 13; the size at birth has been recorded to range from 56 to 81 cm. Males mature at from 157 to 226 cm and females between 180 and 230 cm. Males attain about 300 cm and females may reach as much as 340 cm. This species has long been confused with *C. amboinensis* (see Remarks for this species for the means of separating the two) and also with the Ganges Shark, *Glyphis gangeticus*. The latter appears to be confined to river systems of the Indian subcontinent. Records of it from elsewhere have been shown to be misidentifications of *C. leucas*. Compagno (1984b) has provided a detailed taxonomic separation of *G. gangeticus* and *C. leucas*. *C. zambezensis* (Peters) and *C. nicaraguensis* (Gill and Bransbord) are among the nine synonyms of *C. leucas*.

CLASSIFICATION

Figure 62
Carcharhinus leucas, 51 cm, Cochin, India (J. Randall).

Figure 63
Teeth of *Carcharhinus leucas* (after Garrick, 1982).

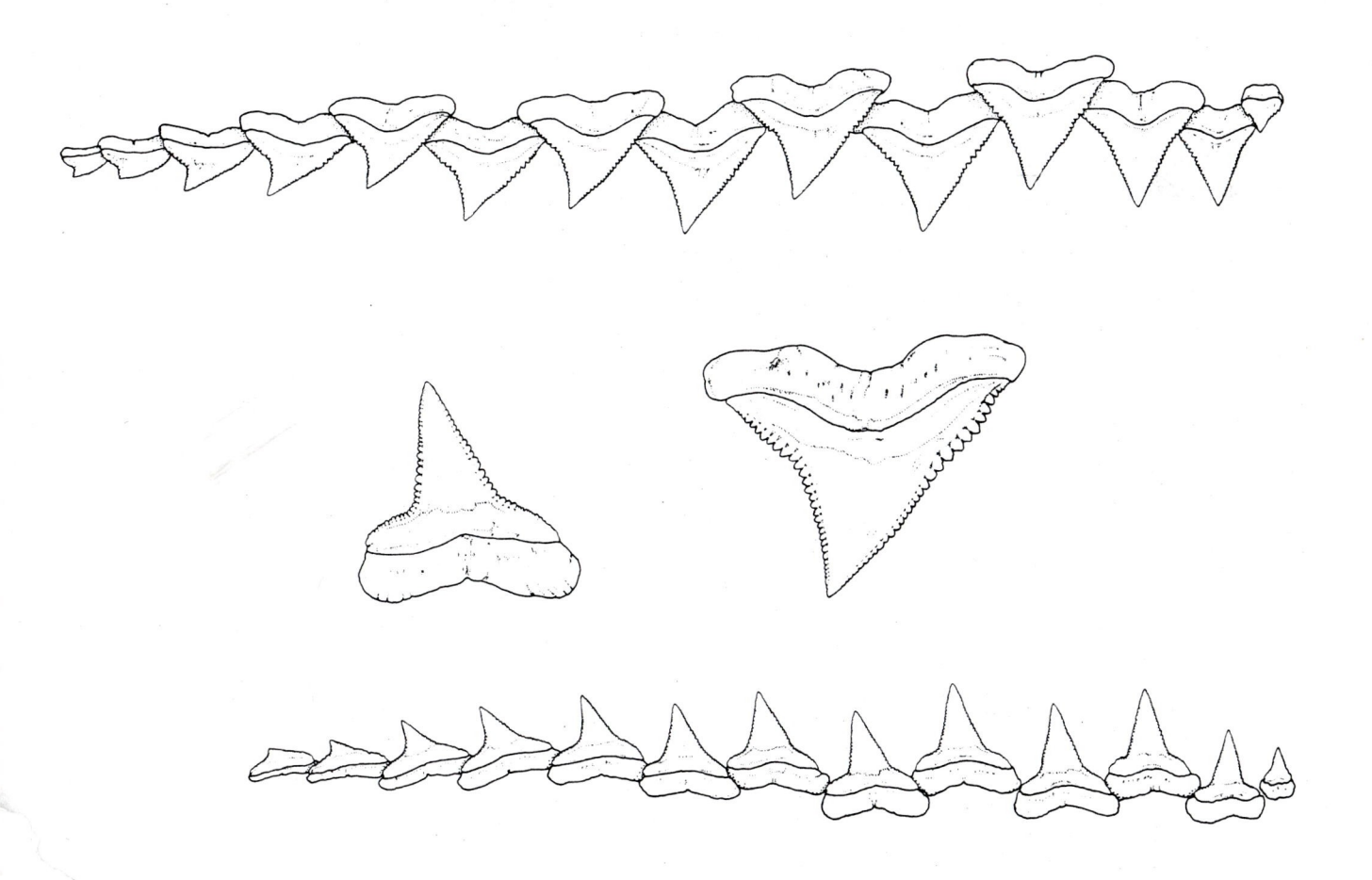

105

Blacktip Shark
Carcharhinus limbatus (Valenciennes, 1839)

Diagnosis
Snout moderately long and pointed, its preoral length 6.3 to 9.0% total length; eyes 1.0 to 2.2% total length; gill openings moderately long, the third 3.8 to 4.9% total length; lateral labial furrows short; 14 to 16 (usually 15) teeth on each side of upper jaw (omitting the small teeth at symphysis) and 13 to 16 (usually 14 or 15) in lower jaw; upper teeth narrow-cusped for the genus, progressively more oblique posteriorly in jaw, the serrations very fine apically, becoming coarse at base; lower teeth with a very narrow, erect, finely serrate cusp; no interdorsal ridge; first dorsal fin moderately large and falcate, its height 8.2 to 13.8% total length, its apex acute, its origin over or slightly posterior to pectoral fin axil; height of second dorsal fin 2.5 to 5.0% total length; anal fin slightly larger than second dorsal fin, its origin below or slightly posterior to origin of second dorsal; pectoral fins moderately large and falcate, the anterior margin 17.2 to 22.2% total length; vertebrae 174 to 203, of which 88 to 102 are precaudal; grey to grey-brown dorsally, shading to white ventrally, with a conspicuous near-horizontal band of grey on midside of body extending into white of upper abdomen; pectoral fins, lower lobe of caudal fin, and anal fin usually tipped with black; the first dorsal fin, pelvic fins, and upper lobe of caudal fin sometimes dusky to blackish at tips, though the upper caudal lobe and apex of the first dorsal fin may have only the edge blackish; attains about 250 cm.

Remarks
This is still another shark described by Valenciennes in Müller and Henle (1839); the type locality is Martinique. The species is worldwide in tropical to warm temperate seas, including the Red Sea. It is found primarily inshore and will enter estuarine and muddy areas; it also occurs somewhat offshore but ordinarily within the influence of land. Active and fast-swimming, it sometimes runs in schools. Feeds primarily on fishes but also on cephalopods and the larger crustaceans. A few attacks on humans have been attributed to this shark, but it is usually not aggressive to man. The number of embryos per female at one time is one to ten; length at birth has been reported from 38 to 72 cm. Males mature at about 135 to 180 cm and females at 120 to 190 cm. Age at maturity in South Africa is believed to be four years. *C. pleurotaenia* (Bleeker) and *C. natator* Meek and Hildebrand are among the eight synonyms of this species.

Figure 64
Carcharhinus limbatus, 171 cm, 31 kg, Marquesas (J. Randall).

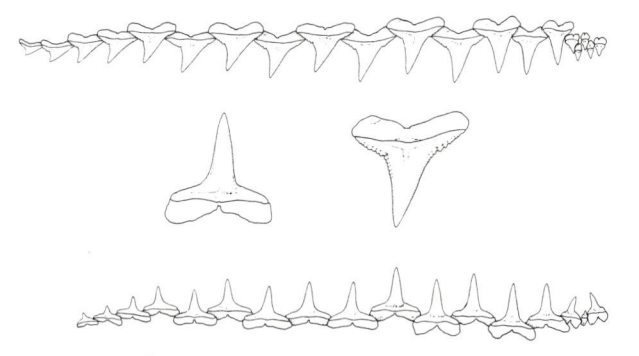

Figure 65
Teeth of *Carcharhinus limbatus* (after Garrick, 1982).

Figure 66
Carcharhinus longimanus, 145 cm, 51 kg, Marquesas Islands. (J. Randall).

Oceanic Whitetip Shark
Carcharhinus longimanus (Poey, 1861)

Diagnosis

Snout moderately short and broadly rounded, the preoral length 5.4 to 7.1% total length; internarial distance 5.2 to 6.2% total length; eyes small, 0.9 to 2.5% total length; third gill opening 3.0 to 4.1% total length; lateral labial furrows short; 13 or 14 (usually 14) teeth on each side of upper jaw (disregarding small symphyseal teeth) and 13 to 15 (usually 14) on lower jaw; upper teeth broadly triangular and strongly serrate, the cusp somewhat oblique posteriorly in jaw resulting in a concave margin on the posterolateral edge of the teeth; lower teeth with narrower cusp (but relatively broad for the genus) which is erect on the most medial teeth but slightly oblique laterally and posteriorly in jaw, the serration moderate; a low interdorsal ridge usually present; first dorsal fin very large and very broadly rounded apically, its height 9.2 to 15.2% total length (average height about 12%), its origin slightly anterior to inner posterior corner of pectoral fins; height of second dorsal fin 2.5 to 3.9% total length; anal fin slightly larger than second dorsal fin, its origin below or slightly posterior to second dorsal origin; pectoral fins very long, broad, and distally rounded, the length of the anterior edge 20.2 to 27.1% total length; vertebrae 228 to 244, of which 123 to 131 are precaudal; brownish grey on back, becoming white ventrally, the usual grey band present within white area of upper abdomen but faint; tips of first dorsal fin, paired fins, and caudal fin lobes broadly mottled white; anal fin usually blackish at tip and second dorsal fin may be dusky at tip; juveniles with most fins tipped in blackish; reaches about 350 cm, but rarely over 300 cm.

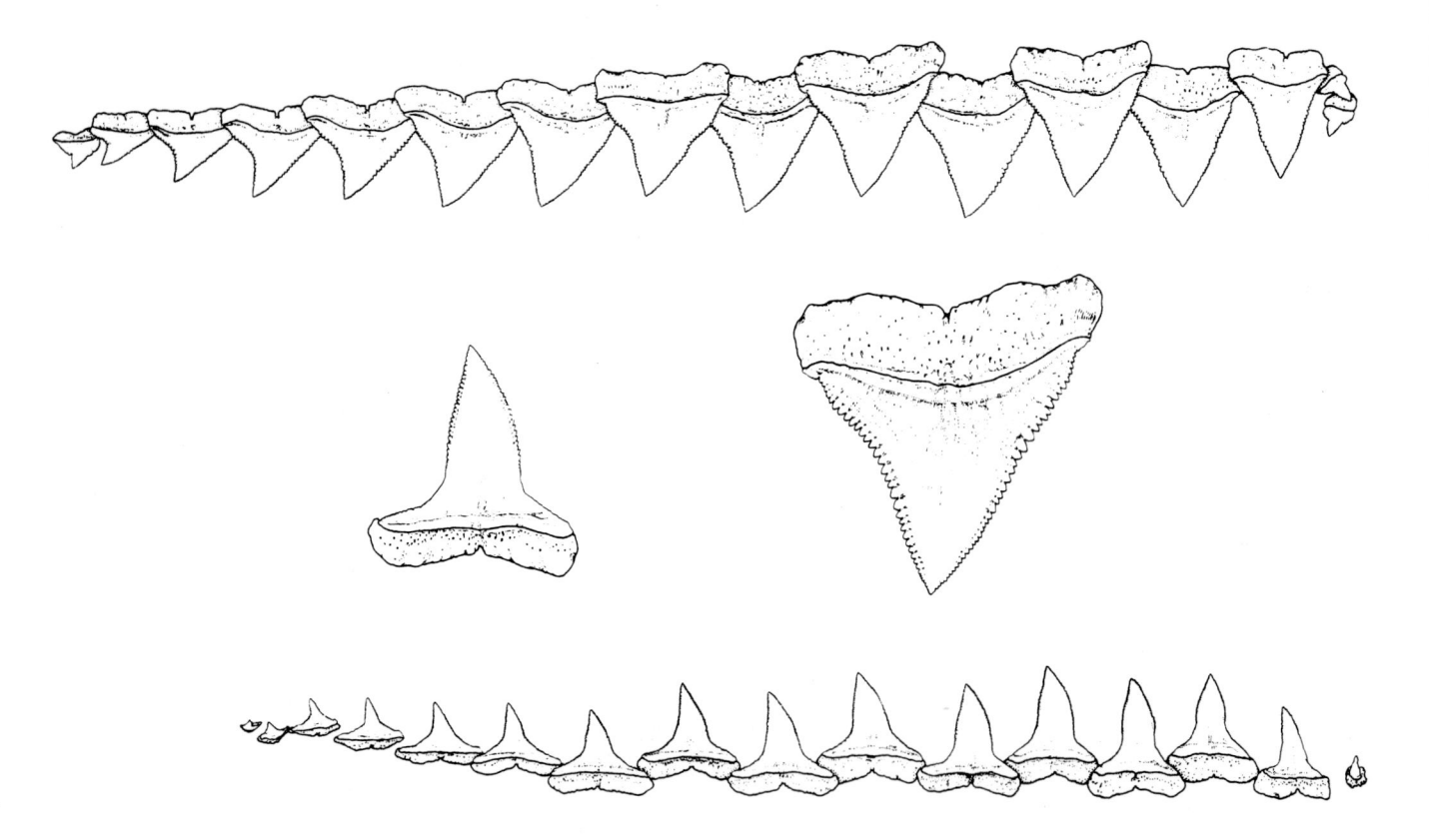

Figure 67
Teeth of *Carcharinus longimanus* (after Garrick, 1982).

Remarks

The type locality for *C. longimanus* is Cuba. This shark has a worldwide distribution in tropical to warm temperate seas, but is most abundant in the lower 20° of latitude (Strasburg, 1958). It is an epipelagic species generally found far from land, though it has been observed over depths as little as 37 m. It is usually encountered near the surface, but has been taken as deep as 152 m. It is often found with the Silky Shark (*C. falciformis*), a faster-swimming species, but it dominates Silkies of about equal size (as when competing for the same food source) by being more aggressive. It feeds on oceanic fishes such as scombrids, lancetfish, oarfish, and dolphins, along with squids, sea birds, sea turtles, and pelagic crustaceans, and gastropods. Its stomachs occasionally contain remains of marine mammals. The illustrated specimen had large pieces of porpoise meat in its stomach, along with squid beaks. It is a dangerous shark known to have attacked man and his boats. When survivors from air and sea disasters in offshore tropical waters have been in the sea for extended periods and shark attacks have resulted, the Oceanic Whitetip is the most likely suspect. It is despised by tuna longline fishermen for the damage it inflicts on their catch of yellowfin and bigeye tuna. *C. longimanus* is one of three Whitetip Sharks, the other two being the Silvertip (*C. albimarginatus*) and the Reef Whitetip (*Triaenodon obesus*). *Triaenodon* is easily distinguished by its slender body, very short blunt snout, large second dorsal and anal fins, and distinctive teeth with a cusplet on each side at the base of the central cusp. *C. albimarginatus* has much smaller and more pointed first dorsal and pectoral fins; its teeth are not so broadly triangular, and the white distally on its first dorsal fin is sharply defined and continues along the entire outer posterior margin (in *C. longimanus* it is broader, mottled, and confined to the tip). As shown by Garrick (1982), the earliest name for the Oceanic Whitetip Shark is *Squalus maou* Lesson (1830); he has given the reasons for retaining *longimanus* for the species: long usage and its placement on the Official List of Specific Names in Zoology (Name 2059) by the International Commission on Zoological Nomenclature. S. Springer (1950) proposed a new genus, *Pterolamia*, for the Oceanic Whitetip Shark (which he changed to *Pterolamiops* in 1951 when he discovered *Pterolamia* is preoccupied). Although this generic name was used by a few authors subsequent to Springer, it is now universally regarded as a synonym of *Carcharhinus*. Female Oceanic Whitetips attain maturity at a smaller size than males which is unusual in sharks. They mature at about 180 to 190 cm whereas males are fully adult at about 200 cm. Litter sizes vary from 1 to 15; the size at birth has been estimated as 60 to 65 cm based on measurements of near-term embryos.

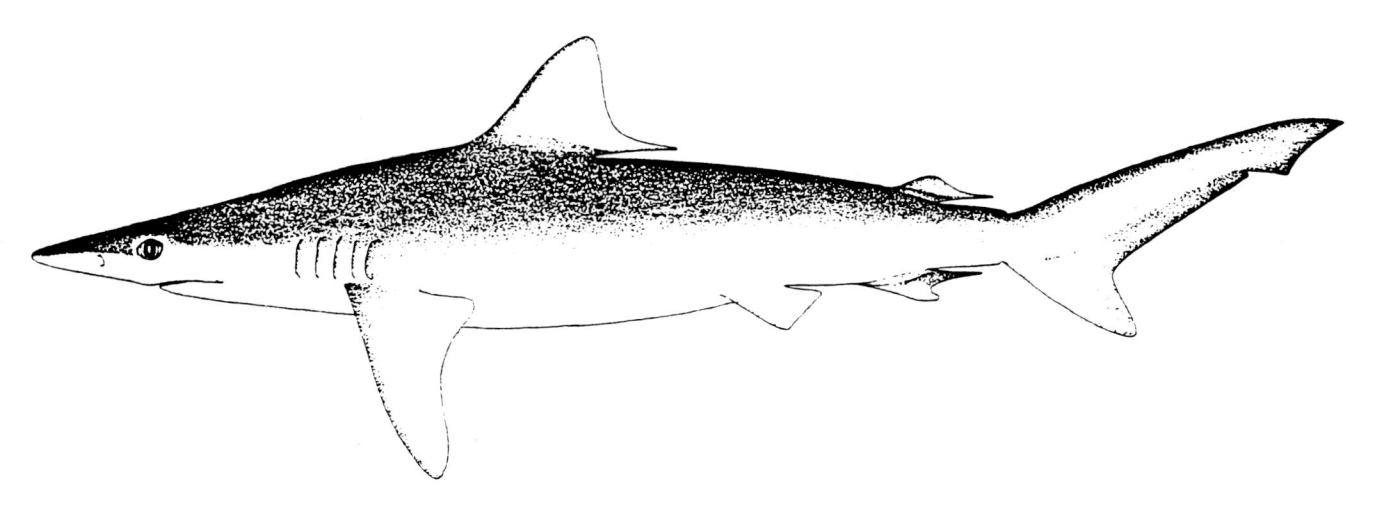

Figure 68
Carcharhinus macloti
(after Compagno, 1984).

Hardnose Shark
Carcharhinus macloti (Müller and Henle, 1839)

Diagnosis

Body slender; snout long and pointed, its preoral length 8.7 to 10.3% total length, with a hypercalcified mass inside; eyes not large, 1.8 to 3.1% total length; gill openings moderate, the third 2.7 to 3.5% total length; nasal lobes slender and moderately long; lateral labial furrows short; 13 to 15 (usually 14) teeth in each side of upper jaw and 13 or 14 in lower (discounting symphyseals); upper teeth with narrow, slightly oblique, smooth-edged, central cusp, the base with about 4 cusplets on each side; lower teeth with a long, narrow, slightly oblique, smooth-edged cusp and no basal cusplets; most specimens with a low interdorsal ridge; first dorsal fin small, its height 7.1 to 8.9% total length, its apex narrowly rounded, the fin origin usually over inner posterior corner of pectoral fins; second dorsal fin long and low, the height 1.6 to 2.1% total length, the inner posterior margin more than twice the fin height; origin of second dorsal fin about over midbase of anal fin; anal fin slightly larger than second dorsal fin, its height 2.2 to 2.8% total length, its posterior tip nearly reaching lower precaudal pit; pectoral fins moderately falcate, 13.5 to 16.1% total length; vertebrae 149 to 154, of which 68 to 71 are precaudal; grey to grey-brown, shading to white ventrally; posterior margin of pectoral fins and margin of lower caudal lobe pale; most individuals with edge of upper caudal lobe and leading edge of second dorsal fin blackish; maximum length probably less than 100 cm.

Remarks

The type locality of this small shark is New Guinea. Known otherwise from scattered records from Taiwan, China, Australia, Viet Nam, Burma, India, Pakistan, Kenya, and Tanzania. Garrick (personal communication) examined a specimen from off Aden, at present the only record from Arabian waters. Additional records can be expected to fill in the discontinuities in its range. Usually one embryo per uterus, the size at birth 45 to 50 cm. Nothing is known of its food habits, but the diet probably includes mainly small fishes and crustaceans. Like *C. hemiodon*, *C. macloti* has been classified by some authors such as Bigelow and Schroeder (1948) in *Hypoprion*, a genus based on the prominent basal cusplets of the upper teeth. Most ichthyologists today regard *Hypoprion* as a synonym of *Carcharhinus*.

Figure 69
Teeth of *Carcharhinus macloti*
(after Garrick, MS).

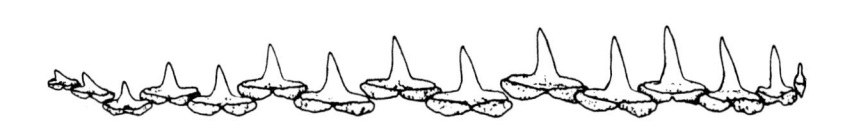

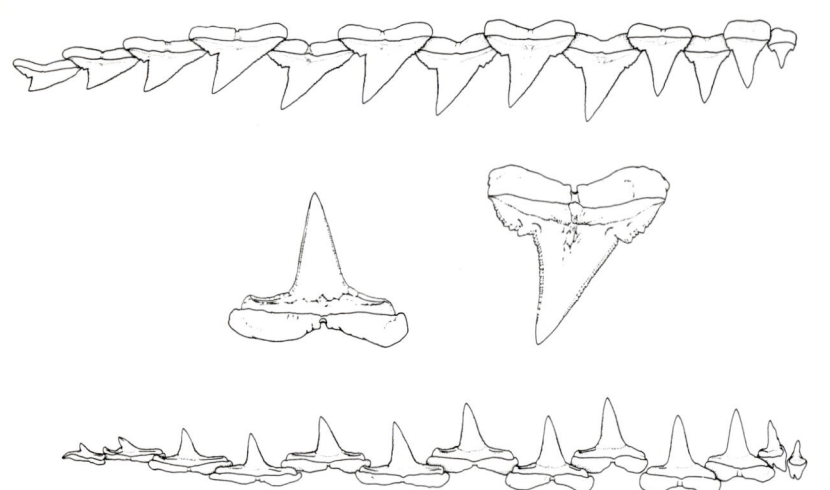

Figure 70
Carcharhinus melanopterus, 52.5 cm, 0.9 kg, Gulf of Oman (J. Randall).

Figure 71
Teeth of *Carcharhinus melanopterus* (after Garrick, 1982).

Blacktip Reef Shark
Carcharhinus melanopterus (Quoy and Gaimard, 1824)

Diagnosis

Snout moderately short and rounded, its preoral length 5.6 to 7.3% total length; eye diameter 1.5 to 3.0% total length; third gill slit 2.6 to 4.7% total length; lateral labial furrows short; 11 to 13 (usually 12) teeth on each side of upper jaw (discounting small symphyseal teeth) and 10 to 12 (usually 11) in lower; upper teeth narrow-cusped, oblique (except first few medial teeth), with a broad angular notch (deeper on posterolateral edge), the serrae at base of cusp on each side enlarged (particularly the first at the angle); lower teeth with a narrow, slightly oblique, finely serrate cusp on a broad base; no interdorsal ridge; first dorsal fin of medium size and falcate, its height 8.0 to 11.4% total length, its origin over or slightly posterior to inner rear corner of pectoral fins; height of second dorsal fin 3.4 to 5% total length; anal fin about equal in size to second dorsal fin and directly below it; pectoral fins moderate, falcate, the length of anterior edge 17.5 to 19.5% total length; vertebrae 193 to 214, of which 111 to 122 are precaudal; greyish to yellowish brown, white below, with a distinct slightly oblique brown band extending from above pectoral fin into whitish area of upper abdomen; all fins conspicuously black-tipped, most broadly on first dorsal fin (where it is often accentuated by a broad submarginal whitish band) and lower caudal lobe and least on pelvic and second dorsal fins; margin of caudal fin black except leading edge of lower lobe; reaches 180 cm.

Remarks

Carcharhinus melanopterus was described from the island of Waigeo off the western end of New Guinea. It is widespread in the tropical Indo-Pacific region from the Red Sea (and into the eastern Mediterranean via the Suez Canal, as reported by Tortonese, 1964), south to Mozambique and Madagascar and east to the Hawaiian Islands and French Polynesia; apparently absent from a few isolated Pacific islands such as Minami Tori Shima (Marcus Island), Johnston Island, Rapa, and the Pitcairn Group. This shark is one of the three most abundant sharks of Indo-Pacific islands and reefs; it is an inshore species which comes into amazingly shallow water on reef and sand flats, often with its first dorsal fin exposed. It feeds on a great variety of reef and inshore fishes and cephalopods, occasionally on shrimps and stomatopods. Although a rather timid species usually frightened away if a swimmer makes an overt movement toward it, it can be dangerous to spearfishermen, and it has been known to bite the feet or legs of persons wading in the shallows (Randall and Helfman, 1973). This is more apt to occur at uninhabited or sparsely populated islands. Litters consist of 2 to 5 pups which are born at a length varying from 33 to 52 cm. Males mature at 91 to 100 cm and females at 96 to 112 cm. Beginning with Whitley (1934), a few authors have used the name *C. spallanzani* (Peron and Lesueur) for this species, but Garrick (1982) has shown that *spallanzani* is a synonym of *C. sorrah*.

Dusky Shark
Carcharhinus obscurus (Lesueur, 1818)

Diagnosis

Snout of moderate size, rounded, the preoral length 5.7 to 8.4% total length; eye diameter 0.8 to 2.1% total length; third gill slit 2.7 to 4.9% total length; lateral labial furrows small; 14 or 15 (usually 14) teeth on each side of upper jaw (not counting small teeth at symphysis) and 13 to 15 (usually 14) in lower jaw; upper teeth broadly triangular, moderately serrate, and slightly oblique with a concavity on the posterolateral edge (slight on medial teeth, marked on posterior teeth); lower teeth with a narrow, finely serrate, slightly oblique cusp on a broad-based root; interdorsal ridge present; first dorsal fin of moderate size, the height 5.8 to 10.4% total length, its apex pointed to narrowly rounded, its origin over or slightly posterior to inner rear corner of pectoral fins; height of second dorsal fin 1.5 to 2.6% total length; anal fin larger than second dorsal fin, its origin below that of second dorsal; pectoral fins long and falcate, the length of the anterior edge 16.8 to 23.0% total length; vertebrae 173 to 194, of which 86 to 97 are precaudal; grey, shading to white ventrally, with a faint, near-horizontal, grey band invading the white of upper abdomen; tips of fins dusky (darker on paired fins of small individuals); reported to 365 cm; maximum length might approach 400 cm.

Remarks

The type locality of this shark is North America (the exact locality not known). It is worldwide in tropical to warm temperate seas. In the western Atlantic it ranges from Massachusetts to Florida and the northern Gulf of Mexico, with records from Nicaragua, Trinidad, Guyana, and southern Brazil; in the eastern Atlantic from Portugal and the Mediterranean to Sierra Leone; in the western Indian Ocean from the Cape of Good Hope to Mozambique; one record from the northern Red Sea (a single specimen reported by Garrick, 1982); west and east coasts of Australia, China, and Japan; in the eastern Pacific from southern California to the Gulf of California; possibly also in Chile. It appears to be absent from equatorial waters. Primarily a species of continental shelves from shallow water to depths as great as 400 m; sometimes encountered at the surface well offshore. It is a migratory species, at least in some areas, moving into higher latitudes during the warm time of the year. Feeds mainly on a great variety of bony fishes, sharks and rays, cephalopods, and larger crustaceans. Although few attacks on man have been recorded for the Dusky Shark (one of a juvenile in Bermuda by Randall in Gilbert, 1963), it is a dangerous species as its size, dentition, and occurrence in shallow water might suggest. Six to 14 young per litter; size at birth 69 to 100 cm. Males mature at about 280 cm and females from 257 to 300 cm. *C. obscurus* has been confused with *C. altimus*, *C. galapagensis*, and *C. plumbeus*. It may be distinguished from *altimus* and *plumbeus* by its smaller first dorsal fin and the origin of this fin over the inner rear corner of the pectoral fins (over axil of pectoral fins in the other two sharks). The Galapagos Shark is more similar externally to the Dusky, but it also has a larger first dorsal and a larger second dorsal fin than the Dusky (the ranges in fin height overlap a little; average height of first dorsal of *obscurus* 8.2%, of *galapagensis* 10.7% total length). There is no overlap in the number of precaudal vertebrae (103 to 109 in *galapagensis*). Knowledge of locality is also helpful, as *C. galapagensis* is primarily a species of oceanic islands in contrast to the continental *obscurus*.

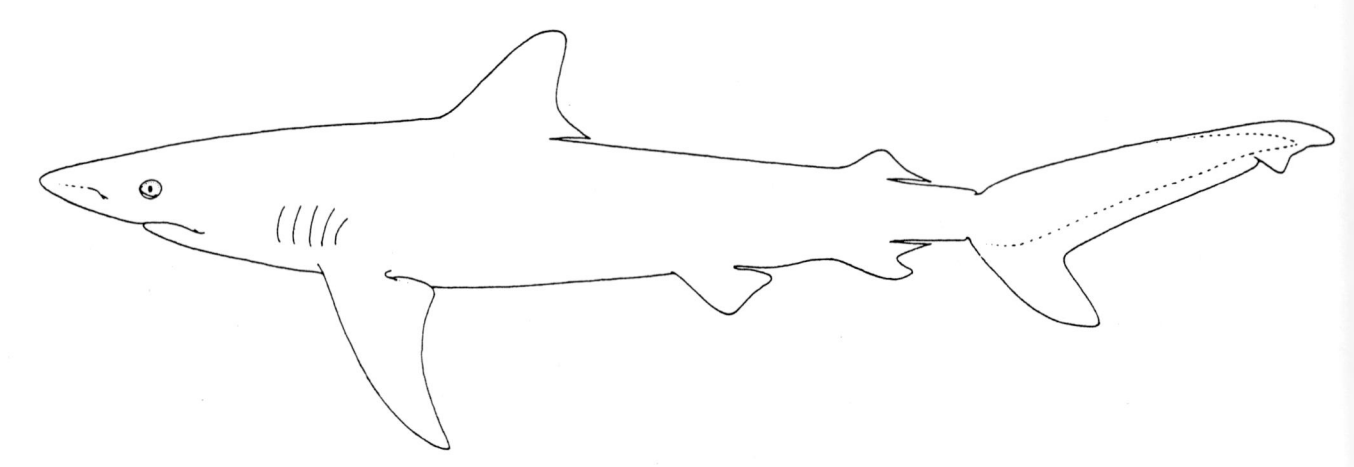

Figure 72
Carcharhinus obscurus, 96.1 cm, Baja California (after Garrick, 1982).

Figure 73
Teeth of *Carcharhinus obscurus* (after Garrick, 1982).

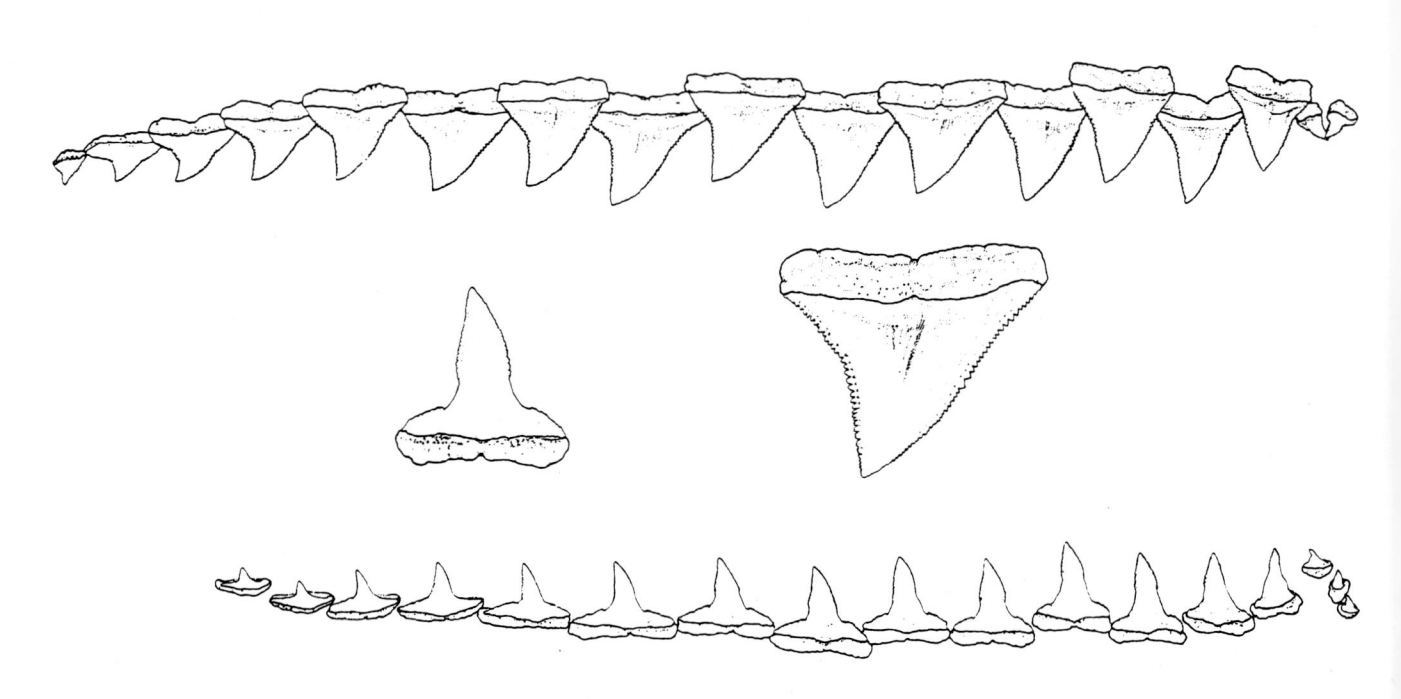

Sandbar Shark
Carcharhinus plumbeus (Nardo, 1827)

Diagnosis

Body moderately heavy; snout rounded and of medium length, the preoral length 5.6 to 8.1% total length; eye diameter 1.4 to 2.9% total length; length of third gill opening 2.4 to 3.7% total length; lateral labial furrows short; 13 to 15 (usually 14) teeth on each side of upper jaw (discounting symphyseals) and 12 to 15 (usually 13 or 14) on lower; teeth shaped almost like those of *C. obscurus*, the cusp only slightly more oblique; interdorsal ridge present; first dorsal fin of mature adults very large, erect, slightly falcate, with a narrowly rounded to pointed tip, the fin height 13.6 to 16.5% total length (height of fin of small individuals ranges as low as 8.4% total length); origin of first dorsal fin over or slightly anterior to pectoral axil; height of second dorsal fin 2.6 to 3.9% total length; anal fin equal in size or slightly larger than second dorsal fin, its origin over or slightly posterior to that of second dorsal; pectoral fins large, slightly falcate, the length of anterior edge 16.9 to 24.0% total length (fins of larger individuals longer, in general); total vertebrae 172 to 189 (except one aberrant individual with 152); precaudal vertebrae 88 to 97; greyish brown dorsally, white ventrally, with a faint brown band in upper part of the white area on midside; tips and trailing edges of fins often dusky; reliably reported to 240 cm.

Remarks

The type locality for *C. plumbeus* is the Adriatic Sea. Until recently most authors have used the name *C. milberti* (Valenciennes) for this species, but Tortonese (1950; 1951) presented arguments for the adoption of *plumbeus* in spite of the poor description of the latter. He was followed by Garrick (1982: 134-135) who presented more evidence for accepting the name *plumbeus*. The Sandbar Shark, like the Dusky, is primarily a continental shelf species of tropical to warm temperate waters, and its distribution is similar to that of the Dusky: Massachusetts to Venezuela and southern Brazil; Mediterranean Sea; Portugal to Zaire; Cape of Good Hope to Tanzania; Madagascar, Mauritius, and Seychelles; Red Sea to Arabian Gulf; western and eastern Australia and New Caledonia; Indonesia, Viet Nam, China, Taiwan, and Japan; and the Hawaiian Islands (the most common shark in the principal islands of this archipelago). The species may be absent from the eastern Pacific. Garrick (1982) examined two newborn specimens from the Revillagigedo Islands taken by the 'Albatross' in 1888 which "appear to be *plumbeus*" (but locality error is possible), and Kato et al. (1967) stated in reference to *plumbeus*, "possibly present at the Galapagos Islands". The apparent gaps in distribution suggest that there may be isolated populations of this shark. S. Springer (1960) has discussed presumed Atlantic populations. An inshore species, but has been taken to depths of 280 m; it may be found from shallow muddy bays to coral reefs; although it occurs off river mouths, it does not ascend rivers. It is normally closely associated with the bottom, feeding mainly on benthic fishes, but also takes crustaceans and molluscs. The number of young per litter varies from 1 to 14; size at birth 56 to 75 cm. Males mature at 131 to 178 cm and females from 144 to 183 cm. This shark has not been implicated in any attacks on man.

OVERLEAF

Figure 74
Carcharhinus plumbeus, 179 cm, Red Sea (J. Randall).

Figure 75
Teeth of *Carcharhinus plumbeus* (after Garrick, 1982).

114

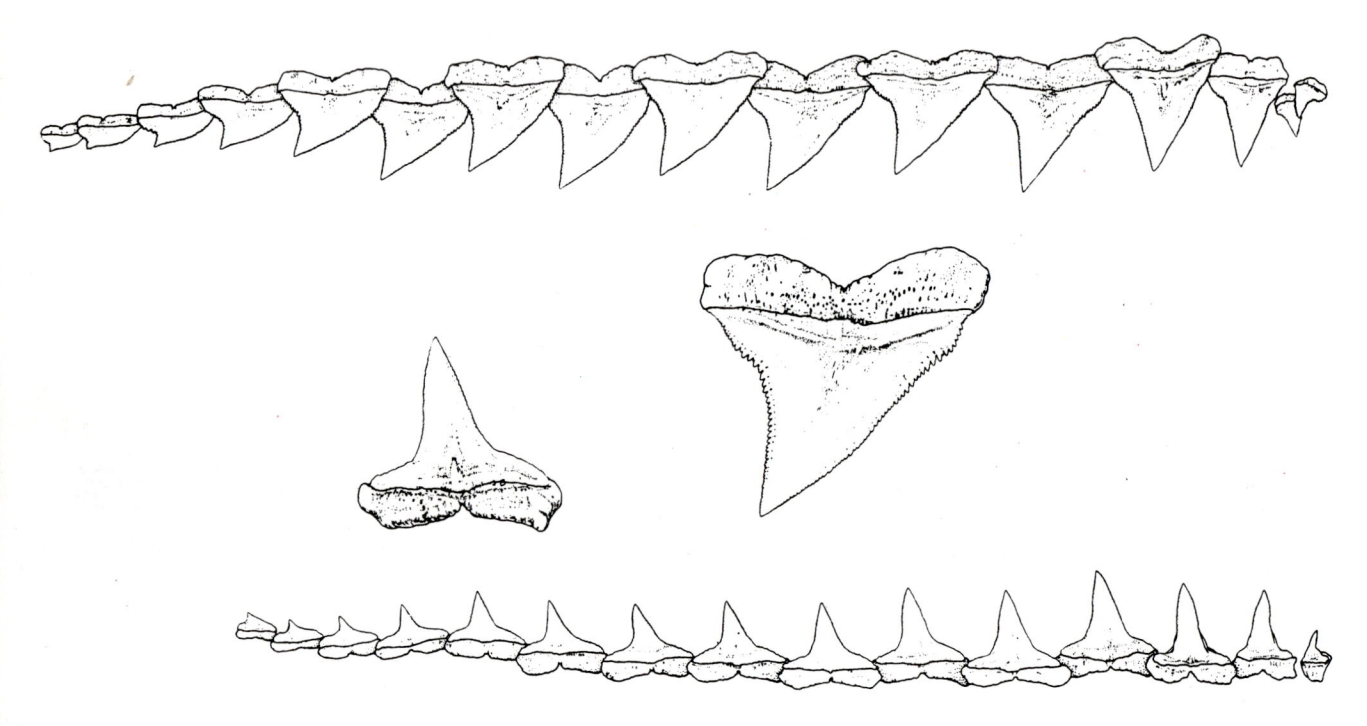

Spottail Shark
Carcharhinus sorrah (Valenciennes, 1839)

Diagnosis
Snout moderately long and pointed, its preoral length 7.1 to 8.4% total length; diameter of eye 1.5 to 2.4% total length; gill slits relatively short, the length of the third 1.8 to 3.3% total length; anterior nasal flap narrow; lateral labial furrows short; 12 or 13 (usually 12) teeth on each side of upper jaw (not counting small teeth at symphysis) and 11 or 12 (usually 12) in lower jaw; upper teeth triangular, slightly to strongly oblique (anteriorly to posteriorly) with a large angular notch on the posterolateral edge, the serrae on the basal half of the notch enlarged (particularly the distal serrae); lower teeth with a narrow, oblique, finely serrate cusp of only moderate height; interdorsal ridge present; first dorsal fin of moderate size, falcate and apically pointed, the height 7.7 to 10.9% total length, the origin over or slightly posterior to inner rear corner of pectoral fins; second dorsal fin small, its height 1.5 to 2.3% total length; anal fin larger than second dorsal fin, its origin distinctly anterior to that of soft dorsal; pectoral fins moderately small, falcate, the length of the anterior edge 14.5 to 19.5% total length; vertebrae 153 to 175, of which 66 to 79 are precaudal; grey above, white below, with a grey horizontal band into upper part of white area on abdomen; lower lobe of caudal fin, pectoral fins, and second dorsal fin broadly tipped with black; first dorsal fin usually with a small blackish spot at tip or just the edge blackish; attains about 160 cm.

Remarks
Carcharhinus sorrah was described by Valenciennes in Müller and Henle (1839) from specimens from India, Java, and Madagascar. Garrick (1982) designated the specimen from Java (in the museum at Leiden) as the lectotype.. He pointed out that the earliest name for this species is *C. spallanzani* (Peron and Lesueur), but he regarded this name as a *nomen dubium* on the grounds of an inadequate original description, lack of a type specimen, and incorrect usage. He was able to determine that it is conspecific with *sorrah* only by seeing unpublished manuscript materials of Peron and Lesueur. *C. sorrah* occurs from the Red Sea and Gulf of Aden south to Mozambique and South Africa and east through Madagascar, Mauritius, Seychelles, and India to western Australia and Indonesia, north in the western Pacific through Viet Nam and the Philippines to China, Taiwan, and southern Japan, and southeast to to eastern Australia and the Solomon Islands. The illustrated specimen from Bahrain herein represents the first record from the Arabian Gulf. This shark is a shallow-water coastal species which feeds mainly on fishes and cephalopods. Litter size varies from 2 to 6; young are born at 45 to 60 cm in length. Males mature at about 106 cm or less, and females at from 110 to 118 cm.

Figure 76
Carcharhinus sorrah, 108 cm, 14.5 kg, Bahrain (J. Randall).

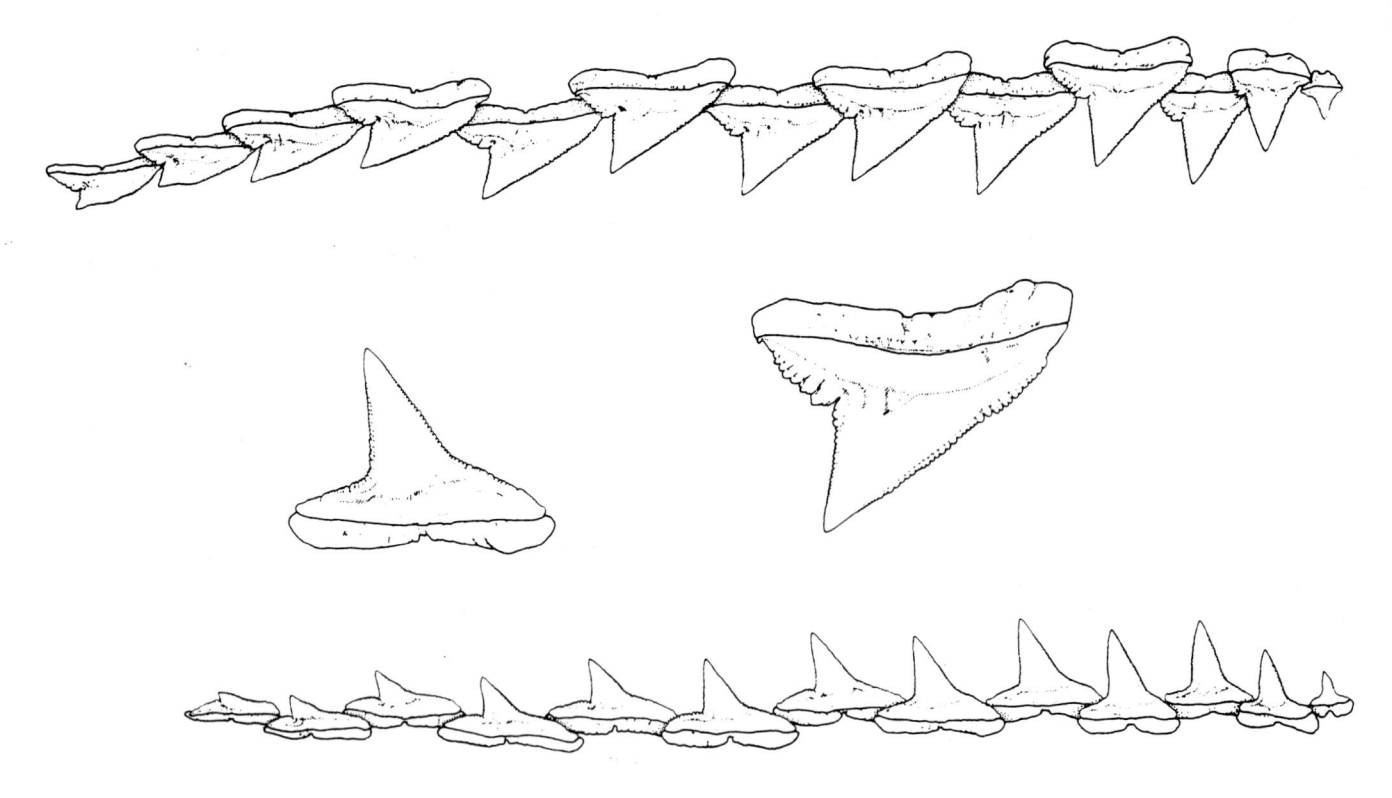

Figure 77
Teeth of *Carcharhinus sorrah* (after Garrick, 1982).

Tiger Shark
Galeocerdo cuvier (Peron and Lesueur, 1822)

Diagnosis

Head, thorax, and abdomen stout, but body becoming very attenuate posteriorly, with a low lateral keel on each side of the narrow caudal peduncle; dorsal part of head only slightly convex; snout very short and slightly rounded, its preoral length 3.7 to 4.8% total length; eyes of moderate size, 0.8 to 2.1% total length; spiracle a narrow slit one-fourth to one-third eye diameter in length, a half eye diameter, or slightly more, behind eye; internarial width 4.6 to 5.6% total length; gill openings small, 1.8 to 2.8% total length; lateral labial furrows very long, twice length of medial, and nearly reaching anterior edge of eyes; usually 10 or 11 teeth on each side of jaws (discounting a symphyseal tooth of medium length) and decreasing greatly in size toward corner of jaws; teeth similar in shape in both jaws, strongly serrate, the anteromedial edge convex and the posterolateral deeply notched, with very large serrae distally on basal part of notch, these larger serrae themselves secondarily serrate; interdorsal ridge present; first dorsal fin not very large, its height 7.5 to 9.3% total length; height of second dorsal fin 2.7 to 3.8% total length; anal fin about equal in size or slightly larger than second dorsal fin, its origin posterior to that of second dorsal; precaudal pits present; upper lobe of caudal fin slender and pointed with a subterminal notch but without a well-developed terminal lobe, the length of the anterior edge 20.8 to 25.2% total length (in the Atlantic up to 30% or more TL); length of lower caudal lobe 11.7 to 14.3% total length; pectoral fins broad and falcate but not long, the length of anterior edge 14.2 to 16.9% total length; vertebrae 216 to 233, of which 100 to 112 are precaudal; grey with darker grey bars or vertical rows of spots on body (faint on large adults), becoming white ventrally; reaches 6 m; unauthenticated reports to 7.4 m or more.

Remarks

The Tiger Shark was described (as *Squalus cuvier*) from the northwest coast of Australia; there is no type specimen. It is worldwide in distribution in tropical to temperate seas, including remote islands of Oceania; its excursions into temperate waters are mainly the result of migrations in warm currents such as the Gulf Stream (an example being a record from Iceland) during summer months. May be found in surprisingly shallow water for such a large shark; it is known from atoll lagoons, harbours and river mouths, often in turbid water. It has also been encountered offshore. Two of six Tiger Sharks tagged off Puerto Rico were recaptured; one was taken near the area of release; the other had migrated to Venezuela (Rivera-Lopez and Randall, MS). Because *G. cuvier* is not often seen at the surface or in shallow water by day but caught there on set lines at night, a pattern of retiring to deeper areas by day and movement to the shallows at night for feeding is regarded as typical. A 400-cm female individual tagged with a telemetric device at French Frigate Shoals, Hawaiian Islands ranged over an area of about 100 km^2 during two 24-hour periods for a horizontal distance of about 82 km per day, at a rate varying from 0.4 to 11.0 km/hour (nighttime average rate slightly slower than day and more area covered by day). 68% of its activity during the day was spent deeper than the reef drop off at 40 m (to at least 140 m during short periods), in contrast to 83% of its nocturnal activity in shallower water than the drop off (Tricas et al., 1981). The Tiger Shark eats a greater variety of animals than any other shark: numerous species of bony fishes, sharks (includng its own species when hooked), rays, sea turtles, sea birds, seals, dolphins, cephalopods, spiny lobsters, crabs, horseshoe crabs, gastropods, and jellyfishes. Feeds readily on carrion. Many different terrestrial animals have been found in its stomach, mostly a result of disposal in the sea by man; in addition, an incredible variety of refuse and garbage, including indigestible plastic, metal, and other items of human origin. Justifiably the most feared sharks in tropical and subtropical seas; more confirmed attacks on man and boats than any other shark except for the Great White Shark. Ovoviviparous, the number of young per litter varying from 10 to over 80; size at birth 51 to 76 cm. Males mature at 226 to 290 cm, and females from 250 to 350 cm. Among the most important commercial species of sharks because of its abundance, quality of its meat and its hide, of its fins for shark fin soup, its jaws and teeth as curios and as sport for anglers. The all-tackle world record is 807.4 kg. *Galeocerdo arcticus* (Faber) is a synonym.

SHARKS OF ARABIA

Figure 78
Embryo of *Galeocerdo cuvier*, 52.7 cm, from a 360-cm female taken in the Marshall Islands (J. Randall).

Figure 79
Teeth of *Galeocerdo cuvier* (after Bigelow and Schroeder, 1948).

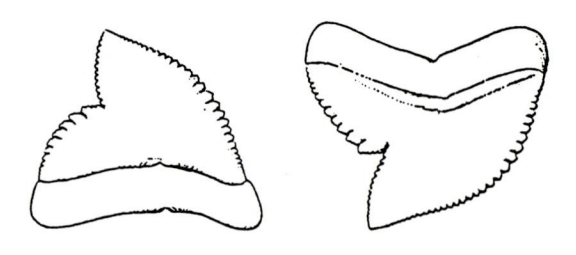

Figure 80
Galeocerdo cuvier, 305.5 cm, 175 kg, Marshall Islands (J. Randall).

Figure 81
Loxodon macrorhinus, 72.3 cm, Red Sea (J. Randall).

Slit-eye Shark
Loxodon macrorhinus Müller and Henle, 1839

Diagnosis

Body slender, the depth about 10 to 14% total length; snout long and pointed, its preoral length 8.1 to 9.8% total length; eyes large, the diameter 2.3 to 3.6% total length, with a characteristic small notch at midlevel in posterior edge of orbit; spiracles minute to absent; gill slits short, the third 1.4 to 2.1% total length; lateral labial furrows short; mouth small, its width 4.9 to 6.5% total length; 12 to 14 teeth on each side of jaws (discounting a medium-sized symphyseal tooth); teeth in both jaws similar, smooth-edged, highly oblique, with a deep notch on posterolateral edge, the basal part of this notch convex; interdorsal ridge absent or rudimentary; first dorsal fin not large, its height 6.2 to 8.7% total length, centered between bases of pectoral and pelvic fins; second dorsal fin small, its height 1.1 to 1.7% total length, its origin over rear base of anal fin; anal fin larger than dorsal fin, its base about twice as long as that of second dorsal; precaudal pits present; upper caudal lobe long, the length of its anterior edge 25.0 to 31.7% total length, with a distinct terminal lobe about one-third length of entire upper lobe; pectoral fins short and broad, the length of the anterior margin 11.3 to 13.9% total length; vertebrae 148 to 191, of which 77 to 106 are precaudal; greyish brown, shading to whitish ventrally, without any prominent markings; front of snout translucent; trailing edges of paired fins often pale; anterior margin of first dorsal fin may be narrowly dark; caudal fin sometimes narrowly dark-edged except anterior margin of lower caudal lobe; maximum length reported 91 cm.

Remarks

The only species of the genus. Type locality is not known. Distributed from the Red Sea to Natal and east through Madagascar, Seychelles, India, and Sri Lanka to Indonesia, north to the Philippines, China, Taiwan, and Japan and south to Queensland. Recorded from depths of 7 to 80 m. Feeds on bony fishes, cephalopods, and crustaceans. Viviparous; two to four young per litter. Size at birth 40 to 43 cm. Males mature between 62 and 66 cm and females at about 79 cm. Probably does not exceed 100 cm. Of commercial importance in some areas as food, especially in southeastern India.

Figure 82
Teeth of *Loxodon macrorhinus*, female (after V.G. Springer, 1964).

Sicklefin Lemon Shark
Negaprion acutidens (Rüppell, 1837)

Diagnosis
Body moderately stout; head broad and only slightly convex dorsally; snout broadly rounded to slightly wedge-shaped, and short, its preoral length 4.6 to 6.5% total length; eye diameter 0.9 to 2.1% total length; spiracles usually absent (occasional individuals with very small spiracles); gill openings large, the third 4.0 to 5.3% total length; labial furrows short; 13 to 16 (usually 14) teeth on each side of jaws (not counting small symphyseal teeth); upper teeth with a moderately long narrow cusp on a broad base, only the most medial tooth erect, the rest progressively more oblique, without serrations (except faintly on basal part of crown of a few teeth); lower teeth similar but with even narrower cusps, less oblique, and without basal serrae; no interdorsal ridge; first dorsal fin falcate, moderate in size, its height 6.9 to 10.9% total length, its origin slightly posterior to inner rear corner of pectoral fins; second dorsal fin nearly as large as first, its height 6.4 to 8.5% total length; anal fin smaller than second dorsal fin, its origin posterior to origin of second dorsal; pectoral fins broad and falcate, the length of the anterior edge 15.7 to 21.2% total length; vertebrae 224 to 227 (three specimens); precaudal vertebrae 139 to 140; yellowish grey to yellowish brown, paler below, the fins more yellowish than body; no dark or light markings; attains at least 310 cm.

Remarks
The type locality of *N. acutidens* is Jeddah, Saudi Arabia. The species is known throughout the tropical Indo-Pacific region, ranging in East Africa to northern Natal, in the western Pacific from the Philippines to Queensland, and in Oceania east to the Line Islands and French Polynesia. It is primarily an inshore species oriented to the bottom, preferring bays, lagoons, and estuaries to exposed outer reef areas. The young may be seen in very shallow water on sand flats where they must compete with juvenile *C. melanopterus*. They feed mainly on reef and shore fishes. They are not as active, in general, as the species of *Carcharhinus*; they are often found resting upon the bottom. Although ordinarily not aggressive to divers, this species has been implicated in attacks on man, particularly following provocation and the stimuli of spearfishing, as has the one other species of the genus, the Atlantic *N. brevirostris* (Poey) (Randall in Gilbert, 1963). The two species of *Negaprion* are very closely related, apparently differing only in the fins of *acutidens* being slightly more falcate and in the lower number of vertebrae of *brevirostris* (197 to 206). Viviparous, the number of pups per litter ranging from 1 to 13; size at birth 45 to 80 cm. Males are reported to mature at 243 cm. *Hemigaleops fosteri* Schultz and Welander in Schultz and collaborators, 1953, is a synonym based on a small specimen from the Marshall Islands. *Odontaspis madagascariensis* Fourmanoir, 1961, is also a synonym.

Figure 83
Teeth of *Negaprion brevirostris* (after Bigelow and Schroeder, 1948). Similar to teeth of *N. acutidens*.

Figure 84
Negaprion acutidens, 178 cm, 31.5 kg, Fanning Island (J. Randall).

Milk Shark
Rhizoprionodon acutus (Rüppell, 1837)

Diagnosis
Body slender, the depth about 11 to 14% total length; snout long and somewhat pointed, the preoral length 7.9 to 10.5% total length; eyes large, 1.5 to 3.0% total length; spiracles absent; length of third gill opening 2.0 to 3.2% total length; labial furrows long, the lateral slightly longer, 1.4 to 2.0% total length; number of hyomandibular pores (series of large pores above corner of mouth on each side) 7 to 15; 11 to 13 (usually 12) teeth on each side of jaws (disregarding a medium-sized symphyseal tooth); upper teeth with a highly diagonal blade-like cusp which is finely serrate in adults, nearly straight on anteromedial edge and strongly notched on the posterolateral, the basal part of the notch convex with larger serrae; lower teeth similar to uppers but the anteromedial edge concave and the serrae smaller; no interdorsal ridge or only a faint low one; first dorsal fin of moderate size, the height 7.2 to 9.6% total length; its origin ranging from slightly anterior to slightly posterior of a vertical through inner rear corner of pectoral fins; second dorsal fin small, its height 1.6 to 2.2% total length, its origin over last half of anal fin base; anal fin larger than second dorsal fin, its base nearly twice as long; pectoral fins short, broad, and slightly falcate, the anterior edge 11.8 to 14.6% total length; vertebrae 121 to 162, of which 55 to 79 are precaudal; brownish grey, whitish ventrally, the upper lobe of the caudal fin often narrowly edged in black; leading edge of first dorsal fin sometimes narrowly blackish; pectoral fins with a pale trailing edge; maximum recorded length 178 cm, but few exceed 110 cm.

Figure 85
Rhizoprionodon acutus, 67 cm, 1.4 kg, Bahrain (J. Randall).

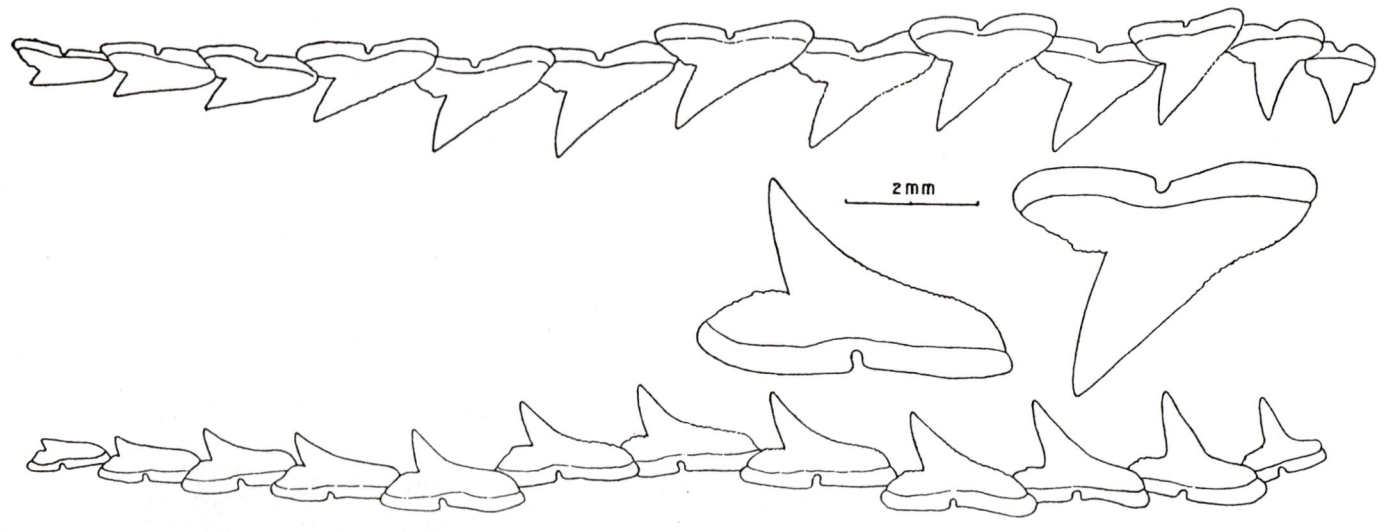

Figure 86
Teeth of *Rhizoprionodon acutus*, male (after V.G. Springer, 1964).

Remarks

This shark was described in the genus *Carcharias* from a specimen taken in the Red Sea off Jeddah. The generic name *Rhizoprionodon* was proposed by Whitley (1929) as a replacement name for *Rhizoprion* Ogilby, 1915. It consists of seven small species, none reaching 180 cm (revision of the genus and the related monotypic *Loxodon* and *Scoliodon* by V.G. Springer, 1964). *R. acutus* occurs in the eastern Atlantic from the Madeira Islands to Angola and in the Indo-Pacific from the Red Sea and Arabian Gulf south to Natal and Madagascar and east through Pakistan and India to Thailand, Indonesia, and Malaysia, north to China, Philippines, Taiwan, and Japan and south to Queensland. It occurs on the continental shelf or around island on or near the shelf in the depth range of 1 to 200 m, generally in turbid water. It may be found in estuaries but not of very low salinity. It feeds on a wide variety of small schooling fishes such as clupeoids, as well as benthic fishes, cephalopods, crustaceans, and gastropods. The number of young per litter varies from one to eight; size at birth 25 to 39 cm. Gestation period about one year. Males mature at 68 to 72 cm and females at 70 to 81 cm. Locally abundant in some areas. The objective of small-scale commercial fisheries in some countries such as India. The common name Milk Shark is in reference to the belief that the flesh of this shark promotes lactation in women. Springer (1964) has listed the six synonyms of *R. acutus*.

Grey Sharpnose Shark
Rhizoprionodon oligolinx Springer, 1964

Diagnosis

Similar in morphology to the preceding but a little heavier-bodied and with slightly shorter but still pointed snout, the preoral length 7.2 to 8.3% total length; eye diameter 2.1 to 3.2% total length; spiracles absent; length of third gill opening 1.8 to 2.6% total length; lateral labial furrow shorter than medial, its length 0.3 to 1.3% total length; number of hyomandibular pores (series of large pores above corner of mouth) on each side 3 to 8 (usually 4 to 7); 11 to 13 (usually 11 or 12) teeth in upper jaw and 10 to 12 (usually 11) in lower; teeth much like those of *R. acutus* but serration irregular and less evident; interdorsal ridge, if present, very faint; width of first dorsal fin 7.3 to 8.6% total length, its origin over or just posterior to inner rear corner of pectoral fins; second dorsal fin small, its height 1.6 to 1.9% total length, its origin over posterior half of anal fin; anal fin larger than second dorsal fin, its base nearly twice as long as that of second dorsal; pectoral fins short, broad, and slightly falcate, the length of the anterior edge 11.7 to 13.3% total length; vertebrae 151 to 162, of which 84 to 91 are precaudal; grey to brownish grey above, rather abruptly whitish below; leading margins of upper caudal lobe and first dorsal fin often narrowly blackish; trailing margin of pectoral fins pale; largest specimen reported, 61 cm; probably reaches about 70 cm.

Remarks

The type locality of this small shark is the Gulf of Thailand. It ranges from the Arabian Gulf along the southern Asian continent to Kampuchea, with records from Sri Lanka, Sumatra, and Java. A record from Angaur in the Palau Islands (Belau) listed by Compagno (1984a) is an unexpected range extension. *R. oligolinx* is very closely related to the Australian *R. taylori* (Ogilby), the latter differing in having 7 to 11 enlarged hyomandibular pores on each side and 73 to 80 precaudal vertebrae. Little is known of the biology of *R. oligolinx*, althouth it is a common inshore species over much of its range. The number of young per litter ranges from three to five; size at birth, 21 to 26 cm. Males mature between 29 and 38 cm and females between 32 and 41 cm.

Figure 87
Rhizoprionodon oligolinx, 47.5 cm, Indonesia. (J. Randall).

Figure 88
Teeth of *Rhizoprionodon oligolinx*, female (after V.G. Springer, 1964).

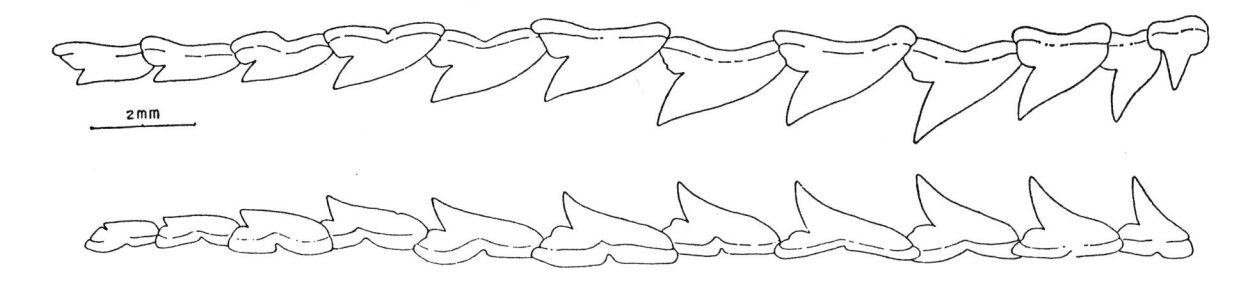

Whitetip Reef Shark
Triaenodon obesus (Rüppell, 1837)

Diagnosis
Body slender, the depth about 11 to 16% total length; head depressed, about twice as broad as deep; snout very short, the preoral length 3.1 to 4.5% total length; eyes horizontally elongate, their greatest diameter 1.3 to 2.4% total length; spiracles absent or minute; third gill slit 2.7 to 3.8% total length; labial furrows very short; teeth small, in at least two function rows in jaws, 20 to 24 on each side of upper jaw (discounting small symphyseal teeth) and 20 to 22 in lower; teeth similar in both jaws, smooth-edged, with a large, oblique, narrow, central cusp and a small pointed cusp basally on each side (two small cusps on each side of lower teeth and two on anteromedial side of upper teeth in about posterior half of jaws); no interdorsal ridge; first dorsal fin of moderate size, its height 8.7 to 11.0% total length, its origin at about midpoint between bases of pectoral and pelvic fins; second dorsal fin relatively large, its height about two-thirds to three-fourths height of first dorsal; anal fin about as large as second dorsal fin, its origin below or slightly posterior to origin of second dorsal; pectoral fins broad, slightly falcate and short, the length of the anterior margin 15.1 to 16.6% total length; precaudal vertebrae 128 to 135; caudal vertebrae 79 to 85; brownish grey, shading to whitish with a yellowish cast ventrally, usually with a few scattered roundish dark grey spots on body (more on ventral half than dorsal); tips of first dorsal fin and upper caudal lobe broadly white; apices of second dorsal fin and lower lobe of caudal fin often white-tipped; maximum length about 175 cm.

Figure 89
Teeth of *Triaenodon obesus*.

Triaenodon obesus is one of five new species of sharks described by Rüppell (1837) from the Red Sea, all of which are valid. His choice of the specific name *obesus* was not appropriate for such a slender shark, however. The genus is monotypic. Compagno (1984a) determined that *T. obtusus* Day from India is probably a late embryo of *Carcharhinus amboinensis*. Until recently, most authors, including Bigelow and Schroeder (1948), have placed the Whitetip Reef Shark in the Triakidae. Gohar and Mazhar (1964a), Kato et al. (1967) and Compagno (1973), however, have classified it in the Carcharhinidae. Although its teeth ar triakid-like with a prominent basal cusp on each side of the large central cusp and occur in more than one functional row, the presence of a nictitating membrane, well-developed precaudal pit, prominent lower caudal lobe, and a scroll-type valvular intestine rather than the spiral form are carcharhinid characters. A. Baranes and G. Dingerkus, however, are planning to shift *Triaenodon* to the Hemigaleidae. The Whitetip Reef Shark is broadly distributed throughout the tropical and subtropical Indo-Pacific region and has extended its range to the tropical eastern Pacific. It is so ubiquitous in the Indo-Pacific that it is simpler to list the few localities where it has not been reported in spite of considerable collecting effort: Arabian Gulf, Easter Island, and Rapa. There are, of course, other localities where it is not yet known, but they are ones from which it could, with some degree of certainty, be expected. This shark is primarily an inshore species, though it was once recorded from 330 m in the Ryukyu Islands (Taniuchi, 1975). It is truly a reef fish in the sense that it not only feeds mainly on reef fishes (and secondarily on octopuses) but resides in reefs. During the day it spends most of its time at rest on the bottom in caves or beneath ledges. With its slender supple body it is able to movethrough the narrow places in reefs that other sharks cannot negotiate. Although thisshark will feed by day when the opportunity arises, it is primarily nocturnal. On only a few occasions has it displayed aggressive behaviour to divers, and then as a result of the stimuls of speared fish or provocation. There is perhaps a greater threat to man from eating this shark, as it has been implicated in ciguatera (though such poisoning is not common and is very localised) (Randall, 1977, 1980). Number of embryos per litter, one to five; size at birth about 52 to 60 cm. Males mature at about 105 cm and females at slightly larger size. Tags were affixed to 124 Whitetip Reef Sharks at Johnston Island, of which seven were recovered, four of individuals at large with tags from six months to a little over one year. These sharks measured 81 to 105 cm precaudal length; they grew at a rate of 2.1 to 4.2 cm per year (Randall, 1977). From the tagging studies and observation of sharks identified by their pattern of spots or other features, it is evident that this species is resident to a relatively small area and probably does not normally undertake long migrations.

Figure 90
Triaenodon obesus, 66 cm, 1.2 kg, Lombok, Indonesia (J. Randall).

FAMILY SPHYRNIDAE (HAMMERHEAD SHARKS)

Diagnosis
Head strongly depressed and greatly expanded laterally into blade-like extensions; eyes circular or nearly circular, one at end of each lateral extension of head; internal nictitating eyelids present; spiracles absent; five gill slits of moderate size, the fifth posterior to origin of pectoral fins; labial furrows absent or rudimentary; mouth small; teeth similar to those of *Carcharhinus* (except one species with molariform posterior teeth), serrate or smooth-edged; no interdorsal ridge; first dorsal fin moderate to large in size, its origin over or anterior to inner rear corner of pectoral fins; second dorsal fin small, its origin posterior to origin of anal fin; upper precaudal pit present; caudal fin much like that of carcharhinids.

Remarks

The Hammerhead Shark family consists of nine species. One, the Winghead, is sometimes placed in a separate genus, *Eusphyra*, though more often this has been regarded as a subgenus of *Sphyrna*, the genus of the remaining eight species. Hammerheads are found throughout tropical to warm temperature seas. Three species occur in Arabian waters. Sharks of this family are unique in the broad lateral expansions of the head. This head shape is believed to function as an anterior plane to give these sharks greater maneuverability. Also, by separating the eyes more broadly, the Hammerheads have better binocular vision, and by having the nostrils farther apart they can find a source of olfactory stimulus more readily than other sharks. They share a number of characters with the Requiem Sharks, and are believed to have evolved from carcharhinid stock. A few authors have regarded them as a subfamily of the Carcharhinidae. Hammerheads, in general, are not aggressive to man in the sea except when enticed into action by speared fish. There are a few documented cases of attacks on humans by large Hammerheads; usually the sharks have not been identified to species. C.R. Gilbert (1967) monographed the family.

Winghead
Sphyrna blochii (Cuvier, 1817)

Diagnosis

Head greatly expanded laterally, its width 42 to 49% total length, each lobe angling posteriorly; nostrils well separated from eyes (nearer median tip of rostrum than eyes); lateral nasal groove present; first four gill slits about equal in length, longer than fifth which lies behind pectoral base; 15 or 16 teeth on each side of upper jaw and 14 (disregarding any symphyseals) on lower; teeth not serrate, the cusp of each strongly projecting posterolaterally; dorsal fin moderately large, its origin above or slightly anterior to axil of pectoral fins; origin of second dorsal fin over posterior third of anal fin, its posterior tip nearly reaching precaudal pit; anal fin base more than 1.5 times longer than second dorsal base; pectoral fin length about equal to height of first dorsal fin; vertebrae 117 to 124 (two specimens), of which 51 to 54 are precaudal; grey to brownish grey, paler ventrally, without any markings on fins; a small species which is not reported to exceed 100 cm.

Remarks

This hammerhead is readily distinguished by its long, narrow, lateral cephalic lobes. The type locality is unknown. Relatively few records exist for this species. It is distributed from the Arabian Gulf through India, Burma, and Indonesia to the western Pacific where it ranges from southern China to northern Queensland. It is not known from any oceanic island.

Figure 91
Sphyrna blochii, 62.2 cm, North Borneo (after C.R. Gilbert, 1967).

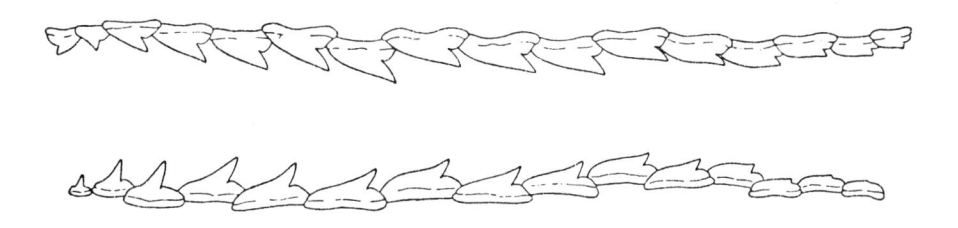

Figure 92
Teeth of *Sphyrna blochii*, female (after C.R. Gilbert, 1967).

Scalloped Hammerhead
Sphyrna lewini (Griffith and Smith, 1834)

Diagnosis

Anterior margin of head broadly convex with a prominent median indentation and another more conspicuous notch laterally near the end, setting off the terminal lobe bearing the eye; a slight indentation in anterior margin between the median and lateral notches on each side, the overall effect being a scalloped edge; preoral length of snout 4.6 to 5.8% total length; prenarial grooves anteromedial to nostrils well-developed; posterior edge of eyes anterior to front of mouth; 15 or 16 teeth on each side of jaws (discounting small symphyseals); upper teeth with a narrow oblique cusp on a broad base, the edges slightly serrate only on large adults; lower teeth with an even narrower cusp, erect to slightly oblique; first dorsal fin moderately large and erect, the outer posterior margin concave, the height 11.9 to 14.5% total length, the origin over or slightly behind axil of pectoral fins; second dorsal fin small, its height 2.4 to 3.2% total length, its origin over midbase of anal fin; inner posterior margin of second dorsal fin long, about twice height of fin, the tip nearly reaching precaudal pit; anal fin nearly twice as

Figure 93
Sphyrna lewini, 252 cm, 77 kg, Hawaii (J. Randall).

large as second dorsal fin; outer posterior margin of paired fins only slightly concave; pectoral fins moderately long, the length of the anterior edge 12.6 to 15.2% total length; vertebrae of 66 South African specimens 191 to 203, of which 91 to 96 are precaudal; brownish grey, shading to white ventrally; underside of pectoral fins tipped with black; attains about 400 cm.

Remarks
The Scalloped Hammerhead was named (as *Zygaena lewini*) by Griffith and Smith in Cuvier, Griffith, and Smith (1834), supposedly from the south coast of Australia. There is no type specimen. The species is circumglobal in all tropical to warm temperate seas; believed to be the most abundant species of the family. The young occur inshore. Kaneohe Bay, Oahu has been shown to be a major pupping and mating ground in the Hawaiian Islands (Clarke, 1971). Adults are found in offshore waters, in general, to depths of at least 275 m. They feed on a great variety of fishes, including other sharks, but also heavily on squids and other cephalopods, and on crustaceans such as shrimps, crabs, and lobsters. Large semi-stationary schools are often seen (as off Baja California), the function of which is uncertain (Klimley, 1982). The number of young per litter varies from 15 to 31; size at birth 42 to 55 cm. Males mature at 140 to 165 cm and females around 212 cm. *S. diplana* Springer is a synonym.

Figure 94
Teeth of *Sphyrna lewini* (after Bigelow and Schroeder, 1948).

Great Hammerhead
Sphyrna mokarran (Rüppell, 1837)

Diagnosis
Anterior margin of head of adults nearly straight with a median indentation; preoral length of snout 5.0 to 6.4% total length; prenarial grooves absent or very small; posterior edge of eyes anterior to front of mouth; 17 teeth on each side of upper jaw and 16 or 17 in lower (discounting small teeth at symphysis); teeth more broadly triangular than the preceding species and serrate at all stages; first dorsal fin large and very falcate, its origin over or slightly posterior to axil of pectoral fins; second dorsal fin large for the genus, its height 4.7 to 6.5% total length; inner posterior margin of second dorsal fin not long, about equal to height of fin, the tip not approaching precaudal pit; anal fin only slightly larger than second dorsal fin, its origin a short distance anterior to that of second dorsal; pectoral fins moderately long, with concave outer posterior margin, the length of anterior edge 13.4 to 18.4% total length; pelvic fins falcate; vertebrae 197 to 212; brownish grey, paler below, without any markings on fins; reaches at least 600 cm.

Remarks
Described from the Red Sea. Worldwide in tropical to warm temperate seas. Some populations are migratory, as indicated by movement to higher latitudes in warmer months. Individuals may be found inshore to well offshore. Feeds mainly on fishes, including other sharks and stingrays (the barbed venomous spines of these rays often found imbedded inside the mouth), squids, and crabs. The number of young per litter ranges from 13 to 42; size at birth 50 to 70 cm. Males mature at 234 to 269 cm and females from about 250 to 300 cm. The largest of the Hammerheads and one of the largest of the predatory sharks. Unauthenticated reports to lengths as great as 8 m. Many authors, including Bigelow and Schroeder (1948), have applied the name *S. tudes* (Valenciennes) to the Great Hammerhead. It is now known that *tudes* is the correct name for the Atlantic species which S. Springer (1944) described as *S. bigelowi*.

CLASSIFICATION

Figure 95
Sphyrna mokarran, 241.5 cm, 62 kg, Red Sea (J. Randall).

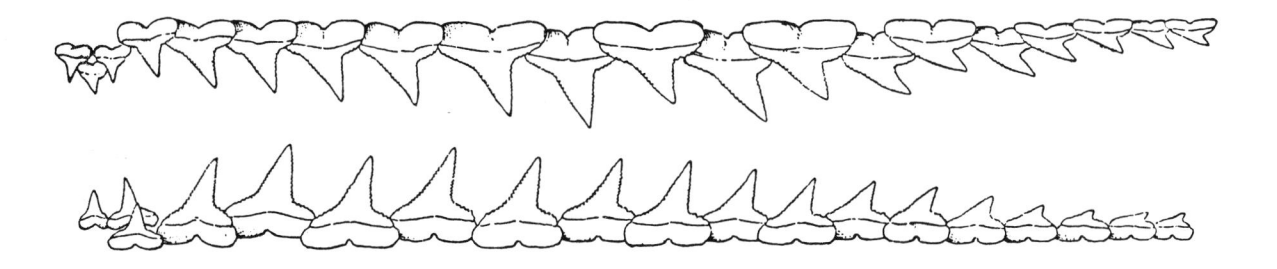

Figure 96
Teeth of *Sphyrna mokarran* (after Bigelow and Schroeder, 1948).

129

Smooth Hammerhead
Sphyrna zygaena (Linnaeus, 1758)

Diagnosis
Anterior margin of laterally expanded head broadly convex with a marked indentation near end of each lobe, a faint one near base of each lobe, (i.e. in line with side of body), but no median indentation; preoral length of snout 4.0 to 5.2% total length; prenarial grooves anteromedial to eyes well-developed; posterior edge of eyes slightly behind front of mouth; 13 to 15 (usually 14) teeth on each side of upper jaw and 12 to 14 (usually 14) on lower (not counting a smaller tooth at symphysis when present); upper teeth triangular and oblique (except the most medial tooth), smooth or finely serrate, nearly straight-edged on anteromedial edge and deeply notched on posterolateral; lower teeth similar to uppers but a little smaller and with a narrower cusp; first dorsal fin moderately large and falcate, its height 12.0 to 15.4% total length, its origin over axil of pectoral fins; second dorsal fin small, its height 1.6 to 2.5% total length, its inner posterior edge not approaching precaudal pit, its origin about over midbase of anal fin; anal fin larger than second dorsal fin, its height 2.5 to 3.3% total length; pectoral fins only slightly falcate, the length of anterior edge 15.4 to 18.0% total length; vertebrae 193 to 206, of which 94 to 102 are precaudal; brownish to olivaceous grey dorsally, paler below, with no dark markings on fins; maximum length about 400 cm.

Remarks
There is no type specimen of the Smooth Hammerhead; the type locality was given by Linnaeus as 'Europe, America'. The common name is in reference to the lack of a median indentation on the anterior margin of the head. This shark is circumglobal in distribution, occurring in the western Atlantic from Nova Scotia (only in summer) to southern Florida, and southern Brazil to southern Argentina; in the eastern Atlantic from Scotland to the Ivory Coast (including the Mediterranean); in the Indian Ocean from southern South Africa to southern Mozambique, the Arabian Gulf, India, Sri Lanka, and Western Australia; in the western Pacific from New South Wales and New Zealand, then from the Gulf of Tonkin to Japan and southern Siberia; in the eastern Pacific from northern California to the Gulf of California, Panama (one record), Galapagos Islands, and Ecuador to Chile. As may be seen from the above, there are noteworthy north-south gaps in its distribution. It has been listed as an antitropical species (Hubbs, 1952); however, some of the above localities (if identifications are correct) are in the tropical zone. Nevertheless, it is clear that *S. zygaena* is primarily a warm temperate species. It is found more inshore, in general, than the previous two Hammerheads, and is frequently seen at the surface with first dorsal fin and upper caudal lobe exposed. Sometimes occurs in large schools off the eastern coast of the United States. It tends to migrate to the north in the summer and the south during winter. It feeds on a variety of small schooling fishes, benthic fishes (including small sharks, skates and rays), shrimps, crabs, and cephalopods. The number of young in a litter varies from 29 to 37, the size at birth 50 to 61 cm. Maturity is attained at a length of about 210 to 240 cm. Gilbert (1967) has listed the four synonyms of *S. zygaena*, the last named in 1848.

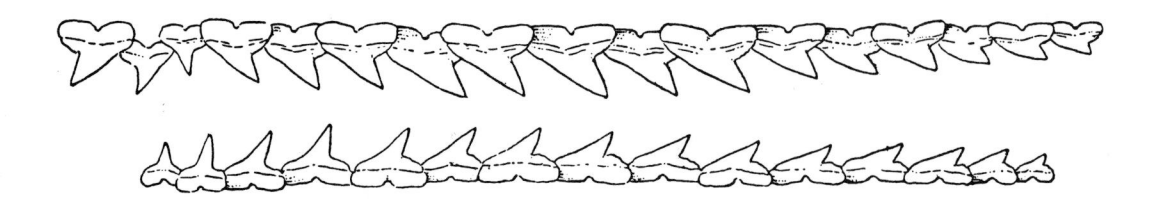

Figure 97
Teeth of *Sphyrna zygaena* (after Bigelow and Schroeder, 1948).

Figure 98
Sphyrna zygaena, 68.7 cm (after Bigelow and Schroeder, 1948). Ventral view of head by H.A. Randall.

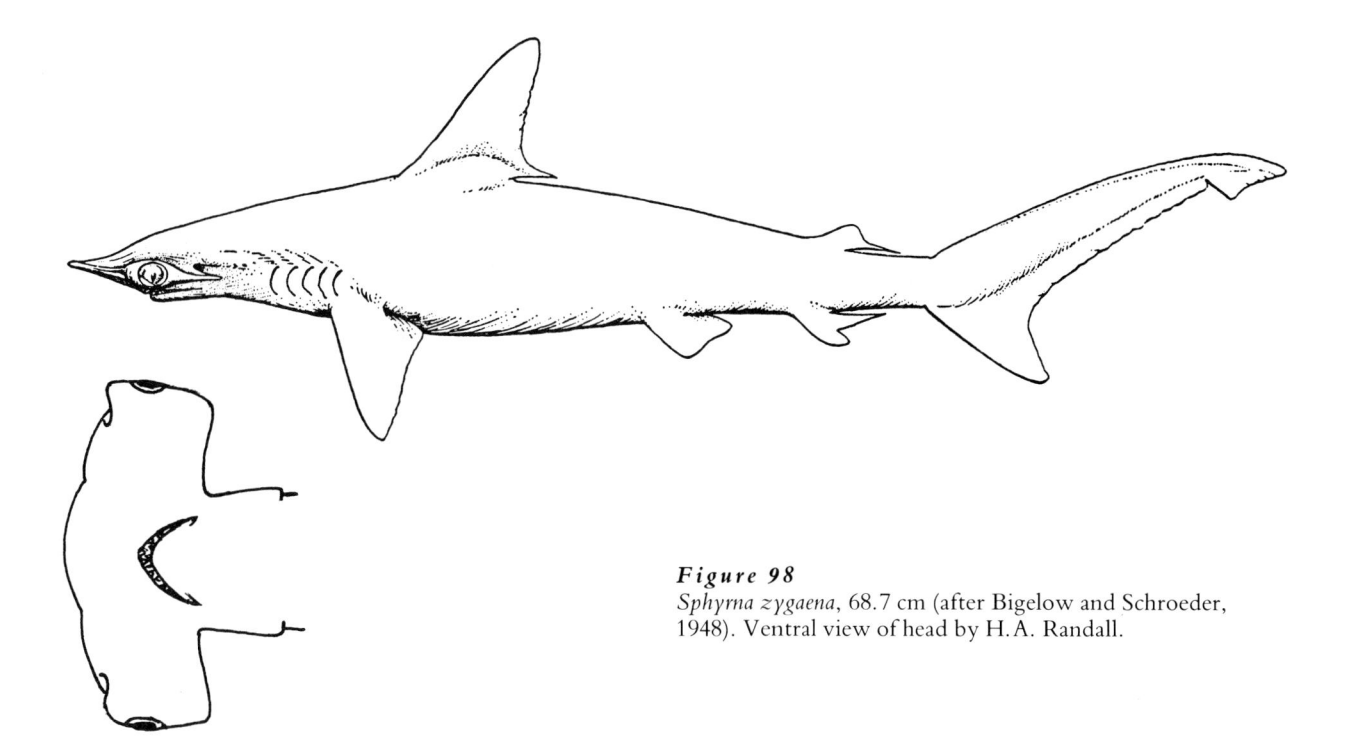

GLOSSARY

The definition of terms below are in reference to fishes – in particular, cartilaginous fishes.

Abductor: a muscle that draws a body or limb part away from the axis of the body or limb (as when one raises ones arm from the side).

Adductor: a muscle that draws a body or limb part toward the axis of the body or limb (adduction is thus the opposite of abduction).

Afferent: in reference to a vessel which leads toward a given position (an artery going to the gills of a fish is an afferent artery).

Allopatric: in reference to species with different geographic distribution; the opposite of sympatric.

Ampulla: a small bladder-like enlargement.

Analogous: referring to similarity in external appearance and/or function but not of origin.

Aorta: a major artery.

Aortic arches: paired arteries in fishes which transport blood to and from the gills from the ventral aorta to the dorsal aorta.

Appendicular skeleton: the pectoral fin and pelvic fin girdles and supporting cartilages of these fins.

Archinephric duct: the name for the duct which transports urine in adult sharks. Derived from the mesonephric duct of the embryo.

Articulation: the point of attachment of a joint.

Auditory: pertaining to the sense of hearing.

Auricle: the thin-walled chamber of the heart which receives the venous blood. Also called the atrium.

Axial skeleton: the vertebral column and chondrocranium of sharks.

Axil: the acute angular region between a fin and the body; usually used in reference to the underside of the pectoral fin toward the base. Equivalent to the armpit of man.

Axis: a line passing longitudinally through a body around which parts are arranged symmetrically.

Band: an oblique or irregular marking (compare 'bar' below).

Bar: an elongate colour marking of vertical orientation, the sides of which are usually more-or-less straight (although they need not be parallel).

Barbel: a slender tentacle-like protruberance of sensory function which is seen on the anterior underside of head of some sharks such as the Nurse Shark.

Benthic: referring to the benthos, the fauna and flora of the sea bottom.

Brachial: referring to the pectoral fins.

Branchial: referring to the gills.

Buccal: referring to the mouth.

Capillary: the smallest of blood vessels.

Cardiac: in reference to the heart.

Carnivore: a flesh-eating animal.

Cartilage: a translucent somewhat flexible structural tissue of embryos of all vertebrates; retained as the skeletal tissue of sharks but largely replaced by bone in higher vertebrates.

Caudal fin: the tail fin. The term tail alone generally refers to that part of a fish posterior to the anus.

Glossary

Caudal peduncle: the part of the body between the posterior basal parts of the dorsal and anal fins and the base of the caudal fin. The usual vertical measurement is the least depth; the length measurement herein is horizontal, and the fin of reference (i.e., rear base of dorsal or anal) is designated.

Centrum: the main central part of a vertebra.

Cephalic: referring to the head.

Ceratotrichia: the slender, flexible, horny fibers which support the outer part of elasmobranch fins.

Cerebellum: the dorsoanterior part of the hind brain; concerned with the synchronization of the sensory systems and body movements, hence with equilibrium.

Cerebrum: the dorsoanterior part of the forebrain in fishes; includes the olfactory lobes. A major part of the telencephalon of the brain.

Character: a characteristic; a distinguishing feature.

Chondrocranium: the cartilaginous braincase of elasmobranch fishes.

Chondrichthyes: a class of the vertebrates which includes the cartilaginous fishes (sharks, rays, and chimaeras).

Chondrocranium: the cartilaginous braincase of elasmobranch fishes.

Chondrichthyes: a class of the vertebrates which includes the cartilaginous fishes (sharks, rays, and chimaeras).

Chordata: the phylum of the Animal Kingdom containing animal groups which possess a notochord. Includes tunicates, cephalochordates (such as amphioxus), and vertebrates.

Clasper: the paired intromittent organ of elasmobranch fishes; develops in mature males along the medial edge of the pelvic fins.

Cloaca: the common chamber receiving the end products of the digestive tract, excretory system, and reproductive system of sharks from whence these products pass to the exterior.

Coelom: the body cavity containing the stomach, intestine, reproductive organs, etc.

Community: the assemblage of animals and plants living in one habitat.

Compressed: laterally flattened; often used in reference to the shape of the body – in this case deeper than wide.

Cornea: the outermost transparent layer of the eye.

Cranial: in reference to the brain or skull.

Crustacean: an animal of the Class Crustacea of the Phylum Arthropoda; includes crabs, lobsters, shrimps, and copepods.

Demersal: living on the sea bottom.

Dentine: calcareous material that makes up the main mass of a tooth.

Depressed: dorsoventrally flattened. The opposite in body shape of compressed.

Depth: a vertical measurement of the body of a fish; most often employed for the maximum height of the body excluding the fins.

Dermal: pertaining to the skin, specifically to the connective tissue layer below the epidermis.

Diplospondylous: referring to a condition of two vertebrae forming per body segment.

Distal: outward from the point of attachment; the opposite of proximal.

Dorsal: toward the back or upper part of the body; the opposite of ventral.

Dorsal fin: a median fin along the back which is supported by rays. There may be two or more dorsal fins, in which case the most anterior one is designated the first.

Ductuli efferentes: small ducts which carry sperm from the testes to the ductus deferens.

Ductus deferens: the duct which transports sperm from the ductuli efferentes to the cloaca (old name: vas deferens).

Duodenum: the anterior part of the intestine.

Echinoderm: an aquatic marine animal of the Phylum Echinodermata; radially symmetrical with a skeleton composed of calcareous plates (may be reduced to spicules); many move via their numerous tube feet; includes starfishes, brittle stars, sea urchins, and sea cucumbers.

Efferent: in reference to a vessel which leads away from a given position (an artery leaving the gills is an efferent artery).

Elasmobranch: in reference to the Subclass Elasmobranchii of the Class Chondrichthyes. Includes all true sharks, skates, and rays.

Emarginate: concave; used to describe the posterior border of a caudal fin which is inwardly curved.

Embryo: a developing young animal before hatching or birth.

Endemic: native; in reference to an animal or plant restricted to a particular area.

Endocrine: in reference to an internal secretion from a ductless gland.

Ephiphysis: the dorsal outgrowth of the diencephalon of the brain. Also known as the pineal body.

Epidermis: the outer layer of the skin.

Epithelium: a layer of cells covering a surface (generally an internal surface).

Esophagus: that part of the digestive tract between the pharynx and stomach.

Family: a major entity in the classification of animals and plants which consists of a group of related genera. Family words end in 'idae', an example Carcharinidae for the Requiem Shark family; when used as an adjective, the 'ae' is dropped, hence carcharinid.

Fascia: a layer of connective tissue which covers an organ; often used in reference to the connective tissue sheathing of muscles.

Foramen: an opening through bone, cartilage, or other tissues, generally for the passage of blood vessels or nerves.

Fusiform: spindle-shaped; used in reference to the body shape of a fish which is cylindrical or nearly so and tapers towards the ends.

Ganglion: a concentration of the cell bodies of neurons.

Gas bladder: a tough-walled gas-filled sac lying in the upper part of the body cavity of many bony fishes just beneath the vertebral column, the principal function of which is to offset the weight of the heavier tissues, particularly bone. The organ is also called the air bladder or the swim bladder.

Genus: a group of closely related species; the first part of the scientific name of an animal or plant. The plural is genera.

Gill arch: the bony or cartilaginous support for the gill filaments and gill rakers. Normally there are four pairs of gill arches in bony fishes.

Gill opening: the opening posteriorly and often also ventrally on the head of fishes where the water of respiration is expelled. Bony fishes have a single such opening on each side whereas cartilaginous fishes (sharks and rays) have five to seven. The gill openings of sharks and rays are also called gill slits.

Gill rakers: stout protruberances of the gill arch on the opposite side from the red gill filaments which function in retaining food organisms. They vary greatly in number and length and are important in the classification of fishes.

Gonad: a reproductive organ (either an ovary or testis).

Haemal: referring to blood.

Hepatic: pertaining to the liver.

Hepatic portal system: veins leading from the digestive tract to the liver.

Herbivore: a plant-feeding animal.

Homologous: referring to structures in different animals which had a common evolutionary origin (thus the pectoral fin of a fish, the wing of a bird, and the arm of man are homologous).

Incisiform: chisel-like; used to describe teeth which are flattened and truncate with sharp edges like the front teeth of some mammals such as man.

Infundibulum: the ventral extension of the diencephalon of the brain leading to the pituitary gland.

Interorbital space: the region on the top of the head between the eyes; measurements may be taken of the least width, either fleshy (to the edges of the orbits) or bony (between the edges of the frontal bones which rim the orbits).

Invertebrate: an animal lacking a vertebral column; includes the vast majority of animals on earth such as the corals, the worms, and the insects.

Keel: a lateral strengthening ridge posteriorly on the caudal peduncle or base of the caudal fin; typically found on swift-swimming fishes with a narrow caudal peduncle and a broadly lunate caudal fin.

Labial: pertaining to the lips.

Lamella: a thin plate-like structure. The gills of fishes have numerous parallel lamellae which contain capillaries that effect the gaseous exchange of respiration.

Lateral: referring to the side or directed toward the side; the opposite of medial.

Lateral line: the major part of the lateralis system that runs along the side of the body.

Lateralis system: a sensory system of fishes which consists of a canal running along the side of the body and a complex of canals on the head which communicate via pores to the exterior; functions in perceiving low frequency vibrations, hence provides a sense which might be termed 'touch at a distance'.

Lumen: the central cavity of a vessel duct, gland or organ.

Lymphatic system: the part of the circulatory system which consists of vessels and spaces between body cells that slowly transports the body fluid known as lymph (which lacks red blood cells) to the veins.

Mandible: the lower jaw of vertebrates.

Medial: toward the middle or median plane of the body; opposite of lateral.

Median fins: the fins in the median plane, hence the dorsal, anal, and caudal fins.

Medulla oblongata: the most posterior part of the brain which leads to the spinal cord. Equivalent to the myelencephalon, contains the nuclei for cranial nerves V to X.

Mesentery: a sheet of connective tissue that suspends organs in the body cavity; continuous with the peritoneum.

Mesonephric duct: the duct which transports nitrogenous waste from kidney tubules of the functional second kidney of the embryo to the cloaca. Also known as the Wolffian duct. Becomes the archinephric duct in adult sharks and the ureter of higher vertebrates.

Mesonephros: literally 'middle kidney', the second kidney to form in the embryo, developing segmentally in the middle part of the body; becomes the adult kidney of fishes (then properly called the opisthonephros).

Metabolic: referring to metabolism, a collective term for all the biochemical processes, both constructive and destructive that take place in the body.

Metanephros: literally 'after kidney'. The last kidney to form in the embryo of reptiles, birds, and mammals; becomes the adult functional kidney of these groups. Not found in fishes.

Molariform: in reference to teeth which are like the molars of mammals, hence very blunt and without sharp cusps; these teeth are used for crushing.

Mollusc: an animal of the Phylum Mollusca; unsegmented with a muscular 'foot' and visceral mass; often protected by one or two shells; includes gastropods (snails and nudibranchs), pelecypods (bivalves such as clams and oysters), cephalopods (such as squids and octopuses), and amphineurans (chitons).

Monotypic: referring to a taxon consisting of a single subsidiary group, such as a genus of one species.

Morphology: a study of the form and structure of animals and plants.

Myotome: the segmental embryonic precursor of the voluntary muscles of the adult.

Nape: the dorsal region of the head posterior to the occiput.

Nephric: pertaining to the kidney.

Nephrostome: ciliated end of a kidney tubule which opens to the coelom.

Neuromast: a cluster of sensory and supportive cells found in the canals of the lateralis system in fishes which is the receptor unit for detecting vibrations in the aquatic environment. Each sensory cell has a tiny terminal hair projecting into the lumen of the canal.

Neuron: a nerve cell, consisting of cell body, dentrites and axon; transports impulses from one part of the body to another.

Notochord: a longitudinal flexible rod which forms the axial support of vertebrate embryos. Persists in the adult cephalochordates (such as amphioxus) and cyclostomes (lampreys and hagfishes).

Olfactory: pertaining to the sense of smell.

Omnivore: an animal which feeds on both plant and animal material.

Oophagy: feeding on eggs; a unique form of embryonic nutrition whereby the developing shark in the uterus feeds on the ova of the mother as they come down from the oviduct. Found in laminiform shark families such as the Mackerel Sharks, Sand Tiger Sharks, and the Threshers.

Orbital: referring to the orbit or eye.

Order: a major unit in the classification of organisms; an assemblage of related families. The ordinal word ending in the animal kingdom is 'iformes'.

Organ: a group of tissues in an animal performing a major function or functions.

Organism: a living entity, whether unicellular or multicellular, animal or plant.

Origin: the beginning; often used for the anterior end of the dorsal or anal fin at the base. Also used in zoology to denote the more fixed attachment of a muscle.

Osmosis: diffusion through a semipermeable membrane.

Ovary: the female reproductive organ that produces eggs.

Oviduct: the tube which recovers the ovum from the body cavity and transports it to the uterus; also known as Müllerian duct.

Oviparous: producing ova (eggs) that hatch after leaving the body of the mother; the mode of reproduction of the great majority of bony fishes and some sharks.

Ovoviviparous: producing eggs which hatch within the body of the mother; the mode of reproduction of most sharks and rays.

Ovum: an egg.

Paired fins: collective term for the pectoral and pelvic fins.

Papilla: a small fleshy protuberance.

Pectoral fin: one of the anterior pair of fins of fishes; in sharks it is found ventral in the thoracic region and is held laterally when swimming.

Pelagic: pertaining to the open sea (hence not living inshore or on the bottom); oceanic.

Pelvic fin: one of the posterior pair of fins of fishes; found ventrally on the body (sometimes called ventral fin); in sharks this pair of fins is near the cloaca, the medial edge in males developing as the clasper.

Pericardial cavity: chamber in which heart lies.

Peritoneum: the thin membrane that covers the walls of the body cavity and the organs therein.

Pharynx: the region of the digestive tract between the mouth and esophagus; in fishes it contains the gills.

Phylogeny: the evolutionary history of an organism or a group of organisms; an extended family tree.

Plankton: a collective term for pelagic animals and plants that drift with ocean currents; though many are motile, they are too small or swim too feebly or aimlessly to resist the sweep of the current. By contrast the animals of the nekton are independent of water movement.

Plexus: a concentration or network of nerves or blood vessels. The plural is plexi.

Pronephros: the primitive anterior kidney; the first kidney to appear in embryos of vertebrates, soon replaced by mesonephros.

Proximal: toward the centre of the body; the opposite of distal.

Pseudobranch: literally 'false gill', referring to the small patch of functional gill filaments associated with the spiracle.

Pterygion: Greek word for fin or wing. Often used in combined form with other words in reference to fin structures of fishes.

Pulp cavity: the central cavity of a tooth or dermal denticle which provides access for blood vessels and nerves.

Radials: parallel rods of cartilage forming the basal support of elasmobranch fins.

Ramus: a branch, as of a nerve.

Ray: the supporting elements of fins. Also flattened elasmobranchs of the Order Rajiformes.

Retina: the cellular layer posteriorly in the eye containing the light receptors (rods and cones).

Rudiment: a structure so deficient in size that it does not perform its normal function; often used in reference to the small nodular gill rakers at the ends of the gill arch.

Sagittal: pertaining to a vertical anteroposterior plane of a bilaterally symmetrical animal. Such a plane in the exact middle of an animal is the median sagittal plane.

Seminal vesicle: the posterior enlargement of the ductus deferens; functions for the storage of sperm.

Serrate: notched along a free margin, like the edge of a saw.

Shell gland: an enlargement in the oviduct of elasmobranch fishes which lays down albuminous material and the shell of the ovum.

Sinus: an enlargement in the circulatory system; a cavity within bone or cartilage.

Sinus venosus: the uppermost part of the heart in fishes which receives the venous blood.

Snout: the region of the head in front of the eye and mouth.

Somatic: referring to the body.

Species: the fundamental unit in the classification of animals and plants consisting of a population of individuals which freely interbreed with one another. The word 'species' is both singular and plural.

Spine: an unsegmented bony process consisting of a single element which is usually rigid and sharply pointed.

Spiracle: an opening between the eye and the first gill slit of sharks and rays which leads to the pharyngeal cavity.

Spiral valve: the internal structure of the shark intestine which resembles a spiral staircase within a closed cylinder. Serves to increase the absorptive surface of the intestine and slow the passage of food.

Stripe: a horizontal straight-sided colour marking.

Suture: the immobile junction of two parts of a skeleton.

Sympatric: in reference to species which live in the same major geographical area.

Symphysis: an articulation, generally immovable, between two bones; often used in reference to the anterior region of juncture of the two halves of the jaws.

Synonym: an invalid scientific name of an organism proposed after the accepted name.

Systematics: the division of a science concerned with the classification of animals and plants. Taxonomy in a broad sense.

Tactile: pertaining to the sense of touch.

Tail: that part of an animal posterior to the anus (disregarding the hind limbs of quadrupeds).

Taxon: a unit in the classification of organisms; the plural is taxa.

Teleost: refers to the Teleostei, the highest superorder of the rayfin bony fishes. The other superorders are the Chondrostei (the sturgeons and paddlefishes are the living representatives) and the Holostei (the bowfin and gars are the contemporary forms). The Teleostei and Holostei may be polyphyletic (of multiple origin), so these superordinal names, though often heard, are usually omitted from recent formal classifications. The great majority of living fishes are teleosts.

Testis: the male reproductive organ which produces sperm; the plural is testes.

Thoracic: referring to the chest region.

Thorax: the chest region, hence between the head and abdomen.

Tissue: a group of cells with the same structure and function.

Total length: the length of a fish from the front of whichever jaw is most anterior to the end of the longest caudal ray.

Truncate: square-ended; used to describe a caudal fin with a vertically straight terminal border and angular or slightly rounded corners.

Umbilical cord: the strand-like structure containing blood vessels which links a developing embryo to the mother within the uterus.

Ureter: the duct which transports urine from the kidney to the cloaca. Some anatomists prefer to call this the archinephric duct in sharks as it is not homologous to the ureter of higher vertebrates.

Uterus: the enlarge posterior part of the oviduct in which the embryos develop.

Valve: folds of tissue in an opening to or from a cavity or within a vessel which permits the passage of material in only one direction.

Vascular: pertaining to blood vessels.

Ventral: toward the lower part of the body, the opposite of dorsal.

Ventricle: the muscular chamber of the heart; also a cavity within the brain.

Vertebra: one of the segmental units of the axial skeleton of a vertebrate animal.

Vestigial: rudimentary. A small structure that once was more fully developed.

Viscera: the internal organs.

Vitrodentine: a very hard, enamel-like form of dentine found as the outer layer of sharks teeth and of the dermal denticles.

Viviparous: producing living young which develop from nourishment directly from the mother.

Yolk: the nutritive material (rich in fatty substances) of an egg.

Zooplankton: the animals of the plankton.

BIBLIOGRAPHY

Agassiz, J.L.R. 1833-1843.
Recherches sur les Poissons Fossiles. 5 vols. Petit-pierre, Neuchâtel.

Alcock, A. 1899.
A descriptive catalogue of the Indian deep-sea fishes in the Indian Museum, collected by the Royal Indian Marine Survey Ship "Investigator". 220 pp., Calcutta.

Backus, R.H., S. Springer, and E.L. Arnold. 1956.
A contribution to the natural history of the white-tip shark, *Pterolamiops longimanus* (Poey). Deep-Sea Res. 3: 178-188.

Bagnis, R., P. Mazellier, J. Bennett, and E. Christian. 1972.
Poissons de Polynésie. 368 pp., Les Editions du Pacifique, Papeete.

Baldridge, H.D. 1973.
Shark attack against man. A program of data reduction and analysis. Office Naval Research, Oceanic Biol. Programs, NR 104-148 Tech. Rep.: v + 122.

Baranes, A. and A. Ben-Tuvia. 1978.
Occurrence of the sandbar shark *Carcharhinus plumbeus* in the northern Red Sea. Israel Jour. Zool. 27:45-51.

Baranes, A. and A. Ben-Tuvia. 1979.
Two rare carcharhinids, *Hemipristis elongatus* and *Iago omanensis*, from the northern Red Sea. Israel Jour. Zool. 28: 39-50.

Bass, A.J. 1973.
Analysis and description of variation in the proportional dimensions of scyliorhinid, carcharhinid and sphyrnid sharks. S. Afr. Assoc. Mar. Biol. Res., Invest. Rep. 32: 1-28.

Bass, A.J., J.D. D'Aubrey, and N. Kistnasamy. 1973.
Sharks of the east coast of southern Africa. I. The genus *Carcharhinus* (Carcharhinidae). Oceanogr. Res. Inst., Invest. Rep., no. 33: 1-168.

Bass, A.J., J.D. D'Aubrey, and N. Kistnasamy. 1975a.
Sharks of the east coast of southern Africa. IV. The families Odontaspididae, Scapanorhynchidae, Isuridae, Cetorhinidae, Alopiidae, Orectolobidae and Rhiniodontidae. Oceanogr. Res. Inst., Invest. Rep., no. 39: 1-102.

Bass, A.J., J.D. D'Aubrey, and N. Kistnasamy. 1975b.
Sharks of the east coast of southern Africa. III. The families Carcharhinidae (excluding *Mustelus* and *Carcharhinus*) and Sphyrnidae. Oceanogr. Res. Inst., Invest. Rep., no. 38: 1-100.

Bass, A.J., J.D. D'Aubrey, and N. Kistnasamy. 1976.
Sharks of the east coast of southern Africa. VI. The families Oxynotidae, Squalidae, Dalatiidae and Echinorhinidae. Oceanogr. Res. Inst., Invest. Rep., no. 45: 1-103.

Bauchot, R., R. Platel, and J-M. Ridet. 1976.
Brain-body weight relationship in Selachii. Copeia, no. 2: 305-309.

Bigelow, H.B. and W.C. Schroeder. 1948.
Sharks in Fishes of the Western North Atlantic, No. 1, Chapter 3: 59-576. Mem. Sears Found. Mar. Res., Yale Univ.

Bigelow, H.B. and W.C. Schroeder. 1961.
Carcharhinus nicaraguensis, a synonym of the bull shark, *C. leucas*. Copeia, no. 4: 359.

Bigelow, H.B., W.C. Schroeder, and S. Springer. 1943.
A new species of *Carcharhinus* from the western Atlantic. Proc. New Engl. Zoöl. Club 22: 69-74.

Bleeker, P. 1852.
Bijdrage tot de kennis der plagiostomen van den Indischen Archipel. Verh. Bataviaasch genoot. Kunsten Wet. 24(12): 1-92.

Bleeker, P. 1856.
Carcharias Prionodon amblyrhynchos, eene nieuwe haaisort, gevangen nabij het Eiland Solombo. Nat. Tijdschr. Ned. Indië. 10: 467-468.

Blegvad, H. 1944.
Fishes of the Iranian Gulf. 247 pp., Einar Munksgaard, Copenhagen.

Böhlke, J.E. and C.C.G. Chaplin. 1968.
Fishes of the Bahamas and Adjacent Tropical Waters. 771 pp., Livingston Publishing Co., Wynnewood, Pennsylvania.

Boeseman, M. 1960.
A tragedy of errors: the status of *Carcharhinus* Blainville, 1816; *Galeolamna* Owen, 1853; *Eulamia* Gill, 1861; and the identity of *Carcharhinus commersonii* Blainville, 1825. Zool. Meded. (Leiden) 37: 81-100.

Bonham, K. 1960.
Note on sharks from Rongelap Atoll, Marshall Islands. Copeia, no. 3: 257.

Brauer, A. 1906.
Die Tiefseefische. I. Systematischen Teil. In C. Chun Wiss. Ergebnisse Deutsch. Tiefsee-Exped. "Valdivia," 1898-99, vol. 15, 420 pp., Jena.

Budker, P. 1947.
La Vie des Requins. 277 pp., Librairie Gallimard, Paris.

Carey, F.G. and J.M. Teal. 1969.
Mako and porbeagle: warm-bodied sharks. Comp. Biochem. Physiol. 28: 199-204.

Castro, J.I. 1983.
The Sharks of North American Waters. 180 pp., Texas A. & M. Univ. Press, College Station.

Clark, E. and K. von Schmidt. 1965.
Sharks of the central Gulf coast of Florida. Bull. Mar. Sci. 15: 13-83.

Clarke, T.A. 1971.
The ecology of the scalloped hammerhead shark, *Sphyrna lewini*, in Hawaii. Pac. Sci. 25(2): 133-144.

Coles, R.J. 1915.
Notes on the sharks and rays of Cape Lookout, N.C. Proc. Biol. Soc. Wash. 28: 89-94.

Compagno, L.J.V. 1970.
Systematics of the genus *Hemitriakis*)Selachii: Carcharhinidae), and related genera. Proc. Calif. Acad. Sci., ser. 4, 38: 63-97.

Compagno, L.J.V. 1973.
Interrelationships of living elasmobranchs. In P.H. Greenwood, R.S. Miles, and C. Patterson (eds.), Interrelationships of fishes, pp. 15-61. Suppl. 1, Zool. Jour. Linn. Soc.

Compagno, L.J.V. 1979.
Carcharhinoid sharks: morphology, systematics, and phylogeny, 2 vols. Dissertation Abstr. Int. (B) 40(2): 629.

Compagno, L.J.V. 1984a.
FAO Species Catalogue, Vol. 4, Part 1, Sharks of the World. viii + 249 pp. United Nations Development Programme and Food and Agriculture Organization of the United Nations, Rome.

Compagno, L.J.V. 1984b.
FAO Species Catalogue, Vol. 4, Part 2, Sharks of the World. 251-655 pp. United Nations Development Programme and Food and Agriculture Organization of the United Nations, Rome.

Compagno, L.J.V. and S. Springer. 1971.
Iago, a new genus of carcharhinid sharks, with a description of *I. omanensis*. Fishery Bull. 69(3): 615-626.

Coppleson, V.M. 1958.
Shark Attack. 266 pp., Angus and Robertson, Sydney.

Cousteau, J.-Y. and P.C. Cousteau. 1970.
The Shark: Splendid Savage of the Sea. xii + 277 pp., Doubleday & Co. Inc., New York.

Cuvier, G. 1834.
The Animal Kingdom ... by the Baron Cuvier ... with Additional Descriptions of Species ... by Edward Griffith, Charles Hamilton Smith (and P.B. Lord), vol. 10, 680 pp., London.

Daniel, J.F. 1934
The Elasmobranch Fishes. 332 pp. Univ. of California Press, Berkeley.

D'Aubrey, J.D. 1964
Preliminary guide to the sharks found off the east coast of South Africa. S. Afr. Assoc, Mar. Biol. Res., Invest. Rep. 8: 1-95.

Davies, D.H. 1965
About Sharks and Shark Attack. 237 pp., Brown, Davis and Platt, Durban.

Day, F. 1878.
The Fishes of India; being a Natural History of the Fishes known to Inhabit the Seas and Fresh Waters of India, Burma, and Ceylon. Vol. 1, 778 pp., Vol. 2, pp. 779-816. Bernard Quaritch,, London.

Dingerkus, G. 1984.
A revision of the orectolobiform shark family Ginglymostomatidae. Abstract, ASIH 32nd Ann. Meet., Norman, Oklahoma.

Dingerkus, G. and T.C. DeFino. 1983.
A revision of the orectolobiform shark family Hemiscyllidae (Chondrichthyes, Selachii). Bull. Amer. Mus. Nat. Hist. 176(1): 1-93.

Dijkgraaf, S. 1963.
The functioning and significance of the lateral-line organs. Biol Rev. 38: 51-105.

Fourmanoir, P. 1961.
Requins de la cote Ouest de Madagascar. Mém. Inst. Sci. Madagascar, sér. F Océanogr., 4: 3-81.

Fourmanoir, P. 1964.
Raies et Requins-scie de la cote Ouest de Madagascar (ordre des Batoidei). Cah. O.R.S.T.O.M. Océanogr. 6 (sér. NOSY-BE 11): 33-58.

Fourmanoir, P. and P. Laboute. 1976.
Poissons de Nouvelle Calédonie et des Nouvelles Hébrides. 376 pp., Les Editions du Pacifique, Papeete.

Fowler, H.W. 1941.
Contributions to the biology of the Philippine Archipelago and adjacent regions. The fishes of the groups Elasmobranchii, Holocephali, Isospondyli, and Ostarophysi obtained by the United States Bureau of Fisheries steamer "Albatross" in 1907 to 1910, chiefly in the Philippine Islands and adjacent seas. U.S. Natl. Mus. Bull. 100(13): 1-879.

Gans, C. and T.S. Parsons. 1981.
A Photographic Atlas of Shark Anatomy. (The gross morphology of *Squalus acanthias*). 106 pp. The Univ. of Chicago Press, Chicago and London.

Garman, S. 1913.
The Plagiostoma (sharks, skates and rays). Mem. Mus. Comp. Zool., Harvard Univ. 36: 1-528.

Garrick, J.A.F. 1962a.
Reasons in favour of retaining the generic name *Carcharhinus* Blainville, and a proposal for identifying its type species as the Indo-Pacific black-tipped shark, *C. melanopterus*. Proc. Biol. Soc. Wash. 75: 84-96.

Garrick, J.A.F. 1962b.
Carcharhinus Blainville, 1816 (class Chondrichthyes, order Selachii); proposed designation of *Carcharhinus melanopterus* Quoy & Gaimard as type-species under plenary powers. Z.N.(S.)920. Bull. Zool. Nomencl. 19: 100-102.

Garrick, J.A.F. 1982.
Sharks of the genus *Carcharhinus*. NOAA Tech. Rep., NMFS Circ. 445: vii + 194 pp.

Garrick, J.A.F., R.H. Backus, and R.H. Gibbs, Jr. 1964.
Carcharhinus floridanus, the silky shark, a synonym of *C. falciformis*. Copeia, no. 2: 369-375.

Gilbert, C.H. 1892.
Scientific results of explorations by the U.S. Fish Commission steamer Albatross. No. XXII – Descriptions of thirty-four new species of fishes collected in 1888 and 1889, principally among the Santa Barbara Islands and in the Gulf of California. Proc. U.S. Natl. Mus. 14: 539-566.

Gilbert, C.R. 1967.
A revision of the hammerhead sharks (Family Sphyrnidae). Proc. U.S. Natl. Mus. 119(3539): 1-88.

Gilbert, P.W. (ed.). 1963.
Sharks and Survival. 578 pp., D.C. Heath and Co., Boston.

Gilbert, P.W. 1972.
Response patterns of porpoises and elasmobranch fishes. Office Naval Research, Contract No. N00014-69-C-0340 Final Rep.: 1-13.

Gilbert, P.W., B. Irvine, and F.H. Martini. 1971.
Shark-porpoise behavioral interactions (Abstract). Amer. Zool. 11(4): 636.

Gilbert, P.W., R.F. Mathewson, and D.P. Rall (eds.). 1967.
Sharks, Skates, and Rays. 624 pp., The Johns Hopkins Press, Baltimore.

Gohar, H.A.F. and F.M. Mazhar. 1964a.
The elasmobranchs of the north-western Red Sea. Publ. Mar. Biol. Sta. Al-Ghardaqa, Red Sea. 13(3): 3-144.

Gohar, H.A.F. and F.M. Mazhar. 1964b.
Keeping elasmobranchs in vivaria. Publ. Mar. Bio. Sta. Al-Ghardaqa, Red Sea 13: 241-250.

Grant, E.M. 1982.
Guide to Fishes. 896 pp., Dept. Harbours and Marine, Queensland Govt., Brisbane.

Gruber, S.H. 1977.
The visual system of sharks: adaptations and capability. Amer. Zool. 17(2): 453-469.

Gruber, S.H. and L.J.V. Compagno. 1981.
Taxonomic status and biology of the bigeye thresher, *Alopias superciliosus*. Fish. Bull. 79(4): 617-640.

Gubanov, E.P. and N.A. Shleib (eds.). 1980.
Sharks of the Arabian Gulf. 69 pp., Minis. Public Works, Agri. Dept., Fisheries Div., Kuwait.

Gudger, E.W. 1940.
Whale sharks rammed by ocean vessels. New England Naturalist, no. 7: 1-10.

Guitart Manday, D. 1966.
Nuevo nombre para una especie de tiburon del genero *Isurus* (Elasmobranchii:Isuridae) de aguas Cubanas. Poeyana Inst. Biol. (Havana), ser. A, 15: 1-9.

Guitart Manday, D. 1968.
Guia para los tiburones de aguas cubanas (con notas adicionales sobre los del Golfo de Mexico, Mar Caribe y Oceano Atlantico cerca de Cuba). Acad. Cienc. Cuba, Ser. Oceanol. 1: 1-61.

Günther, A. 1870.
Catalogue of the Fishes of the British Museum. Vol. 8, 549 pp., Brit. Mus., London.

Harry, E.K., R. Crawford, P. McCracken, and G. Carr (eds.). 1984.
World Record Game Fishes 1984. 320 pp., International Gamefish Association, Ft. Lauderdale.

Heemstra, P.C. 1973.
A revision of the shark genus *Mustelus* (Squaliformes: Carcharhinidae). Ph.D. dissertation, 187 pp., University of Miami.

Hemprich, F.G. and C.G. Ehrenberg. 1899.
Symbolae physicae, seu icones adhuc ineditae corporum naturalium novorum aut minus cognitorum quae ex itineribus per Libyam, Ægyptiam, Nubiam, Dongolam, Syriam, Arabiam et Habessiniam publico institutis sumptu ... studio annis MDCCCXX-MDCCCXXV redierunt. Zoologica. Berlin.

Hodgson, E.S. and R.F. Mathewson (eds.). 1978.
Sensory Biology of Sharks, Skates, and Rays. ix + 666 pp., Office Naval Research, Dept. Navy, Arlington.

Holden, M.J. 1974.
Problems in the rational exploitation of elasmobranch populations and some suggested solutions. In F.R. Harden Jones (ed.), Sea Fisheries Research, pp. 117-137. John Wiley & Sons, New York.

Hubbs, C.L. 1952.
Antitropical distribution of fishes and other organisms. Symposium on problems of bipolarity and pantemperate faunas. Proc. Seventh Pac. Sci. Congr. (Pac. Sci. Assoc.) 3: 324-329.

International Commission on Zoological Nomenclature. 1950.
The official record of Proceedings of the International Commission on Zoological Nomenclature at their session held in Paris in July 1948. Bull. Zool. Nomencl. 4: 269-271, 283-287.

International Commission on Zoological Nomenclature. 1965.
Opinion 723. Repeal of the ruling given in Opinion 47 together with the stabilisation of the generic names *Carcharhinus* Blainville, 1816, *Carcharodon* Smith, 1838, and *Odontaspis* Agassiz, 1838, in their accustomed sense (Pisces). Bull. Zool. Nomencl. 22: 32-36.

Irvine, B., R.S. Wells, and P.W. Gilbert. 1973.
Conditioning an Atlantic bottlenosed dolphin, *Tursiops truncatus*, to repel various species of sharks. Jour. Mammal. 54(2): 503-505.

Iversen, E.S. and H.O. Yoshida. 1956.
Longline fishing for tuna in the central equatorial Pacific, 1954. U.S. Fish Wildl. Serv., Spec. Sci. Rep., Fisheries, no. 184: 1-33.

Johnson, R.H. 1978.
Sharks of Polynesia. 170 pp., Les Editions du Pacifique, Papeete.

Johnson, R.H. and D.R. Nelson. 1973.
Agonistic display in the gray reef shark, *Carcharinus menisorrah*, and its relationship to attacks on man. Copeia, no. 1: 76-84.

Jones, R.S. 1971.
Two nonfatal shark attacks in the Truk District, Eastern Caroline Islands. Micronesica 7: 230-233.

Jordan, D.S. and B.W. Evermann. 1905.
The aquatic resources of the Hawaiian Islands. Part I. – The shore fishes. Bull. U.S. Fish Comm. 23 (part 1): 1-574.

Kato, S., S. Springer, and M.H. Wagner. 1967.
Field Guide to eastern Pacific and Hawaiian Sharks. U.S. Fish Wildl. Serv., Bur. Commercial Fish. Circ. 271: 1-47.

Kauffman, D.E. 1950.
Notes on the biology of the tigershark (*Galeocerdo arcticus*) from Philippine waters. U.S. Fish Wildl. Serv. Res. Rep. 16: 1-10.

Klausewitz, W. 1959.
Ergebnisse der Xarifa-Expedition 1957/58 des Instituts für Submarine Forschung, Vadus (Leitung: Dr. H. Hass). Fische aus dem Roten Meer. I. Knorpelfische (Elasmobranchii). Senckenb. Biol. 40: 43-50.

Klausewitz, W. 1960.
Die Typen und Typoide des Naturmuseums Senckenberg, 23: Pisces, Chondrichthyes, Elasmobranchii. Senckenb. Biol. 41: 289-296.

Klunzinger, C.B. 1871.
Synopsis der Fische des Rothen Meeres. II. Theil. Verh. Zool.-Bot. Ges. Wein. 21: 441-688.

Klimley, A.P. 1981-1982.
Grouping behavior in the scalloped hammerhead. Oceanus 24(4): 65-71.

Kreuzer, R. and R. Ahmed. 1978.
Shark Utilization and Marketing. 180 pp., Food and Agriculture Organization of the United Nations, International Trade Centre, Rome.

Lesson, R.P. 1830.
Zoologie. In L. Duperrey, Voyage autour de monde, exécuté par ordre du roi, sur la corvette de la majesté, La Coquille, pendant les années 1822, 1823, 1824 et 1825. Vol. 2, pt. 1, 471 pp. Arthus Bertrand, Paris.

Lesueur, C.A. 1818.
Descriptions of several new species of North American fishes. Jour. Acad. Nat. Sci. Phila. 1: 222-235.

Lesueur, C.A. 1822.
Description of a *Squalus*, of a very large size, which was taken on the coast of New Jersey. Jour. Acad. Nat. Sci. Phila. 2(2): 343-352.

Linnaeus, C. 1758.
Systema naturae sive regna tria naturae, systematice proposita per classes, ordines, genera et species ... locis. 10th ed., vol. 1, Regnum animales. 824 pp., Holmiae.

Lo, E.Y.-F. 1984.
Where shark fin crowns the meal. The New York Times, Sept. 16, 1984: 6-7.

McCosker, J.E. 1981.
Great white shark. Science 81, July/Aug.: 42-51.

Marshall, T.C. 1964.
Fishes of the Great Barrier Reef and Coastal Waters of Queensland. 566 pp., Angus and Robertson, Sydney.

Masuda,, H., C. Araga, and T. Yoshino. 1975.
Coastal Fishes of Southern Japan. 382 pp., Tokai Univ. Press, Tokyo.

Mathewson, R. and P.W. Gilbert. 1967.
Report on shark-porpoise experiments at the Lerner Marine Laboratory. In Conference on the shark-porpoise relationship. Amer. Inst. Biol. Sci., pp. 17-24, Washington, D.C.

Meek, S.E. and S.F. Hildebrand. 1923.
The marine fishes of Panama. Field Mus. Nat. Hist. Publ. 215, Zoöl. Ser. 15: 1-330.

Melouk, M.A. 1957.
On the development of *Carcharhinus melanopterus* (Q. & G.). Publ. Mar. Biol. Sta. Al-Ghardaqa, Red Sea 9: 229-251.

Miyosi, Y. 1939.
Description of three new species of Elasmobranchiate fishes collected at Hyuga Nada, Japan. Bull. Biogeogr. Soc. Tokyo 9:91-97.

Moreno, J.A. and A. Hoyos. 1983.
Premiere capture en eaux Espagnoles et en Mediterranée de *Carcharhinus altimus* (S. Springer, 1950). Cybium 7(1):65-70.

Moss, S.A. 1977.
Feeding mechanisms in sharks. Amer. Zool. 17(2): 355-364.

Müller, J. and F.G.J. Henle. 1838-1841.
Systematische Beschreibung der Plagiostomen. xxii + 200 pp., Von Veit and Co., Berlin.

Murphy, G.I. and R.S. Shomura. 1955.
Longline fishing for deep-swimming tunas in the central Pacific, August-November 1952. U.S. Fish Wildl. Serv., Spec. Sci. Rep., Fisheries, no. 137: 1-42.

Myrberg, Jr., A.A. and S.H. Gruber. 1974.
The behavior of the bonnethead shark, *Sphyrna tiburo*. Copeia, no. 2: 358-374.

Nakamura, H. 1935.
On the two species of the thresher shark from Formosan waters. Mem. Fac. Sci. Agric. Taihoku Imp. Univ. 14: 1-6

Nardo, J.D. 1827.
Prodromus observationum et disquisitionum ichthyologiae Adriaticae. Oken's Isis 20(6):472-631.

Nelson, D.R. 1974.
Ultrasonic telemetry of shark behavior. Naval Res. Rev. (December): 1-21.

Nelson, J.S. 1984.
Fishes of the World. 2nd edition, xv + 523 pp., John Wiley & Sons, New York.

Norman, J.R. 1939.
Fishes. The John Murray Expedition 1933-34. Brit. Mus. Nat. Hist., Sci. Rep., Zool. 7(1): 1-116.

Norman, J.R. and F.C. Fraser. 1937.
Giant Fishes, Whales and Dolphins, xxii + 375 pp., Putnam, London.

Ogilby, J.D. 1915.
Ichthyological notes (No. 2). Mem. Queensl. Mus. 3:130-136.

Ogilby, J.D. 1916.
Check-list of the cephalochordates, selachians, and fishes of Queensland. Part 1. Mem. Queensl. Mus. 5: 70-98.

Otake, T. and K. Mizue. 1981.
Direct evidence for oophagy in thresher shark, *Alopias pelagicus*. Jap. Jour. Ichth. 28(2): 171-172.

Penrith, M.J. 1972.
Earliest description and name for the whale shark. Copeia, no. 2: 362.

Poey, F. 1858-1861.
Memorias sobre la historia natural de la Isla de Cuba, acompanadas de sumarios latinos y extractos en francés, vol. 2, 442 pp. Viuda de Barcina, Habana.

Quiring, D.P. 1941.
The scale of being according to the power formula. Growth 4: 301-327.

Quoy, J.R.C. and P. Gaimard. 1824-1826.
Zoologie. In L. de Freycinet, Voyage autour de monde exécuté sur les corvettes de S. M. "L'Uranie" et "La Physicienne" pendant les années 1817, 1818,1819, et 1820. 712 pp. Pillet Aîné, Paris.

Rafinesque, C.S. 1810a.
Caratteri di alcuni nuovi generi e nuove specie di animali (principalmente di pesci) e piante della Sicilia, con varie osservazioni sopra i medisimi. 105 pp., Palermo.

Rafinesque, C.S. 1810b.
Indice d'ittiologia siciliana; ossia, catalogo metodico dei nomi latini, italiani, e siciliani dei pesci, che si rinvengono in Sicilia; disposti secondo un metodo naturale e seguito da un apendice che contiene la decrizione di alcuni nuovi pesci siciliani. 70 pp., Messina.

Randall, J.E. 1968.
Caribbean Reef Fishes. 318 pp., T.F.H. Publications, Jersey City.

Randall, J.E. 1973a.
Size of the great white shark (*Carcharodon*). Science 181: 169-170.

Randall, J.E. 1973b.
Expedition to Pitcairn. Oceans 6(2): 12-21.

Randall, J.E. 1974.
Rapa and Beyond. Oceans 7(6): 24-31.

Randall, J.E. 1977.
Contribution to the biology of the whitetip reef shark (*Triaenodon obesus*). Pac. Sci. 31(2): 143-164.

Randall, J.E. 1980.
A survey of ciguatera at Enewetak and Bikini, Marshall Islands, with notes on the systematic and food habits of ciguatoxic fishes. Fishery Bull. 78(2): 201-249.

Randall, J.E. 1983.
Red Sea Reef Fishes. 192 pp., IMMEL Publishing, London.

Randall, J.E. and G.S. Helfman. 1973.
Attacks on humans by the blacktip reef shark (*Carcharhinus melanopterus*). Pac. Sci. 27(3): 226-238.

Randall, J.E. and M.F. Levy. 1976.
A near-fatal shark attack by a mako in the northern Red Sea. Israel Jour. Zool. 25: 61-70.

Randall, J.E., G.R. Allen, and W.F. Smith-Vaniz. 1978.
Illustrated Identification Guide to Commercial Fishes. Reg. Fish. Sur. & Dev. Proj., FAO/FI:DP/RAB/71/278/3: v + 221.

Read, K.R.H. 1971.
Nonfatal shark attack, Palau Islands. Micronesica 7: 233-234.

Romer, A.S. 1945.
Vertebrate Paleontology. 2nd edition. 687 pp., Univ. Chicago Press, Chicago.

Romer, A.S. 1949.
The Vertebrate Body. 643 pp., W.B. Saunders Co., Philadelphia and London.

Rosenblatt, R.H. and W.J. Baldwin. 1958.
A review of the eastern Pacific sharks of the genus *Carcharhinus*, with a redescription of *C. malpeloensis* (Fowler) and California records of *C. remotus* (Duméril). Calif. Fish & Game 44(2): 137-159.

Rüppell, E. 1837.
Neue wirbelthiere zu der fauna von Abyssinien Gehörig. Fische des Rothen Meeres. 148 pp., Siegmund Schmerber, Frankfurt am Main.

Schultz, L.P. 1967.
Predation of sharks on man. Chesapeake Sci. 8(1): 52-62.

Schultz, L.P. and collaborators. 1953.
Fishes of the Marshall and Marianas Islands. Bull. U.S. Natl. Mus. 202, vol. 1: xxxii + 685 pp.

Seba, A. 1758.
Locupletissimi rerum naturalium thesauri accurata descriptio, et iconibus artificiosissimus expressio, per universam physices historiam opus, cui ex toto terrarum orbe collegit, digessit, descripsit et depingendum curavit A. Seba. 4 vols. Amsterdam.

Sivasubramaniam, K. 1969.
New evidences on the distribution of predatory pelagic sharks in the tuna grounds of the Indian Ocean. Bull. Fish. Res. Sta. Ceylon 20: 65-72.

Smith, A. 1829.
Contributions to the natural history of South Africa, etc. Zool. Jour. 4: 433-444.

Smith, H.M. 1913.
Description of a new carcharioid shark from the Sulu archipelago. Proc. U.S. Natl. Mus. 45: 599-601.

Smith, J.L.B. 1949.
Interesting fishes of three genera new to South Africa. Ann. Mag. Nat. Hist. 2(12): 367-374.

Smith, J.L.B. 1952.
Carcharhinus zambezensis Peters, 1852, with notes on other chondrichthyan fishes. Ann. Mag. Nat. Hist., ser. 12, 5: 857-863.

Smith, J.L.B. 1953.
The Sea Fishes of Southern Africa. 2nd edition. 564 pp., Central News Agency, Ltd., Cape Town.

Smith, J.L.B. 1957.
The rare shark *Hemipristis elongatus* (Klunzinger), 1871, from Zanzibar and Mozambique. Ann. Mag. Nat. Hist., ser. 12, 10: 555-560.

Smith, J.L.B. and M.M. Smith. 1963.
The Fishes of Seychelles. 215 pp., Dept. Ichthyol., Rhodes Univ., Grahamstown.

Springer, S. 1944.
Sphyrna bigelowi, a new hammerhead shark from off the Atlantic coast of South America, with notes on *Sphyrna mokarran* from New South Wales. Jour. Wash. Acad. Sci. 34: 274-276.

Springer, S. 1950.
A revision of North American sharks allied to the genus *Carcharhinus*. Amer. Mus. Novit. 1451: 1-13.

Springer, S. 1951.
Correction for "A revision of North American sharks allied to the genus *Carcharhinus*." Copeia, no. 3: 244.

Springer, S. 1960.
Natural history of the sandbar shark *Eulamia milberti*. U.S. Fish Wildl. Serv., Fish. Bull. 61: 1-38.

Springer, S. 1979.
A revision of the catsharks, family Scyliorhinidae. NOAA Tech. Rep., NMFS Circ. 422: v + 152 pp.

Springer, S. and J.D. D'Aubrey. 1972.
Two new scyliorhinid sharks from the east coast of Africa with notes on related species. Oceanogr. Res. Inst., Invest. Rep., no. 29: 1-19.

Springer, V.G. 1964.
A revision of the carcharhinid shark genera *Scoliodon*, *Loxodon*, and *Rhizoprionodon*. Proc. U.S. Natl. Mus. 115(3493): 559-632.

Springer, V.G. and J.A.F. Garrick. 1964.
A survey of vertebral numbers in sharks. Proc. U.S. Natl. Mus. 116(3496): 73-96.

Stevens, J.D. 1984.
Life-history and ecology of sharks at Aldabra Atoll, Indian Ocean. Proc. Roy. Soc. Lond. B 222: 79-106.

Storer, T.I. and R.L. Usinger. 1965.
General Zoology. 4th edition. 741 pp., McGraw-Hill, New York.

Strasburg, D.W. 1958.
Distribution, abundance, and habits of pelagic sharks in the Central Pacific Ocean. Fishery Bull. 58(138): 335-361.

Tanaka, S. and K. Mizue. 1979.
Studies on sharks – XV. Age and growth of Japanese dogfish *Mustelus manazo* Bleeker in the East China Sea. Bull. Jap. Soc. Sci. Fish. 45(1): 43-50.

Taniuchi, T. 1971.
Reproduction of the sandbar shark, *Carcharhinus milberti*, in the East China Sea. Jap. Jour. Ichth. 18: 94-98.

Taniuchi, T. 1975. Reef whitetip shark, *Triaenodon obesus*, from Japan. Jap. Jour. Ichth. 22(3): 167-170.

Taylor, L.R., Jr. 1972.
A Revision of the Shark Family Heterodontidae (Heterodontiformes, Selachii). Ph.D. dissertation, 176 pp., Scripps Inst. Oceanogr., Univ. of Calif., San Diego.

Teshima, K. and K. Mizue. 1972.
Studies on sharks. I. Reproduction in the female sumitsuki shark *Carcharhinus dussumieri*. Mar. Biol. (Berl.) 14: 222-231.

Tester, A.L. 1963.
The role of olfaction in shark predation. Pac. Sci. 17(2): 145-170.

Tester, A.L., G.J. Nelson, and C.I. Daniels. 1968.
Test of NUWC shark attack deterrent device, NUWC-TP-53. 46 pp., Naval Undersea Center, San Diego.

Thomerson, J.E. and T.B. Thorson. 1977.
The bull shark *Carcharhinus leucas*, from the upper Mississippi River near Alton, Illinois. Copeia, no. 1: 166-168.

Thomson, K.S. and D.E. Simanek. 1977.
Body form and locomotion in sharks. Amer. Zool. 17(2): 343-354.

Thorson, T.B. 1971.
Movement of bull sharks, *Carcharhinus leucas*, between Caribbean Sea and Lake Nicaragua demonstrated by tagging. Copeia, no. 2: 336-338.

Thorson, T.B., D.E. Watson, and C.M. Cowan. 1966.
The status of the freshwater shark of Lake Nicaragua, Copeia, no. 3: 385-402.

Tinker, S.W. and C.J. DeLuca. 1973.
Sharks & Rays. 80 pp., Charles E. Tuttle Co., Rutland, Vermont and Tokyo, Japan.

Tortonese, E. 1935-36.
Pesci del Mar Rosso. Boll. Mus. Zool. Anat. Comp. Torino, ser. 3, 45: 153-218.

Tortonese, E. 1950.
Studi sui Plagiostomi. Materiali per una revisione dei *Carcharhinus* Mediterranei. Boll. Pesca, Piscic. Idrobiol. Roma, Nuova Ser., 26: 5-21.

Tortonese, E. 1951.
Studi sui Plagiostomi. V-Ulteriori considerazioni sulle specie Mediterranee dei generi *Sphyrna* e *Carcharhinus*. Doriana 1(20): 1-8.

Tortonese, E. 1964.
The main biogeographical features and problems of the Mediterranean fish fauna. Copeia, no. 1: 98-107.

Tricas, T.C. and J.E. McCosker. 1984.
Predatory behavior of the white shark (*Carcharodon carcharias*), with notes on its biology. Proc. Calif. Acad. Sci. 43(14): 221-238.

Tricas, T.C., L.R. Taylor, and G. Naftel. 1981.
Diel behavior of the tiger shark, *Galeocerdo cuvier*, at French Frigate Shoals, Hawaiian Islands. Copeia, no. 4: 904-908.

van der Elst, R. 1981.
A Guide to the Common Sea Fishes of Southern Africa. 367 pp., C. Struik Publishers, Cape Town.

Wainwright, S.A., F. Vosburgh, and J.H. Hebrank. 1978.
Shark skin: function in locomotion. Science 202: 747-749.

Wass, R.C. 1971.
A Comparative Study of the Life History, Distribution, and Ecology of the Sandbar Shark and the Gray Reef Shark in Hawaii. Ph.D. dissertation, 219 pp., Univ. of Hawaii, Honolulu.

Wass, R.C. 1973.
Size, growth, and reproduction of the sandbar shark, *Carcharhinus milberti*, in Hawaii. Pac. Sci. 27(4): 305-318.

Wass, R.C. 1984.
An annotated checklist of the fishes of Samoa. NOAA Tech. Rep., NMFS Spec. Sci. Rep., Fish., no. 781: 1-43.

Wheeler, A. 1982.
Comment on the proposed suppression of *Rhiniodon* Smith, 1828 (Pisces) in favour of *Rhincodon* Smith, 1829 as the generic name of the whale shark. Z.N.(S.) 2090. Bull. Zool. Nomencl. 39(1):6.

Wheeler, J.F.G. 1953.
In J.F.G. Wheeler and F.D. Ommaney. Report on the Mauritius-Seychelles fisheries survey 1948-1949. Fish. Publ. Colon. Off. 1(3): 1-145.

Wheeler, J.F.G. 1960.
Sharks of the western Indian Ocean – III. *Carcharhinus menisorrah* (Müller and Henle). East Afr. Agric. Jour. 24(4): 271-273.

Wheeler, J.F.G. 1963.
Notes on the three common species of sharks in the Mauritius Seychelles area. Proc. R. Soc. Arts Sci. Mauritius 2: 146-160.

White, E.I., D.W. Tucker, and N.B. Marshall. 1961.
Proposal to repeal the ruling given in Opinion 47 and to use the plenary powers to stabilize the generic names *Carcharhinus* Blainville, 1816, *Carcharodon* A. Smith, 1838, and *Odontaspis* J.L.R. Agassiz, 1838, in their accustomed senses (Class Pisces). Z.N.(S.) 920 Bull. Zool. Nomencl. 18: 273-280.

Whitley, G.P. 1929.
Additions to the check-list of the fishes of New South Wales. No. 2. Austral. Zool. 5(4): 353-357.

Whitley, G.P. 1934.
Notes on some Australian sharks. Mem. Queensl. Mus. 10(4): 180-200.

Wood, F.G., D.K. Caldwell, and M.C. Caldwell. 1970.
Behavioral interactions between porpoises and sharks. In Investigations on Cetacea, II. G. Pilleri, ed., pp. 264-277. Benteli AG, Berne-Bümpliz.

INDEX

English Common and Scientific Names

acanthias, Squalus 16, 25, 26, 38, 40, 62, 63, 64
acanthodian 51
Acanthodii 43, 44
acutidens, Negaprion 120, 121
acutus, Rhizoprionodon 121, 122
Agnatha 43, 44
albimarginatus, Carcharhinus 12, 91, 92, 93, 108
alcocki, Halaelurus 82
Alopias 41, 49, 62, 79
    pelagicus 78
    superciliosus 79
    vulpinus 78
ALOPIIDAE 31, 49, 66
altimus, Carcharhinus 94, 112
amblyrhynchoides, Carcharhinus 95
amblyrhynchos, Carcharhinus 52, 53, 61, 91, 92, 95, 96, 97, 102
amboinensis, Carcharhinus 11, 98, 104, 124
Angelshark 18, 48, 51
anguineus, Chlamydoselachus 32, 37
antarcticus, Mustelus 63
antiarchs 44
Apristurus indicus 82, 83
Arabian Bamboo Shark 75
    Houndshark 87
arabicum, Chiloscyllium 74, 75
arcticus, Galeocerdo 117
arthrodires 44
atripinna, Hypoprion 103
australis, Galeorhinus 63

balfouri, Hemigaleus 89
    Hypogaleus 85, 86
Bamboo Sharks 13, 31, 49, 66
Barbeled Houndshark 51
Basking Shark 22, 49
bigelow, Sphyrna 128
Bigeye Houndshark 86
    Thresher 79
Bignose Shark 94
Blacktip Houndshark 85
    Reef Shark 1, 4, 11, 110
    Shark 106
Blind Shark 49
blochii, Sphyrna 126, 127
Blue Shark 19, 58, 62, 63, 64, 91

Bluefish 61
boesemani, Halaelurus 83
Bonnethead Shark 41
Bony fishes 33, 44, 51
BRACHAELURIDAE 49
Bramble Shark 48
brevipinna, Carcharhinus 99
brevirostris, Negaprion 120
buergeri, Halaelurus 83
Bull Shark 18, 19, 57, 77, 91, 104
Bullhead Sharks 13, 30, 31, 51, 66, 67

canescens, Scyllium 82
CARCHARHINIDAE 12, 25, 31, 66, 88, 90, 91, 124, 126
Carcharhiniformes 12, 48, 49, 82
Carcharhinus 11, 13, 18, 21, 51, 65, 91, 108, 109, 120, 125
    albimarginatus 12, 91, 92, 93, 108
    altimus 94, 112
    amblyrhynchoides 95
    amblyrhynchos 52, 53, 61, 91, 92, 95, 96, 97, 102
    amboinensis 11, 98, 104, 124
    brevipinna 99
    dussumieri 100
    falciformis 62, 91, 97, 101, 102, 108
    floridanus 101
    galapagensis 112
    hemiodon 102, 103, 109
    leucus 19, 57, 77, 91, 104, 105
    limbatus 95, 106
    longimanus 14, 15, 62, 91, 92, 107, 108
    macloti 103, 109
    maculipinnis 99
    melanopterus 1, 4, 11, 41, 97, 110, 111, 120
    menisorrah 97, 100, 102
    milberti 113
    natator 106
    nicaraguensis 104
    obscurus 111, 112
    platyrhynchus 92
    pleurotaenia 106
    plumbeus 112, 113, 114
    radamae 94
    sealei 100

    signatus 103
    sorrah 97, 111, 115, 116
    spallanzani 97, 111, 115
    wheeleri 91, 96, 97
    zambezensis 104
Carcharias 76
    limbatus 103
    melanopterus 91
carcharius, Carcharodon 21, 23, 49, 57, 63, 79
Carcharodon 49, 79
    carcharias 21, 23, 49, 57, 63, 79
    megalodon 49
Cartilaginous fishes 12, 43, 44, 51
Catsharks 13, 31, 49, 66, 82
Cephaloscyllium sufflans 82
uter 18
CETORHINIDAE 49
Cetorhinus maximus 22
Chaenogaleus macrostoma 89
Chioscyllium 49, 74
    arabicum 74, 75
    confusum 75
    griseum 75
    hasselti 75
chimaera 44, 51
Chlamydoselachus 47
    anguineus 32, 37
Chondrichthyes 12, 43, 44, 46
Chordata 33
cladodont 44, 45
Cladodontiformes 44
Cladoselache 23, 45, 46
Cladoselachiformes 45
Collared Carpet Shark 31, 49
concolor, Nebrius 68, 69
confusum, Chiloscyllium 75
Crocodile Shark 49
cuvier, Galeocerdo 6, 11, 64, 91, 116, 117, 118
    Squalus 117
Cyclostome 33, 43, 44

diplana, Sphyrna 128
Dirrhizodon elongatus 89
ditropis, Lamna 63, 79
Dogfish Shark 48, 62
Dugong 61

Dugong dugong 61
dugong, *Dugong* 61
Dusky Shark 111, 113
dussumieri, Carcharhinus 100

ECHINORHINIDAE 48
Elasmobranchii 44
Elf 61
elongatus, Dirrhizodon 89
　Hemipristis 88, 89, 90
Eridacnis radcliffei 84
Eugomphodus 76
　tricuspidatus 76
Eulamia 91
Eusphyra 126

falciformis, Carcharhinus 62, 91, 97, 101, 102
False Catshark 51
fasciatum, Stegostoma 70
ferrugineus, Nebrius 69
Finback Catsharks 51, 66, 84
fishes, bony 33, 44, 51
　cartilaginous 12, 43, 44, 51
floridanus, Carcharhinus 101
fosteri, Hemigaleops 120
Frilled Shark 32, 37, 47

galapagensis, Carcharhinus 112
Galeocerdo 51, 90
　arcticus 117
　cuvier 6, 11, 64, 91, 116, 117, 118
Galeorhinus australis 63
　galeus 51
galeus, Galeorhinus 85
Ganges Shark 104
gangeticus, Glyphis 104
gar 44
Ginglymostoma 21, 24, 35, 49, 68
GINGLYMMOSTOMATIDAE 49, 64, 66, 68, 73
glauca, Prionace 19, 58, 63, 64, 91
glaucus, Isurus 81
Glyphis 90, 91
　gangeticus 104
Goblin Shark 49
Graceful Shark 95
Great Hammerhead 64, 128
Great White Shark 21, 23, 47, 58, 63, 79, 117
Grey Bamboo Shark 75
　Nurse Shark 77, 104
　Reef Shark 52, 53, 61, 62, 92, 96
　Sharpnose Shark 123
griseum, Chiloscyllium 75
griseus, Hexanchus 47

habereri, Proscyllium 84
hagfish 33, 43, 45
Halaelurus alcocki 82
　boesemani 83
　buergeri 83
Hammerhead Sharks 13, 26, 31, 51, 57, 62, 64, 66, 125, 126, 128, 130
Hardnose Shark 109

hasselti, Chiloscyllium 75
hauffianus, Hybodus 46
HEMIGALEIDAE 51, 66, 88
Hemigaleops fosteri 120
Hemigaleus balfouri 89
　microstoma 88
hemiodon, Carcharhinus 102, 103, 109
Hemipristis 51, 89
　elongatus 88, 89, 90
HEMISCYLLIDAE 13, 22, 31, 49, 66
Hemiscyllium 74
Heptranchias 35, 47
　perlo 35, 36
HETERODONTIDAE 13, 31, 66, 67
Heterodontiformes 47, 67
Heterodontus 18, 22, 30, 31, 34, 35, 47, 67
　ramalheira 67, 68
HEXANCHIDAE 47
Hexanchiformes 22, 47
Hexanchus 23, 47
　griseus 47
Holocephali 44
Homo sapiens 61
Hooktooth Shark 89
Horn Shark 67
Houndsharks 31, 51, 66, 85
Hybodontiformes 46
Hybodus 46
　hauffianus 46
Hypogaleus balfouri
　hyugaensis 85, 86
　zanzibariensis 85
Hypoprion 91, 103, 109
　atripinna 103
hyugaensis, Hypogaleus 85, 86

Iago omanensis
Ichthyosaurus 17
indicus, Apristurus 82, 83
Isurus 19, 49, 57, 62, 64
　glaucus 81
　oxyrinchus 58, 63, 79, 80, 81
　paucus 79, 81

Lamna 64, 79
　ditropis 63, 79
　nasus 62, 63, 79
LAMNIDAE 17, 31, 41, 49, 66, 79
Lamniformes 48, 49, 76
Lamniopsis 90
lamprey 33, 43, 45
laticaudus, Squaliolus 48, 84
Lemon Shark 64
LEPTOCHARIIDAE 51
leucus, Carcharahinus 19, 57, 77, 91, 98, 104, 105
lewini, Sphyrna 50, 51, 63, 127, 128
　Zygaena 128
limbatus, Carcharhinus 95, 106
　Carcharias 103
Longfin Mako 79, 81
longimanus, Carcharhinus 14, 15, 62, 91, 92, 107, 108

Loxodon 13, 122
　macrorhinus 119

Mackerel Shark 17, 31, 49, 64, 66, 79
macloti, Carcharhinus 103, 109
macrorhinus, Loxodon 119
macrostoma, Chaenogaeleus 89
maculipinnis, Carcharhinus 99
madagascariensis, Odontaspis 120
Mako 19, 57, 62, 63, 65, 79, 81
maou, Squalus 108
maximus, Cetorhinus 22
megalodon, Carcharodon 49
Megamouth Shark 49
MEGASCHASMIDAE 49
melanopterus, Carcharhinus 1, 4, 11, 41, 97, 110, 111, 120
　Carcharias 91
menisorrah, Carcharhinus 97, 100, 102
microstoma, Hemigaleus 88
milberti, Carcharhinus 113
Milk Shark 121, 122
MITSUKURINIDAE 49
mokarran, Sphyrna 64, 128, 129
Monachus schauinslandi 61
Monk Seal 61
mosis, Mustelus 87
Mustelus 13, 63
　antarcticus 63
　mosis 87

nasus, Lamna 62, 63, 79
natator, Carcharnius 106
Nebrius 24, 68
　concolor 68, 69
　ferrugineus 69
Negaprion 64, 90, 120
　acutidens 120, 121
　brevirostris 120
nicaraguensis, Carcharhinus 104
Notorynchus 47
Nurse Shark 17, 24, 49, 64, 66, 68, 73
obesus, Triaenodon 2, 3, 4, 27, 42, 97, 108, 124, 125
obscurus, Carcharhinus 111, 112
obtusus, Triaenodon 124

Oceanic Whitetip Shark 14, 15, 62, 91, 107, 108
ODONTASPIDIDAE 31, 49, 66, 76
Odontaspis 49, 64, 76
　madagascariensis 120
　taurus 41, 76, 77, 104
　tricuspidatus 77
oligolinx, Rhizoprionodon 123
omanensis, Iago 86, 87
ORECTOLOBIDAE 22, 49
Orectolobiformes 48, 49, 68
Orectolobus 49
Osteichthyes 33, 51
Ostracoderm 43, 44, 45, 51
OXYNOTIDAE 48
Oxyrinchus, Isurus 58, 63, 79, 80, 81

INDEX

Paleospinax 48
PARASCYLLIDAE 31, 49
paucus, Isurus 79, 81
Pelagic Thresher 78
pelagicus, Alopias 78
perlo, Heptranchias 35, 36
Pigeye Shark 98
placoderm 44, 45, 51
Placodermi 43, 44
platyrhynchus, Carcharhinus 92
Pleuracanthiformes 46
Pleuracanthus 46
pleurotaenia, Carcharhinus 106
Pliotrema 22
plumbeus, Carcharhinus 112, 113, 114
Pomatomus saltator 61
Pondicherry Shark 103
Porbeagle 62, 63, 79
Poroderma 82
Prionace 90
   glauca 19, 58, 63, 64, 91
Pristiophoriformes 48
Pristiophorus 48
Propristiophorus 48
PROSCYLLIDAE 51, 66, 84
Proscyllium hebereri 84
PSEUDOCARCHARHINIDAE 49
PSEUDOTRIAKIDAE 49
Pterolamia 108
Pterolamiops 91, 108
Pygmy Ribbontail Catshark 84

Queensland Shark 95

radamae, Carcharhinus 94
radcliffei, Eridacnis 84
Ragged Tooth Shark 77
ramalheira, Heterodontus 67, 68
rays 44, 48, 51
Reef Whitetip Shark 108
Requiem Sharks 13, 17, 25, 31, 64, 66, 90, 126
Rhincodon 49, 73
   typus 22, 72, 73
Rhineodon 73
Rhiniodon 73
RHINCODONTIDAE 31, 49, 66, 73
Rhizoprion 122
Rhizoprionodon 13, 90, 122
   acutus 121, 122
   oligolinx 123
   taylori 123
Rough Shark 48

Salmon Shark 63, 79
saltator, Pomatomus 61
Sandbar Shark 113
Sand Tiger Shark 31, 49, 64, 66, 76, 77
sapiens, Homo 61
sawfish 48
Sawshark 22, 48, 51
Scalloped Hammerhead 63, 127, 128
schauinslandi, Monachus 61
School Shark 63

Scoliodon 13, 90, 122
SCYLIORHINIDAE 13, 31, 49, 66, 82
Scyllium canescens 82
sealei Carcharhinus 100
Seven-Gill Shark 35, 36, 47
Shark, Arabian Bamboo 75
   Arabian Houndshark 87
   Angelshark 18, 48, 51
   Bamboo 13, 31, 49, 66
   Barbeled Houndshark 51
   Basking 22, 49
   Bigeye Houndshark 86
   Bigeye Thresher 79
   Bignos 94
   Blacktip 106
   Blacktip Houndshark 85
   Blacktip Reef 1, 4, 11, 110
   Blind 49
   Blue 19, 58, 62, 63, 64, 91
   Bonnethead 41
   Bramble 48
   Bull 18, 19, 57, 77, 91, 104
   Bullhead 13, 30, 31, 51, 66, 67
   Catsharks 13, 31, 39, 82
   Collared Carpet 31, 49
   Crocodile 49
   Dogfish 48, 62
   Dusky 111, 113
   False Catshark 51
   Finback Catsharks 51, 66, 84
   Frilled 32, 37, 47
   Ganges 104
   Goblin 49
   Graceful 95
   Great Hammerhead 64, 128
   Great White 21, 23, 57, 58, 63, 65, 79, 117
   Grey Bamboo 75
   Grey Nurse 77, 104
   Grey Reef 52, 53, 61, 62, 92, 96
   Grey Sharpnose 123
   Hammerhead 13, 26, 31, 51, 62, 64, 66, 125, 126, 128, 130
   Hardnose 109
   Hooktooth 89
   Horn 67
   Houndsharks 31, 51, 66, 85
   Lemon 64
   Longfin Mako 79, 81
   Mackerel 17, 31, 49, 64, 66, 79
   Mako 19, 57, 62, 65, 79, 81
   Megamouth 49
   Milk 121, 122
   Nurse 17, 24, 49, 64, 66, 68, 73
   Oceanic Whitetip 14, 15, 62, 91, 107, 108
   Pigeye 98
   Pondicherry 103
   Pygmy Ribbontail Catshark 84
   Queensland 95
   Ragged Tooth 77
   Reef Whitetip 108
   Requiem 13, 17, 25, 31, 64, 66, 90, 126

   Rough 48
   Salmon 63, 79
   Sandbar 113
   Sand Tiger 31, 49, 64, 66, 76, 77
   Sawshark 22, 48, 51
   Scalloped Hammerhead 63, 127, 128
   School 63
   Seven-Gill 35, 36, 47
   Shortfin Mako 58, 59, 79, 81
   Sicklefin Lemon 120
   Silky 62, 91, 101, 108
   Silvertip 12, 91, 108
   Six-Gill 132, 49
   Slit-eye 119
   Smallbelly Catshark 82
   Smalltooth Thresher 78
   Smooth Hammerhead 130
   Snaggletooth 89
   Soupfin 85
   Speckled Catshark 83
   Spinner 99
   Spiny 44
   Spiny Dogfish 16, 25, 26, 38, 63
   Spottail 115
   Swell 18
   Tawny Nurse 69
   Thresher 31, 62, 66
   Tiger 6, 11, 61, 62, 65, 91, 116, 117
   Variegated 31, 49, 66, 70, 73
   Weasel 51, 66, 88
   Whale 22, 31, 49, 66, 73
   Whitecheek 100
   Whitespotted Bullhead 67
   Whitetip 108
   Whitetip Reef 2, 3, 4, 27, 42, 56, 124, 125
   Winghead 126
Shortfin Mako Shark 38, 59, 79, 81
Sicklefin Lemon Shark 120
signatus, Carcharhinus 103
Silky Shark 62, 91, 101, 108
Silvertip Shark 12, 91, 108
Six-Gill Shark 23, 47
skates 51
Slit-eye Shark 119
Smallbelly Catshark 82
Smalltooth Thresher 78
Smooth Hammerhead 130
Snaggletooth Shark 89
Somniosus 48
sorrah, Carcharhinus 97, 111, 115, 116
Soupfin Shark 85
spallanzani, Carcharhinus 97, 111, 115
Speckled Catshark 83
Sphyrna 51, 57, 62, 126
   bigelowi 128
   blochii 126, 127
   diplana 128
   lewini 50, 51, 63, 127, 128
   mokarran 64, 128, 129
   tiburo 41
   tudes 128
   zygaena 130, 131
SPHYRNIDAE 13, 26, 31, 66, 125

147

Spinner Shark 99
Spiny Dogfish 16, 25, 26, 38, 63
Spiny Shark 44
Spottail Shark 115
SQUALIDAE 48
Squaliformes 48
Squaliolus laticaudus 48, 84,
Squalus 48
  acanthias 16, 25, 26, 38, 40, 62, 63, 64
  cuvier 117
  maou 108
  varius 70
  Squatina 18, 35, 48, 49
  SQUATINIDAE 49
  Squatiniformes 48
  STEGOSTOMATIDAE 31, 49, 66, 70
  Stegostoma fasciatum 70
  tigrinum 70
  varium 70, 71
sufflans, Cephaloscyllium 82
superciliosus, Alopias 79
Swell Shark 18
taurus, Odontaspis 41, 76, 77, 104
Tawny Nurse Shark 69
taylori, Rhizoprionodon 123
Thresher Shark 31, 62, 66
tiburo, Sphyrna 41
Tiger Shark 6, 11, 61, 62, 64, 65, 91, 116, 117
tigrinus, Stegostoma 70
Triaenodon 90, 108
  obesus 2, 3, 4, 27, 42, 97, 108, 124, 125
  obtusus 124
TRIAKIDAE 31, 51, 66, 85, 124
tricuspidatus, Eugomphodus 76
  Odontaspis 77
tudes, Sphyrna 128
typus, Rhincodon 22, 72, 73
uter, Cephaloscyllium 18
Variegated Shark 31, 49, 66, 70, 73
varium, Stegostoma 70, 71
varius, Squalus 70
vulpinus, Alopias 78
Weasel Shark 51, 66, 88
Whale Shark 22, 31, 49, 66, 73
wheeleri, Carcharhinus 91, 96, 97
Whitecheek Shark 100
Whitespotted Bullhead Shark 67
Whitetip Reef Shark 2, 3, 4, 27, 42, 56, 124, 125
Whitetip Sharks 108
Winghead 126
Wobbegongs 49
zambezensis, Carcharhinus 104
zanzibariensis, Hypogaleus 85
Zygaena lewini 128
zygaena, Sphyrna 130, 1312

148